THE INDOOR LIGHT
GARDENING BOOK

By the Same Author
HOUSE PLANTS

The Indoor Light

GARDENING BOOK

BY

GEORGE A. ELBERT

CROWN PUBLISHERS, INC., NEW YORK

To Jinny

LIBRARY OF CONGRESS CATALOG CARD NUMBER: 72-84298
ISBN: 0-517-500957
ISBN: 0-517-524511 pbk
PRINTED IN THE UNITED STATES OF AMERICA
PUBLISHED SIMULTANEOUSLY IN CANADA BY GENERAL PUBLISHING COMPANY LIMITED
DESIGN: SHARI DE MISKEY AND NEDDA BALTER

Fifth Printing, February, 1976

Contents

Chapter 1

LIGHT GARDENS
THE FIRST EFFECTIVE MEANS OF FLOWERING PLANTS INDOORS

BRINGING THE GARDEN INDOORS

Before the industrial revolution plants were not commonly raised indoors. In the southern countries of Europe, where pot culture was universal, they adorned courtyards and balconies but were not considered subjects for the house. In the north, except in the great houses, small windows were the rule in order to conserve heat in winter. Cities, then, were not large by modern standards and the country was always accessible, so that there was no pressing reason to go to the trouble of growing plants indoors.

In our own country the situation changed during the industrial revolution with the use of soft coal whose smoke enshrouded the ever-increasing cities. Open register heating spewed coal gas into apartments making even foliage plants difficult to grow. In the stuffy, crowded rooms people felt the need for some reminder of the natural environment. Perhaps it was this sense of deprivation which gave rise to the floral decorations of Art Nouveau. And there was an

1

attempt to grow something—anything would do—which was green and lived. But the choices were few for the smogs and gas fumes were fatal to most plants. So the people of those days settled for Aspidistras, Potted Palms, Rubber Plants, and tolerant Ferns.

Estates in the country had their conservatories, and these were superseded by greenhouses once the means was developed to warm them properly in winter. The middle class of the cities had no such amenities. But when railroads made possible commuting to and from work, more and more people left the centers and found it more comfortable to live in detached homes in the suburbs.

Window areas in these homes became bigger and, instead of greenhouses, which were both expensive and troublesome, bay windows and sun porches were added. The latter were intended as light areas in inclement weather and in winter. They have survived till today as standard features of suburban homes.

Central heating created conditions which permitted the growing of plants indoors. On the windowsill sunlight is sufficient only within a few inches of the panes. Sunporches and bays provided longer hours of bright light, and the other requirements of culture could be more effectively controlled. Still the majority of plants which would do well in these conditions produced only foliage.

Numerous books have been written about window and sunporch horticulture. Reading them one gets the impression that there is no end to the number of plants which can be grown and bloomed in this way. And it is true to this extent—that a completely devoted hobbyist can work wonders with plants. Nevertheless the lists recommended to the amateur strike a note of exaggeration. Not a few of the specimens illustrated and described were actually grown in greenhouses and dubbed houseplants when they had been moved indoors for display. Very few, in writing about the subject, have been willing to stick to the sober realities or confess the limitations. If all the recommended varieties could be bloomed by the average amateur, indoor light gardening would not have added so greatly to the potential. Now we can raise all those windowsill plants, and many more, without benefit of any sunlight.

EARLY PLANT INTRODUCTIONS

Plant introductions have played a great role in the expansion of indoor gardening. In the early days of exploration the chief objectives were economically valuable fruits and vegetables. In the nineteenth century, as sea travel became safer and more rapid, it was possible to send back from far places all kinds of plants and seeds for trial. Among these, first of all, were flowering plants for garden and greenhouse. Among them a selection was made which could tolerate house conditions.

The increase for the indoor grower was mainly in foliage plants, notably among the Arums and succulents. Begonias became popular early on and, though they were principally prized for their leaves, they bloomed splendidly in country windows. Gloxinias had a vogue and spring bulbs were introduced for forcing. Windowsill growing of Orchids is quite a modern accomplishment.

THE MIRACLE FAMILY (THE GESNERIADS)

The African Violet (*Saintpaulia*) became popular in this country from 1936 on and fluorescent lighting was introduced in 1938. Experiments with incandescent lamps had already taken place in the twenties but gave out too much heat for efficient growing. Shortly after fluorescent lights began to be used in offices it was learned that the illumination was sufficient to maintain foliage plants without supplementary sunlight. But it took a while before it was fully realized that when plant and fluorescent light were brought into a proper relationship the essential precondition was created for flowering plants anywhere indoors.

The African Violet was the first beneficiary. This "Miracle Plant," discovered in the 1890s, became the first to be raised under lights on a commercial scale because of the experience that it grew better than in sunlight. And it may be because of this success that the further progress in indoor gardening has taken place so quickly. The popularity of this flower became immense and led to extensive experimentation with other plant material.

Growers soon became aware that indoor gardening demanded plants meeting certain specifications. They had to be of tropical or subtropical origin, principally perennials or tuberous, medium in size, and able to bloom in artificial light. Plant exploration and introduction then went forward with these qualifications in mind. Interestingly, the family of the African Violet, the Gesneriaceae, was found to be rich in candidates for the method. In fact, the concentration in this one family has been so great that we are only now beginning to break the spell and look about us for other possibilities. In doing so we are finding that the range of blooming plants which we can grow under lights is far greater than we formerly imagined.

POTENTIAL OF LIGHT GARDENING

What has been accomplished thus far with artificial light in indoor gardens is only a beginning. The potential is limitless. As city people come to realize that it is the only practical way to raise plants in an apartment, the number of devotees will grow rapidly. Without any encouragement from industry, and although indoor light gardening equipment is often not available in major stores across the country, immense numbers of people are adopting the hobby, being driven to engage in it by inner need and the sterility of urban living.

Institutional use of the method is expanding. Teachers are acquiring fixtures for their classrooms, hospitals are including light gardening in their recreational therapy programs, and apartment communities have discovered that they can

grow the plants for the beautification of their open spaces more economically indoors, while supporting their projects through sales of houseplants grown with
the same equipment.

The efficiency of fluorescent light in plant growth will lead to changes in
greenhouse construction and operation, revolutionizing commercial plant growing. In the home the light garden, as a piece of living furniture, may soon become as ubiquitous as the television set. People will have exquisite garden rooms
without a window. Never before could we grow so many and such beautiful
plants.

The essential fact which has changed everything is that we have learned for
the first time in history to grow flowering plants without sunlight.

Chapter 2

LIGHT

INTRODUCTORY

The author is not an electric or lighting engineer and is quite incapable of understanding the more complex features and formulas connected with the science of illumination and electronics. Thus his information is drawn from publications, especially those issued by the manufacturers of fluorescent lamps. The following discussion is intended to be of help to people like himself who are handy enough to build and wire a light garden and sufficiently educated to comprehend those aspects of the subject which can be expressed verbally or visually.

EFFECTIVENESS THE CRITERION

The important matter for most light gardeners is the relative effectiveness of equipment and the best way of arranging it. Engineers of the electrical equipment manufacturers deal largely with commercial installations and specific crops, where the problems presented are quite different from those faced by the home gardener. Thus figures of certain light intensities are of little significance or use to the amateur. What he needs to know is the amount of and the place-

5

ment of available equipment to produce a certain effect on *his* plants. Certain light arrangements possible for commercial installations and experimental ones are, from his point of view, impractical. Finally the information provided by the engineer-scientists often represents theoretical ideals which have little relationship to the actual behavior or effect of equipment.

If he could modify light intensity at will the amateur would indeed be very concerned with measurements. But this is not the case. The choice is limited and cannot be modified in any way. It is this equipment, specifically the fluorescent and incandescent bulbs, which is his true standard of measurement. In other words, our criterion of efficiency is not lumens or footcandles but tubes of a certain length and bulbs of a certain wattage and their actual effect on the type of plants we intend to grow in our light gardens.

The difference between the needs of the amateur and the engineer or commercial grower have been dramatically highlighted by the change in attitude of most light gardeners in the last year or two. Originally a great deal of attention was given to calculations and to the spectral formulas of tubes provided by the manufacturers and each new growth tube was greeted with reports of remarkable results in actual growing. With time and experience it became apparent that the enthusiasm was only the result of observing the behavior of certain plants. The first reaction of a grower, when a plant which has not previously bloomed suddenly performs, is that the new light source is the cause. But when he finds that other plants in his garden react less well than formerly the euphoria evaporates.

This is what has happened. And the disillusionment has been so great that many amateurs have gone back to the original commercial fixtures and are now proceeding to the other extreme of asserting that they are as good or better than the growth lights. Certainly the manufacturers have exaggerated the benefits of the "improved" lights and probably the reaction of the amateurs is overdone. But the whole incident, stretching over several years, indicates that the amateur gardener has certain needs and that all the scientific figures, graphs, charts, and diagrams do not make a plant grow any better. The amateur gardener's first basis of judgment should always be within the area of his understanding— how his plants grow.

Scientists and engineers *are* making progress in the study of photosynthesis and other effects of light on plants and manufacturers are attempting to improve their product. In due time this will lead to substantial progress in light gardening.

THE WAY PLANTS REACT TO COLOR IN LIGHT

The handicap of the amateur in dealing with information supplied by scientists is that he accepts every latest pronouncement as final and complete. There isn't really much else he *can* do, for he usually does not realize what the scientist takes for granted—that knowledge is capable of constant refinement and extension, and that most scientific statements have a narrowly specific application.

Ever since light gardening started the amateur has been subjected to positive statements about the effect of light on photosynthesis and plant growth as well as the growth efficiency of fluorescent lamps. In each instance he has adapted his equipment and culture to the latest information. The results have usually been rather less satisfactory than if he had depended on his own experiments and observations. Particularly misleading has been the assumption that blue and red light are all that are needed to produce a healthy flowering plant.

We know that light produces photosynthesis in plants which supplies the material for growth, just as digestion of food maintains human energy. Discoveries regarding the relationship between certain wavelengths, in the blue and red ranges, and photosynthesis, have therefore been accepted by the amateur as summing up everything we need to know about the effect of light on plants. Dependence on this piece of knowledge has resulted in the installation of many inefficient light gardens.

There are any number of other plant reactions to light besides photosynthesis. What we have learned by experience in the last few years is that fluorescent tubes emitting a spectrum containing some part of all the ranges, and not especially strong in either the blue or red zones, work out very well in practice.

THE SPECTRUM

Below is a simple illustration of the colors of the visible spectrum, their corresponding wavelengths and their position in relation to the total spectrum.

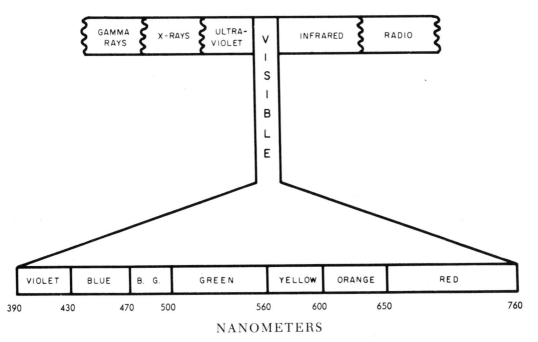

NANOMETERS

Much research has been carried on regarding the relative importance of different wavelengths of the spectrum on photosynthesis in plants. Fluorescent tubes have been formulated which meet most if not all the characteristics of sunlight and which have been considered effective in plant growth. Nevertheless, results, in a number of ways, are not comparable. Knowledge acquired thus far has, therefore, only restricted application, and scientists must go further afield to fill in the gaps between performance and theory. An inkling of what may be the problem may be derived from a consideration of part of the spectrum which is outside the range of vision.

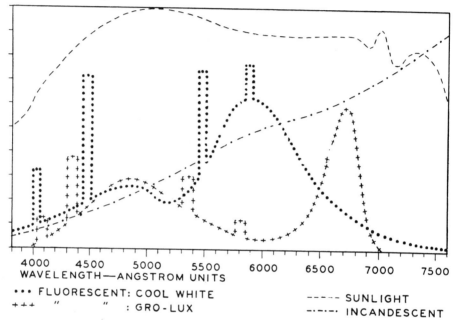

THE EMISSION OF VISIBLE LIGHT FROM THE SUN AND FROM THE THREE MOST COMMONLY USED SOURCES OF ARTIFICIAL LIGHT.

On this chart the graphs of Cool White and Gro-Lux are shown as on two previous charts. In addition we see at the top the curve of the sun's spectrum. Finally, starting in the left-hand lower corner and moving in an almost straight line to the upper-right-hand corner is the graph for incandescent light. It shows that the development of intensity is continuous toward the red end of the spectrum—quite different from the spectral distribution of any of the fluorescent lamps.

It should be repeated here that these charts are only approximations of the true distribution of spectrum intensities and that all lamps show gaps, which may or may not be significant for plant growth, between narrow bands of high intensity. We know next to nothing about the selectivity of plants in regard to wavelengths of light and their intensities or what effect any particular bands may have on the subtler plant processes.

(Wavelengths are usually expressed in Angstrom units. One Angstrom is equal to one ten-billionth of a meter.)

COLORS OF THE SPECTRUM

ULTRAVIOLET LIGHT

The Angstrom wavelengths below 3900 and above the X rays is ultraviolet light, a light which appears black, therefore invisible, but whose effect can be observed on fluorescent materials. Part of this range, from 2900 to 3900 or 4000, penetrates our atmosphere from the sun and is called "near ultraviolet." Until recently all ultraviolet light was considered harmful to plants and animals.

When the discovery was made of the special role in photosynthesis and growth control played by red radiation (see below) manufacturers of fluorescent tubes hurried to bring on the market ones which were formulated with an especially strong emission in the red range along with blue. The other colors were considered unimportant to photosynthesis and useless, if not necessarily harmful, to other plant processes.

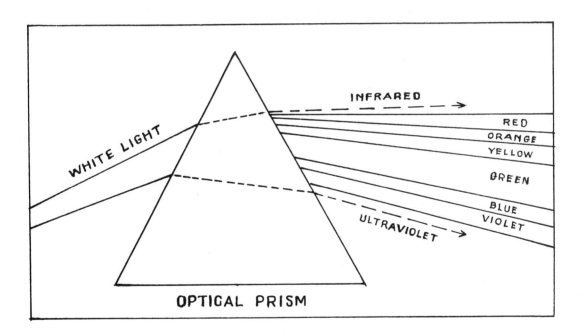

INFRARED

WHITE LIGHT

RED
ORANGE
YELLOW

GREEN

BLUE
VIOLET

ULTRAVIOLET

OPTICAL PRISM

Ultraviolet light has been considered harmful to organic life. The spectral graphs of a number of lamps on the market show ultraviolet emissions in the 3000–3500 range. Growers have been advised to interpose a plastic filter between these tubes and the plants. I have used the tubes without apparent ill effects to my plants.

The question of whether wavelengths other than red and blue are vital to plant life and function has recently been publicized by the studies of Dr. John Nash Ott. Dr. Ott agrees that ultraviolet below 2900 Angstroms is harmful to life. But he believes that the black light range between 2900 and 4000 Angstroms is not only beneficial but essential in triggering bloom in certain plants. He also has been in favor of lamps which emit light of balanced intensity in all the visible color ranges.

BLUE LIGHT

The still primitive state of our knowledge about the effect of light on plants is apparent from our ignorance about blue light. All that we do know is that it is essential to photosynthesis and that it induces phototropism (the turning of plants toward a light source). Beyond that there is a suspicion that under certain circumstances blue light can take over some of the functions of red. We have almost no specific details. There is a good possibility that we will find out that certain plants react in specific ways to very narrow bands of the spectrum.

GREEN AND YELLOW-ORANGE LIGHT

Since the chlorophyll in leaves, by means of its green color, filters out the green light from the sun, it is believed that green light is ineffective in photosynthesis and harmful in large doses. Yellow light is considered neutral. We have virtually no knowledge regarding the importance, or unimportance, for plant function of these ranges as supplements to others. It is difficult to believe that they are entirely useless. And we may find out in the end that a certain proportion of this large section of the visible spectrum contributes to the full function of those ranges to which we have attributed the greatest role in plant growth.

RED LIGHT

Red light has attracted the most attention partly, at least, because this is where the principal scientific discoveries have been made. Scientists at the USDA Plant Industry Station in Beltsville, Maryland, have isolated a pigment in plants which is called phytochrome. It is a protein, a blue pigment, which acts as an enzyme triggering growth changes in plants. There are two forms. One absorbs red light at about 6600 Angstroms. The other absorbs far red light at about 7350 Angstroms. Far red is only faintly visible to the human eye. The red light response is active growth in plants. The far red is negative and causes growth to cease. In a way which is by no means fully understood these two forms of the enzyme and two light wavelengths react in a pattern, probably specific for each plant, which controls its rate and form of growth which we call its habit.

A balance between red and far red light in fluorescent lamps is therefore highly desirable. Unfortunately, despite exaggerated claims, none of the available fluorescent lamps emit light in sufficient intensity at far red.

Chapter 3

TUBES, BULBS,
AND FIXTURES

THE FLUORESCENT TUBE

Since its introduction in 1938 the chief usage of fluorescent lamps has been industrial, commercial, and institutional. Its widespread acceptance has been due to its incomparable efficiency and economy. Nevertheless it has never found its way into the average home principally because of its long rectangular shape which adapts poorly to interior design. Most people are familiar with the workings of an incandescent lamp fixture but few have any experience with the fluorescent lamp.

The catalogs of the major manufacturers list numerous types and sizes of lamps. There are white, blue, green, gold, and red lights. There are tubes emitting colors which are flattering to patrons in restaurants, which make fresh meat appear more appetizing, and which enhance the appearance of clothing on display. Until recently the growth effect of fluorescent light was only coincidental and the largest manufacturer continues to describe his "growth lamps" as plant enhancing.

Two smaller manufacturers have introduced a whole line of "growth lamps." Their efficiency for the purpose has always been a subject of controversy in the trade, and independent research remains noncommittal regarding claims of superiority.

Among light gardeners there are all shades of opinion, and experiences differ. The one thing we know for a certainty is that most blooming plants which have received some attention from light gardeners have been brought to flower. The categories of tubes used have been relatively limited. Thus, without going into all the aspects of an extremely difficult, complex, and largely unexplored subject, we can impart some practical advice regarding the types of tubes which seem best to achieve success in various aspects of light gardening.

The fluorescent lamp is a glass tube or bulb which is coated within with a fluorescent material called a phosphor. Sealed within the tube are a gas—argon or argon with neon—and a small amount of mercury which vaporizes during operation. Extending from the closures which seal the tube at each end are single or double pins which act as contacts.

THE PINS

Med. Bipin   Single Pin   Recessed Double Contact

The medium bipin is used on the tubes, and fits into the fixtures, most often used in the home. They are usually the lower wattage tubes with lengths up to 48 inches. Starters (see page 29) are required.

The single pin is standard equipment with Slimline tubes. Special fixtures are required. There are no starters.

The recessed double contact tube is of higher wattage, requiring special ballasts and fixtures. Lengths of tube are up to 96 inches, and wattage reaches 215 in the superhigh output tubes. No starters are required.

FLUORESCENCE

A number of chemicals are known which, when excited by radiant energy in the form of ultraviolet rays, emit light of a specific wavelength. Displays by manufacturers often include cases containing little piles of these chemicals.

When subjected to ultraviolet light, each one will be seen to glow with a different color. They are the phosphors, and when used singly or in combination, produce the light which is emitted by your fluorescent tube. The proportions of each phosphor in the combination create a light containing various parts of the spectrum with different intensities. In this way the manufacturer can produce a tube emitting a kind of light which is adapted to particular uses.

COLOR

The visible color of the tube has little bearing on the question of whether its phosphors emit a greater or lesser quantity of those blue and red parts of the spectrum which are considered particularly effective in plant growth (see Wave Length and Photosynthesis, above). Moreover, at either end of the spectrum, toward ultraviolet and toward far red, the color is less visible to the human eye. The rays themselves are, of course, invisible, as is all light. Light is only a form of energy which becomes visible when it strikes an object.

The reader need only consider a red-coated incandescent bulb, which seems to emit quantities of very dark red light. Actually there is very little of this light being emitted, and what is there is inefficient for plant growth. A tube which appears nearly white may be very effective in the blue and high red ranges of the spectrum.

The reason is that the eye cannot measure intensities in a mixture. You will remember that a mixture of primary colors produces white light. Yet the red rays are there and so are the blue. It is a widely held fallacy among amateurs that a red-colored fluorescent tube is just what their plants need for flowering. Other colors are a no better indication.

This leaves us just three criteria for judging the efficiency of a tube in plant growth and blooming; lumen output (see below), the spectrum, and practical experience.

Instead of complicating matters this simplifies our problem of choosing the proper fluorescent lamp for our light garden. Of the three, practical experience has been the most reliable guide. Where success with plants has been achieved it has been partly related to sufficient lumen output and a satisfactory spectrum, but neither of the first two criteria alone has been sufficient thus far to "prove" the excellence of a lamp for plant growth.

HOW MANUFACTURERS LABEL THEIR TUBES

Manufacturers label their tubes according to certain color designations. They have little relationship to "true" color but are simply a convenient way of telling them apart. I am giving the terms because they are the ones used in manufacturers' catalogs for all standard commercial tubes. The ones I list are the only names at the present time of interest to light gardeners. They are Sign White, White, Cool White, Deluxe Cool White, Soft White, Natural, Daylight, Warm White, and Deluxe Warm White. The term Deluxe merely means that the phosphors of that tube include a special fluorescent chemical emitting more red.

LUMENS

You are more likely to forgive me for leaving out definitions of some terms and to use them as a way of expressing relative differences if I give, verbatim, a definition of lumens: "the unit of luminous flux, equal to the luminous flux emitted in a unit solid angle by a point source of one-candle intensity."

In their catalogs manufacturers indicate the light output of their lamps in lumens. It is an arbitrary measure of *visible* light and the figure used is for the total output of the lamp. It varies according to the radiance of the phosphors, the length of the tube or its surface area, and the rated wattage.

The ambiguity of many such terms of measurement becomes clear if we consider that they have a special practical use. Lumens are a practical measurement in all situations where visible light is being considered—and that applies to most situations where fluorescent lights are used.

When a manufacturer includes phosphors emitting invisible rays, the apparent lumen output drops rather drastically. But this does *not* mean that growth efficiency of the illumination is less. For this reason manufacturers often leave out the listing of lumen output for lamps in this category.

For example a 30-watt, 36-inch Cool White tube may rate 2300 lumens. The same length lamp in Deluxe Cool White, containing red phosphor, will rate 1530 lumens. All the "growth" lights, such as Gro-Lux, Gro-Lux WS, and Vita-Lite emit less visible radiance and therefore fewer lumens.

In spite of this, the lumen measurement is now considered by many to be more significant for the light gardener than footcandles. And that is because we are finding out that, provided the spectrum of the tube is reasonably well distributed, the greater the intensity of the light output, the more effective the lamp will be for plant growth and bloom. If we use "growth" tubes with a low lumen output we must use more of them closer together to achieve sufficient illumination for the flowering of the more light-demanding blooming plants.

This concept considerably simplifies the problems of the light gardener who no longer has to be so concerned with the details of spectrum, or the exact quantities of blue and red light. And it also means that standard commercial tubes and the high output tubes in standard colors can be as effective as specifically designed "growth" tubes. What light gardeners want from the manufacturer is a cool tube producing more lumens with the same wattage as at present—in other words, a more efficient tube.

FOOTCANDLES

Footcandles are an arbitrary measure of the light striking an object. Your tubes *emit* so and so many lumens. Your plant *receives* so and so many footcandles. Footcandles vary according to the distance of an object from the light source. You can readily see, therefore, that in terms of the same footcandles, your plants can be farther away from the tubes with high lumen output than from those with low lumen output. (For light requirements of plants see pages 31–40.)

Footcandles are also a measure of visible light. An ordinary light meter can only measure footcandles by a complicated conversion process. General Electric produces a Footcandle Meter which makes it easier.

The advantage of footcandles as a measurement is simply the fact that the amateur *can* measure them. For the average grower the knowledge that he has installed two or more high illumination tubes and that, therefore, his plants at a distance of 4 or 5 inches are receiving five or six hundred footcandles, is sufficient. Many of our houseplants will bloom under these circumstances. Should it be desirable to bloom very high light-demanding plants, then 1000 to 1200 footcandles may be needed, or even more. In that case we require tubes emitting more lumens.

LAMP SIZES

The principal fluorescent lamp lengths in use are:

20 watts	24-inch medium bipin
40 watts	48-inch medium bipin
55 watts	72-inch recessed double contact
73 watts	96-inch recessed double contact

These are wattages for standard commercial tubes, and the list indicates the progressive increase in wattage with length of tube. Tubes of one designated color emit proportionately more lumens as they increase in length.

Tubes are available in increments of 2 inches from 6¾ inches all the way to 96 inches. Some sizes are special order tubes. So also are high output tubes of the same length as those listed above.

Circleline lamps are circular fluorescent tubes useful in small square or round light gardens. They have diameters of 8¼, 12, and 16 inches.

CATEGORIES OF TUBES

Standard Commercial Tubes

These are very efficient low wattage tubes produced by all the principal manufacturers and designated by a standard terminology in catalogs, some of which we have mentioned above. They are the tubes you normally see in offices, set into the ceiling.

They are used with relatively inexpensive commercial fixtures available at electrical supply stores. Electrical equipment—wiring, plugs, etc.—are the same as for other equipment in the home.

The tubes are medium bipin equipped and use starters.

These are at the present time overwhelmingly the most common tubes in use and the least expensive, most efficient for the average light gardener.

Slimline Instant Start

These are narrow tubes in various sizes up to 96 inches in length. A Slimline 48-inch tube is 1½ inches in diameter compared with 2 inches for the standard commercial tube. They are equipped with single pins and do not require a starter.

Reflector Lamps

Lamps are available which have a reflector built into the tube itself. They are useful where no other type of reflector can be installed. But the system is not very efficient since the radiation is reflected back through the phosphors in the bottom side of the tube. A good overhead reflector is far more effective.

Power Groove and Power Twist Tubes

Molded or twisted fluorescent tubes, having a greater amount of exposed surface, radiate more light for the same length. Most of these have higher wattages and require special fixtures but they are useful where more light intensity is required within a restricted space.

HO, VHO, and SHO Lamps (High, Very High, and Superhigh Output)

These designations represent lamp series with progressively higher wattages. All are recessed double contact equipped. All require special fixtures and wiring.

Although this equipment is much more expensive to buy and maintain, it is growing in popularity because the light output is so much greater. Light gardeners who install floor gardens or small rooms as gardens, or grow such light lovers as the more showy orchids have found that these lamps are the only ones which produce consistent results.

The most efficient standard commercial Cool White, 48-inch tube emits about 3200 lumens. Compare this with the following:

110-watt	96-inch HO	Warm White	8900	lumens
215-watt	96-inch SHO	Warm White	16,000	lumens

"Growth" Tubes

The principal growth tubes are:

Gro-Lux	Sylvania
Gro-Lux Wide Spectrum	Sylvania
Naturescent/Optima	Duro-Test
Vita-Lite	Duro-Test

Gro-Lux

This was the earliest of the growth lamps and the most popular. Although it is efficient for seedling growth and for the blooming of the less demanding exotic plants, it is quite ineffective with plants requiring more intense illumination. The purplish glow imparts glamor to flowers (and tropical fish) but is distasteful to most growers.

Gro-Lux Wide Spectrum

Less restricted to the blue and red ranges of the spectrum, this tube is fairly efficient. But, in the experience of the author and based on reports from many amateurs, no more so than standard commercial tubes.

Naturescent/Optima

The labeling of these lamps, which are essentially the same, has changed periodically. Optima was originally developed as a full spectrum range tube which would approximate natural light and permit the comparison of cloth samples under artificial illumination. It is probably more long lasting and is certainly more expensive than the same length and wattage commercial lamp.

Although rated a good general growth lamp, Optima has achieved its greatest triumph among Bromeliad growers who believe that it is the most effective in blooming their plants.

Vita-Lite

This lamp was produced in response to the theories of Dr. John Nash Ott which have been discussed in the section on Wave Length and Photosynthesis. A rather expensive tube, it has not been much used by light gardeners. However, here again, one group, the Cactus and Succulent growers, report good results.

THE CHOICE OF A FLUORESCENT LAMP

I do not wish to finish this discussion without giving the reader some suggestions regarding the right lamp to purchase for growing and blooming plants in the house.

For the average grower of a mixed collection of tropical flowering plants the standard commercial lamps and fixtures are economical and very efficient. G.E. or Westinghouse lamps in the following combinations are excellent: Warm White with Daylight or Natural, Deluxe Cool White with Daylight or Natural. Another good combination is Gro-Lux Wide Spectrum and Cool White.

The grower requiring greater intensities but not desiring to install the most expensive fixtures or highest wattages should use the Power Twist and Power Groove tubes.

Those needing maximum intensities can invest in superhigh output tubes.

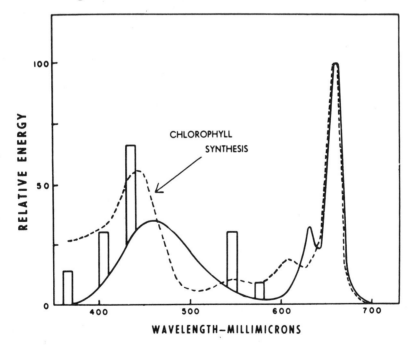

Spectral energy distribution for GRO-LUX fluorescent lamps, designed especially to enhance vegetative plant growth, in comparison to the spectral requirement for chlorophyll synthesis.

Courtesy GTE–Sylvania

The chart is a typical example of the way spectral energy distribution is represented. It shows the presence and the relative intensity of different wavelengths of light emitted by a fluorescent tube. The base line is expressed in millimicrons of a meter of wavelength, sometimes called nanometers. If Angstrom units are used, the figures are multiplied by ten, and 700 becomes 7000.

The solid curved line is that of the fluorescent tube. The dotted line represents the wavelengths and relative intensities that are most active in promoting photosynthesis of chlorophyll in plants. The true spectrum should be imagined as a series of extremely narrow vertical lines, concentrated in some areas and spaced apart in others. The curved lines express the areas of greatest concentration and connect them graphically. They do not indicate the gaps between the areas of concentration.

The vertical posts are an exaggerated expression of narrow bands of especially high intensity. Nothing in this chart tells you whether the tube emits much or little light.

The relationship between the fluorescent tube line and the chlorophyll synthesis line suggests that the lamp is nearly perfect for carrying on photosynthesis in plants. The following charts, in which the energy distribution does *not* appear to be particularly favorable to photosynthesis, represent types of tubes which have been found quite as satisfactory for plant growth and blooming in practice.

The following seven spectral energy distribution charts cover most of the colors of interest to light gardeners among commercial fluorescent tubes on the market.

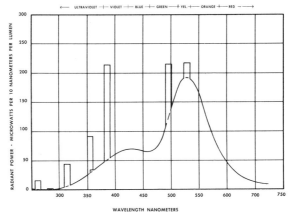

APPROXIMATE INITIAL SPECTRAL ENERGY DISTRIBUTION
COOL WHITE FLUORESCENT   Courtesy General Electric

The 40-watt Cool White tube shows its greatest strength in yellow and orange. It looks as if this would be a tube unsuitable for plant growth. However, with Warm White, it rates highest in lumens. One of the greatest authorities on light and plant growth in the country claims that Cool White is as good for growing plants as any other.

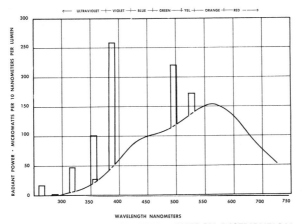

APPROXIMATE INITIAL SPECTRAL ENERGY DISTRIBUTION
COOL WHITE DELUXE FLUORESCENT   *Courtesy General Electric*

The distribution of a Cool White Deluxe tube shows the higher intensities in red from which it derives the Deluxe designation. This is a favorable distribution in the red ranges.

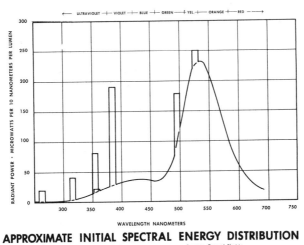

APPROXIMATE INITIAL SPECTRAL ENERGY DISTRIBUTION
WARM WHITE FLUORESCENT   *Courtesy General Electric*

The distribution of Warm White is even more in the yellow range, yet I have found this to be an excellent tube for blooming in combination with either Daylight or Natural.

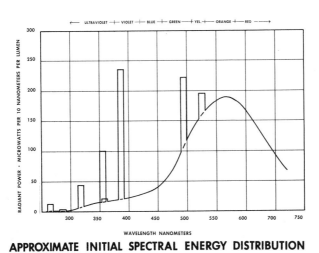

APPROXIMATE INITIAL SPECTRAL ENERGY DISTRIBUTION
WARM WHITE DELUXE FLUORESCENT   *Courtesy General Electric*

Like Deluxe Cool White, the graph for Deluxe Warm White favors the orange-red area of the spectrum.

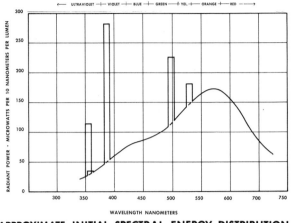

← ULTRAVIOLET —|← VIOLET —|← BLUE —|← GREEN —|← YEL.—|← ORANGE —|← RED — →

APPROXIMATE INITIAL SPECTRAL ENERGY DISTRIBUTION
SOFT WHITE NATURAL FLUORESCENT   *Courtesy General Electric*

Soft White–Natural has the same peaks as the others in the violet range and reaches more into the red than Warm White.

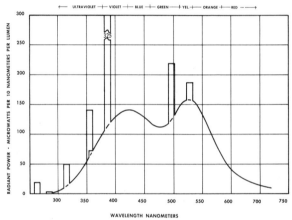

← ULTRAVIOLET —|← VIOLET —|← BLUE —|← GREEN —|← YEL.—|← ORANGE —|← RED — →

APPROXIMATE INITIAL SPECTRAL ENERGY DISTRIBUTION
DAYLIGHT FLUORESCENT   *Courtesy General Electric*

Only Daylight Fluorescent seems to have the strong violet-blue area which would match the orange-red graphs of the charts above.

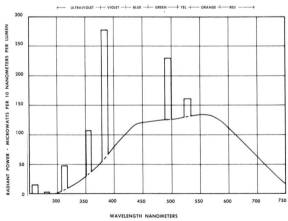

← ULTRAVIOLET —|← VIOLET —|← BLUE —|← GREEN —|← YEL.—|← ORANGE —|← RED — →

APPROXIMATE INITIAL SPECTRAL ENERGY DISTRIBUTION
CHROMA 50 FLUORESCENT   *Courtesy General Electric*

Chroma is a relatively new tube which has considerable promise as an inexpensive growth lamp.

THE SPECTRUM AND THE FLUORESCENT LAMP

Much of the confusion and error of light gardeners on the subject of the fluorescent lamp is connected with their mistaken notion that the spectrum is continuous. They think that a reddish tube occupies a solid block of wavelengths in the red range and that the same is true if it emits other colors. This fallacy has been fostered unintentionally by the kinds of charts and graphs supplied by manufacturers of fluorescent tubes. One type shows blocks of color of different heights, indicating intensity. The other employs a curved line which connects the points of greatest intensity in each color range.

No radiation known covers the whole range of the spectrum, not even the sun. Chemicals, such as the phosphors, radiate intensely in very narrow bands. A combination of phosphors, if represented as a spectrograph—an actual photograph of the spectrum—would be incomprehensible to the layman.

The charts and graphs therefore are only a schematic representation which is convenient and suggestive but by no means tells the whole story. The suggestion that any lamp approximates a complete visible spectrum is misleading.

Lamp Life and Efficiency

VARIATIONS IN THE LIGHT FROM TUBES

Lamp Length

Because about three inches at the ends of the tubes give out very little light and the greatest intensity is concentrated near the center, dropping off gradually toward the ends, longer tubes are more efficient than short ones. For its length the 48-inch tube is the most effective. Because it is sold in the greatest quantities manufacturers have put more research into its development.

Quality Control

Control of the phosphors and the coating of the tube is not perfect, so variations do exist between lamps of the same type produced at a different time or a different factory. The most effective controls are maintained on lumen output. Color, on the other hand, may change somewhat from tube to tube or between different lots. This is often quite visibly noticeable looking down a row of tubes.

Age

Standard medium bi-pin tubes have a rated life of about 9000 hours, or about one and a half years of 16 hours operation per day. Slimline tubes rate

12,000 hours, or about two years of operation. Nevertheless, light growers are urged by manufacturers to change their tubes every six to eight months.

I believe that a common cause of poor plant growth reported by amateurs is a reduction of illumination through an aging of the tubes. On the other hand, some growers have reported the use of tubes with great success right up to the time that they cease to light up. This contradiction is only apparent. When the light garden is equipped with an ample, or even excessive, amount of illumination, through the use of a large number of tubes, or more powerful ones, the reduction of effectiveness through age is often hardly noticeable. But when the light provided is barely sufficient any diminution will be damaging to the plants.

Replacing Lamps

I do not know of any study which has been made of the effect in practice of different systems of replacing tubes. There are three principal methods: (1) Starting with brand new tubes we keep them all burning for six to eight months and then replace them all with new lamps. (2) Starting with brand new tubes, after six to eight months we replace those which appear to have lost the most brilliance, and the others some months thereafter. (3) We replace lamps only when they burn out.

What we would like to do is maintain a high average level of illumination and, though there is a steady reduction of intensity using method (1), it is not very great. Method (2) gives us no control at all and (3) has the drawback that, toward the end of the life of the tubes, intensity is much lower than at the beginning. In practice they do not all go out at the same time so that method (3) is much the same as (2) with almost certain lower average illumination. Thus (1) is the best but none is perfect.

Whenever a number of tubes are replaced in the light garden, care should be taken to space installation at least a few days apart in order not to subject the plants to a drastic change of illumination without time for adjustment.

The following two charts show (1) the loss of intensity through time and (2) the rate of lamp mortality. They are taken from General Electric's bulletin TP-111-R.

With 100 percent performance in the first hours the lamps lose an average of approximately 5 to 12 percent intensity in the first 2000 hours. Toward the end of their rated lives of approximately 12,000 hours they have lost between 10 and 45 percent with an average of about 25 percent.

The chart indicates that up to 40 percent of the rated life of a tube there is little or no chance of its failing. At 80 percent of rated lamp life about 18 percent of the lamps burn out. Fifty percent give up the ghost at 100 percent, and 82 percent at 120 percent of rated lamp life.

This means that rated lamp life is an average. In a large batch some will burn out sooner than the rated lamp life and some later. This is a pretty big spread and accounts for the observed irregularity of failure.

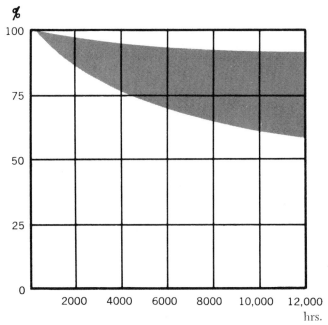

Loss of intensity through time.

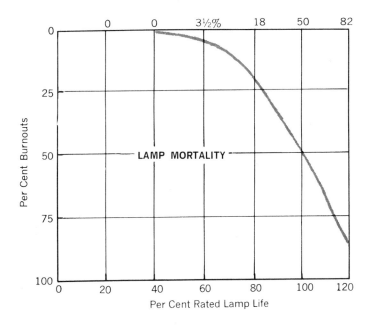

0   0   0   3½%   18   50   82

Per Cent Burnouts

LAMP MORTALITY

Per Cent Rated Lamp Life

The fewer starts to which the lamp is subjected the greater the expected life of the lamp. Frequent starts reduce its efficiency more rapidly.

INCANDESCENT BULBS

Unlike the fluorescent tube, which has a somewhat curvaceous energy chart in the various wavelengths, the incandescent bulb starts low in the violet-blue range and rises steadily on through green, yellow, and red into the far red. It is the only lamp at present which has sufficient far red. Some claim that only when the plant reacts to *both* red and far red is its flowering assured.

By themselves incandescent bulbs have two particular disadvantages. They are low in the blue range and much of their energy is given off as heat. In addition they give out far fewer lumens for the same wattage than a fluorescent lamp and cover a more restricted area with their radiation.

Unbeknownst to most light gardeners, a solution has existed for some time to part of the problem of heat from these bulbs. The ones we normally buy are rated 110–120 volts. Recently some well-informed soul and unsung hero brought to the attention of light growers a type of lamp, used in theatre marquees, which is much cooler. This bulb is rated 130 volts and is made in a number of wattages. It can only be bought from electrical specialty shops. Your electrician should help you order these bulbs.

Combinations

Whether the combination of incandescent with fluorescent lamps offers any substantial increase in efficiency is open to question. Some growers have found combinations of the lamps quite successful; others think that they have done just as well with growth lamps or combinations of commercial tubes, as discussed above.

Combination fixtures usually have two fluorescent tubes with two incandescent sockets between them. The wattage of the fluorescent and incandescent lamps is usually in a relation of one to one. If two 40-watt fluorescent lamps are used, two 40-watt bulbs are set between them.

I have often heard a light gardener report that he had instant success in blooming plants when he added two incandescent bulbs to his fluorescent fixture. Almost invariably he attributed the change to the specific action of the incandescent bulbs rather than to an increase in illumination. To his own thinking he still had only a two-tube fluorescent fixture with a modest addition—the bulbs being much smaller in size than the tubes. Actually he has doubled the wattage and has not asked himself the question: What would happen if I had four fluorescent tubes instead of two? The wattage would be the same as in the fluorescent-incandescent .combination but the illumination would be much greater. Personally I prefer four fluorescent tubes to two fluorescent tubes and two incandescent bulbs. I have never felt a lack of the latter in my growing.

Flood and Spot Lamps

The General Electric Cool Beam Flood Lamp is very useful for lighting large plants from a ceiling or giving side light to a fluorescent light garden. The front of the lamp is a glass filter which allows the cooler rays to pass through but reflects back the warmer ones. Because the heat generated is intense, ceramic sockets should be used. But the light reaching the plants is much cooler than the normal incandescent light of the same size, thus eliminating the risk of leaf burn. The spectrum does not suggest good growth efficiency but the lamps prove satisfactory with foliage plants. The lamp is available in 75-, 150-, and 300-watt models.

Other lamps made by GE with built-in reflectors are available in a range from 75 to 1000 watts. They are principally used in greenhouses to extend day length.

Duro-Test makes the Plant Lite bulb in 75 and 150 watts. These are claimed to have a good growth spectrum. Reports on their use have been favorable on indoor foliage plants and as an exterior light directed into a fluorescent light garden for added illumination. For example, an amateur growing orchids on shelves attached to the wall found that the addition of the Plant Lite to her fluorescent installation improved bloom.

Lucalox and Multivapor Lamps

Both of these lamps are used in street lighting. Multivapor lamps start at 400 watts and emit initially over 30,000 lumens. The 1500-watt lamps produce 132,500 lumens. Lucalox produces 25,000 lumens with 250 watts and 47,000 lumens with 400 watts.

These enormously powerful (and expensive) lamps have potential in the greenhouse and in very large room gardens. A combination of the two lamps gives a spectral distribution favorable to plant growth.

Chapter 4

THE FLUORESCENT FIXTURE

THE LAMPHOLDER

The lampholder is a metal box, slightly longer than tube length and wide enough to accommodate one or more tubes. The mounts, in which the pins of the tubes fit, project downward at either end.

The box is in two parts, the upper containing the ballast (see below), and the lower, called the pan, attached to it by means of two wing nuts.

THE BALLAST

The ballast is a kind of transformer enclosed in an oblong metal case, which serves the purpose of adjusting house current to the requirements of a fluorescent lamp. When the lampholder is in position for operation the ballast is attached off center to the upper surface of the box.

WIRING

When the pan of a new fluorescent fixture is unscrewed and removed you will find a label pasted inside giving directions for connecting the loose wires to the cable which will go to the house electrical outlet. Your extension cord or

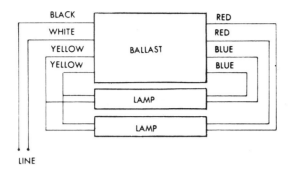

cable is passed into the box through one of the holes bored at either end. Follow the diagram in splicing the loose wires inside the box to your cable.

MOVING THE BALLAST

Usually the ballast is left in place. However, it is the chief source of heat in fluorescent fixtures. Where a large number of fixtures are hung close together there can be a considerable heat buildup harmful to plants. Should that be the case the ballast can be removed by unscrewing it from the box and extending the wires which attach it to the mounts. It can be moved up to 15 feet away without reducing its efficiency but should be stored in a metal box or attached to a metal plate where it cannot start a fire in case of a short circuit.

ATTACHING THE FIXTURE

The fixtures are made with several holes in different positions along the top and ends of the box. These facilitate attachment either by hanging from hooks or screwing to the undersurface of shelves. Additional holes can be drilled into the metal with an electric drill.

After the top of the box is in position you can screw the pan into place.

THE STARTER

The starter is a small metal cylinder which preheats the lamp electrodes. It fits into a hole at one end of the base of a lamp holder. There are two contact posts at one end. These are inserted into the hole, and the cylinder twisted part of a turn with pressure from below.

The starter is required equipment for most standard household size bipin fluorescent tubes with the designation "rapid start." Higher wattage tubes with single pins are mostly "instant start," requiring no starter, but they require different fixtures.

Starters usually have a life longer than that of a tube but not dependably so. When a tube less than a year old fails to light, the cause is almost always the failure of the starter.

Replacements can be bought at any electrical supply store. Always ask for the starter rating the same wattage as your tubes.

REFLECTORS

Because of their tubular shape half of the radiance from a fluorescent tube is emitted in the opposite direction to the area or object we wish to illuminate. There is no solution to this except through the use of reflectors.

Many types of commercial fixtures are equipped with reflectors attached to the lamp holder. They are usually angled or curved down on either side of the tube. The best reflective materials are highly reflective flat white paints—the MMM company makes an industrial paint which is rated 95 percent reflective—and machine polished aluminum.

When fixtures are hung under shelves in a position where separate reflectors cannot be used, the underside of the shelf should be painted with flat white.

Oddly enough, mirrors have been little used as reflectors with fluorescent lighting. They should be very efficient. Where cabinets are lined with the mirrors there should even be an increase in total illumination. Unfortunately nothing positive can be reported at present. The author intends to experiment with this intriguing possibility.

Chapter 5

THE LIGHTS AND
THE PLANTS

LIGHT REQUIREMENTS OF PLANTS

It may be stated as a general rule that foliage plants with low light requirements can be grown with 50 to 300 footcandles. They do very well in an office with banks of ceiling fluorescent lights.

Flowering plants require a minimum of 400 footcandles for 16 hours per day to bloom. This minimum is not absolute but a good guide figure. Most blooming houseplants will perform at 1000 footcandles. The availability of more light is, of course, an advantage and means that the tops of most plants need not be so close to the lights.

At the lower range of light requirement is *Saintpaulia* and some of the miniature Gesneriads. At about 800 footcandles Gloxinias will bloom as will most of the tropicals. With 1000 footcandles, providing other conditions are ideal, we can bloom annuals and other light loving plants.

These figures seem very low when we compare them with sunlight which climbs to over 10,000 footcandles on sunny days. But we are compensating in two ways—by increasing the day length and ensuring the plants light of the same intensity every day of the year.

Our problem, then, is to provide, if we can, equipment which will deliver 1000 footcandles to the plants.

The table below gives an approximation of the information we need. It was developed by the USDA at Beltsville, Maryland.

FOOTCANDLE ILLUMINATIONS OF COOL, WHITE FLUORESCENT LAMPS AT DIFFERENT DISTANCES

Distance from lamps (inches)	(1) Two lamps used for 200 hours	(2) Four lamps used for 200 hours	(3) Four lamps New
1	1100	1600	1800
2	860	1400	1600
3	680	1300	1400
4	570	1100	1260
5	500	940	1150
6	420	820	1000
7	360	720	900
8	330	660	830
9	300	600	780
10	280	560	720
11	260	510	660
12	240	480	600
18	130	320	420
24	100	190	260

This table is a most useful one for light growers. The columns list the footcandles of light reaching a plant first from two Cool White Fluorescent lamps used for 200 hours, second for four lamps used 200 hours, and third for four lamps when new.

The difference between using two and four lamps is striking. With two lamps, over 1000 footcandles are delivered only when the plants are within an inch of the lights, and the drop is considerable with 2 inches. Considering that the lamps will continue to lose efficiency with time, the average footcandles of light reaching the plants at 4 inches will be on the average no more than 500.

On the other hand, the plants are receiving more than 1000 footcandles of light at 4 inches distance under four lamps. On average they will receive about 900 footcandles at 4 inches.

The table does not tell us how far apart the lamps are, nor the position of the plants. But we must assume that the plants are centered under the lights and that the distance between the tubes is no more than 3 inches.

The special interest of this table is its calculation and demonstration of the reduction in light on both sides of a two-tube fixture with reflector. For instance, the bottom line shows that 6 inches in the center remain constant and that light drops off on either side. Closer to the lights, where the angle of the arc is narrower, the reduction is much more rapid within a short distance toward the sides. The table does not show what would happen to the light reaching the plants if placed toward either end of the tubes and to the side. Obviously the figures would be lower. These figures represent the maximum.

The USDA table shows lower footcandle ratings directly under the center than does the G.E. table. The latter may be a bit high, but part of the difference is accounted for by the G.E. table being of a later date when lamps had been somewhat improved.

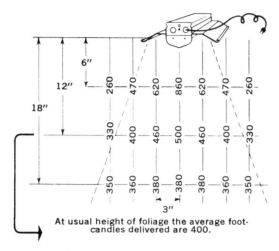

At usual height of foliage the average foot-candles delivered are 400.

PROVIDING ENOUGH LIGHT

From both the previous tables it is apparent that we do provide enough light for blooming plants even with 48-inch tubes with reflectors. But this presumes the use of Cool White with approximately 6400 lumens combined output and that the plants are within a couple of inches of the tubes at all times. Also the drop-off in light with two tubes is quite drastic with the result that foliage at the bottom of a plant may well have very insufficient light.

Thus a two-tube arrangement proves to be just adequate and, because of the narrow area of maximum intensity, only for a relatively few kinds of plants.

INCREASING THE NUMBER OF TUBES

When four Cool White tubes are used with reflectors, delivering some 12,500 lumens, the situation improves considerably. The two additional tubes contribute light to the center, and the center contributes to the sides. About 1000 footcandles are available 6 inches from the tubes. The situation is now much more comfortable for the plants as they have room for maneuvering and the lower foliage will receive adequate light.

The overlapping effect of the lights will extend as far as the arc from the reflectors intersects—narrower near the tubes and broader toward the bottom— until the point is reached where there is only a small reduction of light at 12 or 15 inches from the tubes. As we increase the number of tubes and raise the level, more area is covered and, with more overlapping, higher footcandles are achieved. When the ceiling of a room is completely covered with fluorescent tubes with 6-inch centers, the overlapping is continuous and the plants at floor level receive about the same amount of light at their tops as at pot level.

WITH GROWTH TUBES

The growth (Gro-Lux, Vita-Lite, etc.) and Deluxe tubes emit about 30 percent less visible light than Cool White and Warm White. Theoretically growth tube radiation is more effective for plant growth but this is not confirmed by results with blooming houseplants. It is particularly noticeable that tall plants lose their lower leaves when they are grown under lamps emitting fewer lumens. In order to provide plants with comparable amounts of illumination, growth tubes must be placed closer together than Cool White and Warm White lamps.

WITH HIGH OUTPUT TUBES

Because they emit so much more radiation High Output and Super High Output tubes can be suspended farther above the plants, allowing much more variation in their height. The emissions from the individual tubes in a row overlap more the higher they are set. But the maximum effect is not attained unless the length of the row and the number of tubes are considerable. Unless you have ample space, much of the effectiveness of HO tubes is lost.

Both in terms of original cost and higher electrical bills, an installation of HO tubes of sufficient size involves a major expense. Because of the greater heat output ballasts must be removed and exhaust fans installed. However, those who wish to install room gardens providing maximum lighting conditions for such plants as Orchids and Bromeliads may feel that the large investment is justified.

PLACING PLANTS UNDER THE LIGHTS

One of the most persistent questions from neophyte light gardeners is "How far away from the lights should I place my plants?" It would resolve many doubts if we had some cut-and-dried answer to offer. Unfortunately there are too many variables to arrive at any precise answers. We do know the foot-candle requirements of a few houseplants but not for most of them. And even if we had them all, the answers would be misleading.

Some of the factors to be considered are: the kind of fluorescent lamp, its length and wattage, its age in terms of use, the period of illumination in summer and in winter. Plants themselves are variable in their reactions, even the same species or cultivar. Also every home and every room is more or less humid, warm or cold, drafty or airless, possessing clear or polluted air. All of these have a bearing on the amount and kind of light required for blooming.

I would like to remind those who have ever had a flower garden that, though plants are more or less sun loving, successful placement is often a matter of lengthy experimentation. And the location in which a plant ends up by doing best often conforms not at all with the rules laid down in garden books. The same applies to indoor light gardening. In my own growing I am constantly moving plants around under the lights to find the spot where they will flourish.

A small shift up or down, toward the center or toward the end of the tubes, may make a world of difference in bloom, for reasons I am unable to discover. Plants that are resting need less light and can be placed toward the ends, making room for those whose blooming is imminent. In winter and summer, temperature change may be as important as illumination. It is cooler away from the ballast which is off center in the fixture.

Space under the lights is almost always limited due to our inevitable desire to grow as many plants as possible. We cannot give them all the best positions at the same time. Favor will be given to those we are most anxious to bloom. The center area will be reserved for them. Plants not yet ready, foliage plants, and those which we have previously found do well with little light, will be placed at the ends.

Many species suffer leaf burn if they are too close to the tubes. Others, which appear equally tender, can touch them without damage. Some will raise their leaves toward the light when they are too far away but this is by no means a dependable indication. Proper placement of plants will occur when you give them daily attention, watch the nature of their growth and bud formation, and gradually learn their likes and dislikes.

More often than not I have found that being close, within 4 inches of the lights, is beneficial when plants are recalcitrant. But this rule will not hold with those plants which suffer from heat in summer.

Give your plants a minimum of 16 hours of light indoors. If you still have trouble blooming, be sure to remember to check the age of your lamps. If they are over the eight month mark, replacing them usually helps.

The loss of light at short distances influences the ideal specifications for a light garden plant. Obviously one which is tall, with numerous lower leaves, is likely to suffer. The top leaves will grow well while the lower ones will be deprived. Therefore we prefer the plants to be compact and broad topped.

Plants *can* touch the lamps—not all of them, of course, but some of the best of our houseplants do not suffer any damage. And maximum illumination is needed in so many instances that it should be tried. If the leaves start to brown it is evident that the particular plant cannot endure the heat.

EFFECTIVE AREA COVERED BY A FLUORESCENT TUBE

The usual formula given is the length of the tube and 3 inches on either side. Thus, a 40-watt tube will serve an area 48 inches long and 6 inches wide plus the width of the tube. For blooming plants the channel of effectiveness is certainly narrower. If we have two tubes, say an inch apart, they will cover relatively less area by the above definition but be more effective within the range.

In building light gardens with tubes 48 inches long or more it is a good idea to allow 6 inches of space beyond the ends of the tubes. This is seldom usable space for blooming but very convenient for placing plants that are resting.

If large batteries of tubes are installed—say 20 or more in a row—the plants can grow farther from the lights and, because of the overlap of the beams, the lower parts of taller plants will be adequately illuminated.

Photoperiodism

In the culture and especially the blooming of many plants their photo-periodic responses are of the utmost importance. Photoperiodism is the reaction of a plant to light duration. The specific effect of light duration which concerns us here is blooming. For if certain plants do not receive the correct number of hours of light and darkness they will neither set buds nor bloom.

Because the withdrawal of light at night is presumed to be absolute while days may be sunny or cloudy, night length has been chosen as the criterion. The plants also draw this distinction. They will tolerate alternations of sunny and cloudy days with little effect on blooming but if there is only a minor interruption of darkness they can immediately be affected and fail to produce buds. The sensitivity in this regard is such that for some plants a few minutes of illumination at night may be sufficient to inhibit bloom—a table lamp in a living room or the light shining through a window from a streetlamp.

Very little is known so far about this phenomenon but it has been definitely established that plants are divided into three categories. Some are *short* night plants which require long hours of light to flower. Others are *indeterminate*—they are relatively indifferent to the photoperiod. Finally there are *long* night plants which will bloom only if the day length is drastically diminished and the night is uninterrupted.

Since the light gardener generally maintains a day length of 14 to 16 hours, the indeterminate and short night plants present no difficulty. It is with the long-nighters that he has trouble. Whenever a plant, which is otherwise adapted to indoor culture, refuses to set bud or bloom it is suspect of being a long night plant. We are finding out that there are many of these, though fortunately, not a majority.

Examples of long night plants are the Christmas Cactus and Kalanchoes. The first can be grown with long days of 16 hours but to trigger bloom these must be followed by 8 weeks of 9-hour days. Kalanchoes must receive 4 weeks of short days but once buds are set day length becomes unimportant. Some other long night plants are Asters, Chrysanthemums, and Poinsettias.

The foliage species Begonias and their cultivars have always been considered indeterminate plants. Recent experiments by Jack Golding of the Begonia Society reveal marked differences in the photoperiod required for flowering. Undoubtedly we will find that the secret of blooming many other plants under lights will lie in an understanding of this factor.

Short or long night is not the only factor in the equation. From the above example and Mr. Golding's experience we know that some plants can be released from the long night after budding, others not. Also the short day length may be required after a definite period of longer day length, in other words, must take place at a particular time of year. Certain plants will start to set buds at any time that we lengthen the nights.

The light gardener may well be perfectly happy with his repertoire of long day plants. What can he do, though, if he becomes interested in some family which has many long night members? Most foliage Begonia growers are not too much concerned if their plants do not bloom in the house even though they know that in a greenhouse, where seasonal day length prevails, they do. But still it comes as a shock that he can achieve bloom only by varying the night length under lights. Although the photoperiodism of only a few of the enormous family of orchids is definitely known, it is almost certain that a considerable number are long night plants. Nobody has bothered about the question with Gesneriads (except Kohleria and a couple of others) but here, too, it seems that a number have this difficult requirement.

At least in the present state of knowledge all solutions to this question are exclusive. You just can't raise a mixed collection of long and short night plants together. The indeterminate ones generally do well at the same day length as the long night plants (although, this, as we see, is beginning to be questioned) but the long night plants must be separated.

If we install an astronomical timer (see page 39) we can mimic the day length changes of the seasons. In that case most of our long day plants will stop blooming when the days become shorter. There is one thing to be said for this method, though. Many of our long day plants stop blooming in any event after a certain time, as much from a reaction to calendar time as to photoperiod. Even in the present state of light gardening knowledge of plants, a large repertoire can be bloomed in this way.

Those who introduce long night plants to their long day gardens will have to find some means of segregating them every night for a period. Removing the plant to a dark room, covering it with an opaque material, or some such device is the only solution. Theoretically it is possible to put two levels of a shelf light garden on different time cycles. But one would have to be thoroughly sealed against light from the other during the period of darkness. In a cellar garden it is possible, of course, to divide the area up into separate rooms having gardens with different photoperiods. Light gardeners who have the means to do so should be encouraged. That is one way of finding out at last the true photoperiodic reactions of our many houseplants.

Two Sensational Breakthroughs:
The Twenty-Four-Hour Day and Continuous Bloom

Fluorescent light permits us to grow and bloom plants anywhere in the home without sunlight. This certainly rates among the major achievements in the history of horticulture. But even this is not the whole story, and the two other discoveries about fluorescent light which I discuss below are additional important breakthroughs.

THE TWENTY-FOUR-HOUR LIGHT DAY

It has always been assumed that plants, like people, had to rest at night. I don't think anybody went to the trouble of proving it but rather that it was taken for granted as a law of nature, applying to all the higher organisms. The common viewpoint was that plants subjected to continuous light would sicken because they were not permitted to carry on biological processes which were assumed to occur only at night.

Within the last five years brave souls took the chance of subjecting their plants to continuous light. Lo and behold, their plants prospered. The George J. Ball Company of West Chicago, Illinois, started to grow plants from seed that way. The result was a considerable reduction in the length of time needed to grow young plants for nurseries.

A couple of years back the manager of a very large orchid nursery asked me whether I thought that orchid seedlings could be grown with 24-hour light. He guessed it was possible but was not yet sure enough to risk thousands of valuable plants. He took the plunge and since then he has done it with success and shortened the growth period to maturity.

In New York City a light gardener has been raising Marigolds and Petunias by the hundred with full day length light. They bloom just as well as in the garden, and the plants are just as sturdy.

Within a few years we should know the full range of cultivated plants which will bloom with continuous light. In the meanwhile anybody who wants to grow young plants more rapidly, and without the benefit of natural light, can do so.

CONTINUOUS BLOOM

It is a commonly held theory that a plant can "bloom itself to death." In every instance where this has been asserted, experience has shown in the long run that bloom does not kill a plant.

Even more tenacious has been the idea that all plants must rest after a burst of blooming. Our respectably long list of plants which are in constant flower is sufficient evidence to the contrary.

The gardener in the north expects his plants to die off or go dormant in the fall. With a house in the country he has enough nature around him to feel no great impatience with the lack of plants or flowers. The greenhouse grower has so many plants that something is always in bloom. But it can be imagined what a boon it is for the apartment dweller with few plants to have some which never stop blooming, especially throughout the winter.

All the plants which light gardeners now grow for continuous flowering took a seasonal rest period in their original homes. The cause of the change in behavior can only be guessed, but the guess seems logical. I assume that these plants are accustomed to some change in environment taking place which triggers partial or complete dormancy. Whether this is due to temperature, light, humidity, day length, or something else I do not know. And since many plants continue to go dormant under lights, one or more of the possible influences must still exist in the light garden. What is reasonable to believe is that the stability of conditions indoors under lights is such as to "fool" some plants into continuing the unbroken process of budding and blooming. These are the Miracle Plants we describe in a later section.

Timers

Other than the fluorescent fixture and the tubes, the only significant piece of equipment needed for the lighting installation itself is a timer.

Timers are electric clocks with an exposed dial which are connected midway between the house wiring and the cable leading to the fluorescent fixture. On the face of the dial are two movable levers which can be set at any time of day or night. When the timer is activated one lever will cause a connection in the current so that the lights go on and the other switches them off. If you set the clock for On at 8:00 A.M. and Off at 12:00 P.M. you are assured of a 16-hour light day for your plants without any attention.

In buying a timer be sure that the rated wattage is 10–20 percent greater than the total wattage of all the tubes and other equipment (fans, humidifiers) which may be attached to it.

If you want your fluorescent light day to match the seasons—long summer days and short winter days—you can purchase an astronomical timer. These gadgets are still used to turn street lights and billboard signs on and off according to the time of year and the length of the night. The timer is set, according to directions, at the day of the year and time of day when it is started. From then on it adjusts itself daily to normal day length and night length summer and winter. Paragon Time Control, Three Rivers, Wisconsin, is a major producer of these instruments.

HOW TO MAKE LIGHT GARDENS WITHOUT GLARE

While providing growth light for plants, fluorescent tubes also emit intense illumination which is a visual disturbance, interfering with the enjoyment of the plants, unless it is shielded in some way. To have a garden which is the most blindingly lighted area of a room at night is annoying and causes some people to give up the whole idea.

When a tabletop unit is provided with a well-constructed reflector, one that is turned down vertically along the edge, the light source is not visible from a standing position, although it is only partly shielded when sitting. The same applies to reflector units set in bookshelves or a plant stand at 4 feet above the floor or less. However, when the tubes are 5 or 6 feet high, 6-inch valances are necessary on the front of the shelf. Box gardens with broad frames also close in the source of light quite adequately.

PARAWEDGE LOUVERS

Recently, a means has been discovered of shielding a source of light above eye level which is even more efficient though not yet applicable to small units. It makes possible large hanging batteries of lamps over floor gardens, complete ceilings of fluorescent lighting, nonglare spot lighting, and many other special situations using powerful light sources.

The new material is the parawedge louver. It is a plastic crate or waffle, like that recommended for lining light garden trays, except that the sides of the squares are molded in a mathematically calculated parabolic curve and then metalized to a mirror finish. It is manufactured in 2-by-4-foot and 3-by-4-foot sheets slightly more than ½ inch thick.

When set below fluorescent lights the louver causes the light source to become invisible except when directly under it and looking up into it. At an angle it appears to be black. Thus a black ceiling can be supplied to a room which is flooded with illumination. Racks of fluorescent tubes in a frame, hung over a floor garden, can be lifted above eye level while lighted without causing glare.

This result cannot be achieved with ordinary light diffusers, and plastic sheet reduces efficiency considerably.

Parawedge insets are also available for spotlights. They are fitted on the interior of the cone and eliminate glare beyond a 45-degree angle.

Chapter 6

ARTIFICIAL LIGHT
GARDENS

PREFABRICATED UNITS

The number and variety of prefabricated light gardens on the market have grown rapidly in the last few years. From a utilitarian point of view these are quite adequate but we have not yet seen one which is both attractive and efficient. The cause for this inadequacy is, I think, that all of them are turned out by fixture manufacturers or fabricators. No real thought has been given to making them match the furniture of the average home, to say nothing of an attempt at elegance in form or finish. That is why the sale of these units has been relegated to hardware and electrical fixture stores and houseplant supply mail-order houses. This means that the would-be indoor light grower cannot find equipment in furniture stores or the furniture departments of department stores where he would expect to shop for such an item. It means, very often, that he must buy from a catalog, judging the product only by description and a small photograph. Light gardening equipment will become truly popular when it becomes furniture for the home rather than a gadget for growing plants. Before this text is published the transition may already have been made. But until styled equipment is available, anyone who is handy with tools is far better off

41

to design his own unit, while those who cannot will have to be satisfied with one or another of the products described below and illustrated on pages 42–50.

TABLETOP UNITS

A number of manufacturers produce simple fluorescent light units with reflectors and stands. They are mostly two-tube and come in the 24-, 36-, and 48-inch lengths. Some are adjustable in respect to height, and some are also equipped with trays. The less expensive models are unfinished metal while others are enameled. A so-called Fruit Ripener, made of plastic, consists of a circle line fluorescent tube over a shallow bowl and will accommodate just one medium-size plant. Another model which is larger and of metal provides considerably more space. However, a circular design accommodates few plants.

These units are adequate for the beginner and are not costly. A coat of enamel on the outer surfaces will tone them into the color scheme of a room. Not being very high, the reflectors usually shield the glare fairly well at tabletop level except when seen from a sitting position. Since we do sit in rooms where these units are set on tables it becomes a tussle between the discomfort of the bright lights and the pleasure of the plants. This is a handicap of all prefab units at present.

As growth fixtures they are efficient. In accordance with the general rule of tube efficiency, the longer fixtures are the most effective. These sturdy and dependable units can be used wherever esthetic considerations are secondary.

TABLETOP UNIT

This is a standard two-tube fixture with reflector. There are a number of similar models on the market. The drawing shows the arrangement of the tubes and sockets for incandescent bulbs which are usually not necessary. The fixture is adjustable for height. Position and depth of a suitable tray are also shown.

Drawing by Helen Matsubu

This two-tube, 24-inch tabletop unit, a product of Sylvania, has a gold-colored reflector and a black bent metal stand. By means of the knobs at either end the reflector can be raised or lowered some eight inches.

Photo courtesy GTE–Sylvania

A two-tube, 48-inch adjustable unit with simplified metal stand, finished in black, is shown with some of the supplies for a small light garden. These include a timer, plastic and peat pots, plastic trays, small self-watering trays, fertilizer, a large bag of milled sphagnum moss, labels, and even plants in various stages from seedling to bloom.

Photo courtesy Park Seed Company

MULTISHELF GARDENS

The multishelf garden consists of two to five shelves with two to four two-tube fixtures, usually provided with reflectors. The supporting structure consists either of four metal standards or two, one at each end, which are bent in an inverted **U** or **V**. The fixtures are either supported on the frame or suspended from shelving or metal crosspieces. One manufacturer uses four metal tubes at the corners and shaped wooden clamps on both the long and short sides. The trays fit on one set and the lights on the other. When adjustments in height are desired it is only necessary to loosen the wing nuts and raise or lower the clamps. Many of the units are not adjustable. Those which are not equipped with casters can be fitted with them. The price of these units varies according to size and sturdiness.

Standard equipment is two 36-inch or 48-inch tubes for each shelf. The top shelf can be utilized as a growth level in some units by extensions of the frame from which lighting fixtures are suspended. A few are provided with a pair of incandescent light sockets between the tubes of each fixture.

At the present time only two of the products are of sturdy, long-lasting construction. I presume that the lack of esthetic appeal has retarded demand for the more expensive ones. In most instances people who want larger gardens build their own or purchase the less expensive equipment. This will change, I believe, when more attractive structures are available.

The Tube Craft Company's Floracart was one of the earliest and has proved among the most reliable of multitier units. Sturdiness and mobility are features. The trays are 18 inches wide.

Photo courtesy The Tube Craft Company

STEEL MULTITIER SHELVING

This Hirsh shelving is described in the text and is the same as the one the Metropolitan Chapter of the Indoor Light Gardening Society adapted for its exhibits. The metal unit continues to function in the author's plant room. Note that the 36-inch shelving can be placed at different levels and that the center area has been reserved for small supplies. The installation is purely utilitarian and should be used in a growing rather than a living area.

Photo by the author

The Gro-Cart, made by The Green House, is quite similar to the Floracart. The reflectors can be adjusted more easily.

Photo courtesy The Green House

WARDIAN CASES

The Wardian case was invented by Nathaniel Bagshaw Ward (1791–1868), an English botanist, principally for the purpose of preserving plants during transportation. It is a covered glass terrarium in which plant and soil moisture are precisely balanced. Provided the case is maintained in an environment which gives sufficient but not excessive light and heat, plants can grow within it for long periods without any attention whatsoever. The case quickly became popular for growing houseplants and the name is used for any large terrarium.

When fluorescent lights are suspended above or laid on top of the glass of a Wardian case, one of the requirements of the system is violated. Heat from the lamps is excessive, especially during warm spells in summer, and adequate ventilation must be provided. Homemade terrariums have a glass pane on top which can be removed completely if necessary. But manufactured Wardian cases often have sliding glass panels on the front of the case which give far less effective ventilation (warm air rises). One model has a permanent cover and relies on a thermostat to turn off the lights when temperature rises to the setting.

A recent model is supplied with an interior fan, thermostat, and humidistat, and a controlled supply of CO_2. The equipment does not seem to function efficiently for growth and the CO_2 additive is, if anything, unsuitable since the indoor gardener does not normally desire rapid growth in his plants.

These Wardian cases are relatively high priced and can easily be reproduced in essentials for far less money by using standard aquarium equipment and lighting fixtures as described in the section in terrariums (pages 72–80).

LIGHTED WARDIAN CASE

The glass tank is lighted by a two-tube 48-inch fixture with reflector which rests on the glass. Handsome but not very adaptable and inclined to overheat. Overlapping glass panes in front slide apart.

Photo courtesy Emerson Industries

SEED STARTER

For those who have hundreds of seeds to start for planting out of doors the most efficient unit on the market is the Park Seed Starter. This is a metal unit with 2 × 4 foot shelves which can be stacked as high as one can reach. A five-shelf unit has 32 square feet of growing area. It is also ideal for the growing of large numbers of cuttings.

The Garden Case is a partially controlled environment. This is a well built import but rather low on illumination.

Photo courtesy Shaffer's Tropical Gardens

SEED STARTER

The seed starter accommodates several hundred small pots and is efficient in producing seedlings for outdoor planting. It is very compact and efficient but the trays are too near each other to be used as a decorative light garden. Additional trays with lighting fixtures can be added to any height desired.

Drawing by Helen Matsubu

BUILD-THEM-YOURSELF

It is far more satisfactory in every respect to make your own light garden. The process can be as simple or complicated as you desire or your skill permits. The cost is considerably less, and the result at least as efficient as the presently available finished products.

The Components

1. One or more tube fluorescent fixtures with or without a reflector.
2. A shelf, frame, or ceiling to which the fixture is attached or from which it is suspended.
3. Trays usually filled with plastic crate* or pebbles.
4. An automatic on-and-off timer.

This is all that is required to start with. Nobody should be daunted by the mechanical or electrical problems, as they are of the simplest. Although none of the local shops may carry equipment specifically manufactured for the light gardener, this is no major stumbling block. Standard commercial fluorescent fixtures will do very well. As for the horticultural materials, the variety stores and garden supply centers usually carry them.

The Lamp Garden

A fluorescent desk lamp makes a small light garden at low cost and without any trouble at all. These usually carry a single tube and have a reflector. The flexible stand is an advantage in adjusting the distance of the light from the plants.

Purchase a tray which is about the length of the lamp and 8 inches to a foot in width, fill it with pebbles or plastic crate—and you are in business. The range of blooming plants which you can work with is small, of course. But you can have color with the small Gesneriads and a number of other plants with relatively low light needs and compact growth. A good many miniatures can be arranged in this small space.

UNDERSHELF GARDENS

The principle of the undershelf garden is exactly the same as for multitier units or cabinet gardens. I consider it in a different category only because installation of the equipment is made under existing structures—kitchen cabinets, bookshelves, end tables, coffee tables, or any other furniture with suitable space below which can be converted into a light garden area.

The fluorescent lamp holder always has holes for attachment and for ventilation of the ballast. When the bottom plate, which fits around the sockets, is unscrewed, the interior wiring and the ballast are laid bare. The metal box into which they fit has some small open holes on the upper surface. By means of

---

* Plastic crate is the name for sheets of plastic ½ inch to ¾ inches thick in an openwork waffle design used as a light diffuser and available from plastic supply retailers. It can be cut to size with a light saw.

UNDER SHELF HERB GARDEN

A simple two-tube 24-inch reflector unit is hung by S hooks from screw eyes in the bottom of the cabinet. Many herbs grew well under the lights and the tomato plant fruited and ripened. Although hardly a meal for the family it's a good stunt and the tomatoes are decorative. Flowering plants will do as well.

Photo by The New York Times

these you can screw the lamp holder into any overhead surface. After the lamp holder has been fixed to the shelf, the bottom plate is screwed back on.

The lamp holder usually has two holes at the top of either end plate. A number of other almost complete circles have been cut lower down on the end plates and in the upper surface of the lamp holder. They can be punched out with a hammer and screwdriver.

These holes permit various methods of attachment. For instance, you can suspend the fixture rather than fixing it permanently to the overhead surface. The combination of eye screws and S hooks or chain serves to make the fixture adjustable in height.

If the undersurface to which the lamp is attached is painted white, a reflector is not absolutely necessary, though it always gives more efficient lighting. Should neither solution be acceptable it would be advisable to invest in tubes with built-in reflectors.

When shelving is supported by metal bracket arms, the supporting chains can be hooked over them or through holes drilled in the brackets.

MULTITIER GARDENS

When undershelf gardens are built into existent stacked shelving such as bookcases, étagères, or metal storage frames, the procedure is exactly the same as for a single undershelf unit.

Simple metal frame shelving comes in many sizes and weights. It is delivered knocked down and is assembled by means of screws and bolts. Usually these units are adjustable in increments of 1 inch.

Shelving can also be made of wood using 2 × 4 uprights and crosspieces.

52

DESIGNER'S UNDER SHELF GARDEN

Shelving in a room corner has been covered with white opaque vinyl. The vertical end pieces are thick sheets of acrylic resin. The installation was designed by Mr. Crosby Smith for Mrs. Jane Maurice of New York. Mrs. Maurice is particularly successful with orchids. The apartment is air conditioned and a humidifier faces the garden during the day and is removed at night. Paphiopedilums, Phalaenopsis, and Ascocendas are a few of the orchids she blooms successfully and continuously.

Photo by Marc Neuhof

A community light gardening project in Village View Apartments, New York City. Tenants built the units and maintain the extensive seeding program which provides decorative area plantings in summer and house plants in winter.

Photo by James Fryer

Those who have the equipment can do it with pipe and standard plumbing joints. Anyone who is able and willing to tackle this kind of construction certainly needs no specific instructions.

Heavier built units belong rather in a cellar than a living room. Even the lightweight metal shelving is not very attractive but it is not ponderous and, painted to match walls or furniture, can be relatively unobtrusive.

Following are the specifications for the room divider or wall garden built by members of the Metropolitan Chapter of the Indoor Light Gardening Society of America, Inc., for their display at the International Flower Show in 1970 and reused, with changes, in the Gimbel's Flower Show of 1971. It is probably the first light garden furniture of its kind for it combines the use of light gardens with other spaces devoted to books or objets d'art. Although only the front was left open it could serve just as well as a room divider. The beauty of the installation attracted considerable attention from the public and the press. The same principles of construction and installation can be used with any kind of shelving and with any suitable materials.

The wall garden looks quite different in the International Flower Show display of the Indoor Light Gardening Society. The two sections have been arranged at right angles.

MULTITIER LIGHT GARDEN CART

This sturdy unit is much like the Floracart, made by the Tube Craft Company, and the Gro-Cart from The Green House. The latter has the reflectors suspended by chains. Both have casters. The two 48-inch tubes provided with each fixture are inadequate for light-loving plants. They are both well made and long lasting, though hardly beautiful.

Drawing by Helen Matsubu

WALL GARDEN

Two 6-foot shelving units have been set side by side and faced with plywood valances. Designed by F. Vance Fazzino, this handsome light garden, library, and display wall was the first of its kind. It has been widely publicized and those who have seen it in the author's home have been enchanted by it. Future years will see the adaptation of light gardens to many furniture designs. Ultimately these will become an integral feature of interior design. *Photo by* The New York Times

The photograph shows a light metal shelving unit of a type available in most major department stores. This one is 72 inches high, 72 inches long, and 12 inches deep. It consists of 36-inch-long components which lock together. The upright standards are 72 inches high and come apart in the middle so that the unit can be converted easily into two 36-inch-high sections. The two lengths of the standards lock together by means of a fitted insert.

The 36-inch shelving is attached to the standards by a screw and triangular metal clip which fits into the corners and gives rigidity to the structure. The standards are provided with holes for screws and clips at intervals of 1 inch, permitting numerous arrangements of the shelving. Of course shelving must be carried across top and bottom, but in between it can be set at any level. The unit is shipped knocked down along with hardware and instructions. Assembly is quick and simple.

The bare metal frame can be used as a light garden by attaching fluorescent fixtures under the shelves. But first it is advisable to apply an extra coat of paint to all shelf surfaces. Finish the undersides with two coats of highly reflective white paint. Surfaces on which pots or trays are to stand need waterproofing. Epoxy paint is expensive but very good for the purpose.

Because the 36-inch-long shelves have a turned down edge for reinforcement, 24-inch fixtures will fit snugly against the undersurfaces while fixtures longer than 36 inches must be hung a bit lower to pass under them. Thirty-six-inch and 72-inch fixtures are a rather tight fit, allowing no leeway for wiring and installation of siding for the unit. I have used 48-inch fixtures for a utility light garden but for the display unit, where greater flexibility in shelf arrangement was desirable, 24-inchers were chosen. Other types of shelving (one-piece wood for instance) do not present this problem and the fixtures can be attached flush to the bottoms of the shelves.

In the display, two of these units were set side by side so that they filled 12 feet of wall. This created a more decorative effect but a similar design works very well with a single unit. You must first decide just which areas should be assigned to light gardens and which to other purposes. In our plan, consideration was given to the placing of furniture near the unit. If an upholstered chair or a table partially hides one of the squares of shelving near the floor it is far better to use it for books or storage.

The light gardens, each 36 inches long, were distributed in an irregular pattern. Height was an arbitrary esthetic choice. Fourteen shelf spaces were used; seven in each unit. There were four gardens in one and three in the other. Any number of other combinations is possible.

The holes provided in the lamp holder can be used for attachment. However, it was easier in this case to drill two holes at either end and matching holes in the shelf, and then attach by means of nuts and bolts. The pan of the fixture was then screwed on.

When several light fixtures are used, the wires of each must be extended to reach a multiple plug fixture placed anywhere on the frame as inconspicuously as possible. As we wanted the two shelving units to be independent for future use and rearrangement, each one was provided with a four-way plug fixture and wires from the individual fixtures were extended to reach them. The two multiple plugs were connected by a cable, and one of them attached by an extension cord to the timer connected to the nearest wall plug. The seven gardens together used only about 300 watts.

The unit at the show was faced with wood in order to shield the glare from the fixtures and make a more presentable appearance. The directions given below apply to just one 72-by-72-inch unit and should be doubled for the 12-foot wall unit. The following lumber should be cut very carefully to size. Three-eighth-inch plywood was used throughout.

Six 2-by-36-inch pieces are used to mask the standards. You can use 2-by-72-inch pieces if you do not wish to provide for separating the two 72-by-36-inch sections. By using 36-inch strips you can always convert the 12-foot double unit into four low ones or one high (72-inch) and two low (36-inch) ones.

All the strips between the pieces masking the standards are 33 inches long to allow for the strips masking the outer standards, overlapping more inward than outward, providing framing for the sides of the unit and just sufficient overlap on the outside to cover the thickness of the siding. The different widths of the valances vary according to their height in the unit. They will effectively shield the glare of the lights for a person sitting in a normal chair or couch a few feet away from the unit.

Two 2-inch-by-33-inch pieces run along the bottom, at floor level between the standards.

Two 7-by-33-inch valances attach to the top shelf of the unit.

Count the number of shelves between the top and bottom shelving. The total will be the number of valances still required.

Shelves without fixtures should have 5-inch-wide valances.

Shelves with fixtures higher than 4 feet from the floor should be 6 inches wide.

Shelves with fixtures below 4 feet from the floor can be 5 inches wide.

ATTACHING THE FACING

In setting the height of the valances in relation to the shelving, follow this rule: Where shelves are to be used for books or display objects, the valance top should be flush with the top of the shelf. Where the shelf is to be used for pots or trays, the valance should project ½ inch above the top of the shelf.

Attach the strips for the standards and valances by means of flat-headed screws. An electric drill will pierce wood and metal easily. To set the wood strips in place, start with the strip for the center standard which should have exactly the same overhang on both sides and be perfectly straight. Then attach the valances tightly to the center strip and, finally, fit the vertical end strips snugly to them. Now you can paint, stain, or otherwise finish the wood, plug in the wall socket, and have a light garden.

Two methods of sheathing the back and sides of the unit were used in the two shows. At the International Flower Show the front facing was stained walnut and the other sides were filled with panels of thin plywood. The front, or visible side of these panels was painted with pastel colors and white, each display or garden area being assigned one of four colors. At the Gimbel's Show the back and sides were made of thin wallboard painted inside with Kraftex, a sandy surfaced paint, in pure white and the facing was in flat black. In this latter treatment the plants and display objects were the only spots of color and the effect was most dramatic.

There are a few other matters worth noting. For instance, the display areas will seem very dark if the valances are too short over the gardening areas. This is caused by the glare, and the moment the excess illumination is tamed the display areas will seem to be lighter. In the home very short nails can be attached at intervals along the top front edge of the units. Plastic drop cloth can be fitted with grommets and the cloth hung from the nails. The light cloth can be stored in one of the compartments when not in use. But on days when humidity is low it can be dropped over the front of the unit, greatly improving the plant environment. The maximum effect of the unit is attained when plants and objects are arranged in a planned overall design. The unit has functioned in a New York apartment for some time and plants have grown and bloomed surprisingly well without special humidifying or ventilating equipment. Apparently the lighting is sufficient for most houseplants.

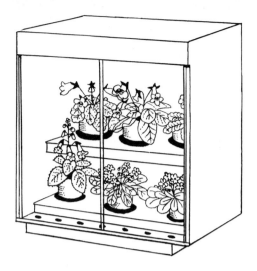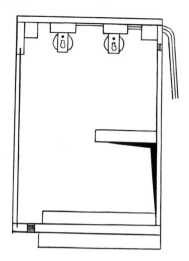

CABINET GARDEN

The drawing shows far better than any photograph the principle of cabinet light garden construction. The size can be increased in any direction and more fluorescent tubes can be used but essentially this garden is an open-fronted box. The shelf is a nice feature which raises small plants in the rear of the cabinet into a visible position. The overlap of the framing is sufficient to prevent glare.

Drawing by Helen Matsubu

LIGHTS ON PULLEYS

Fixtures under shelves can be adjusted with pulleys and counterweights. The system does work but is ugly and cumbersome—at least those we have built and seen. If shelving is set at different levels plants can be distributed according to size, and in some cases where a few inches are involved, supported on up-turned pots.

THE CABINET GARDEN

I call this type of light unit a cabinet garden because it is essentially a box with an open or transparent front, so framed that the effect is of a shadow box. It is particularly useful at floor level along walls and under windowsills. If placed on a stand, it can be carefully finished as a cabinet. Ceramics or glass may be displayed on the upper surface. The simple basic design may be adapted to any style of furniture so that it becomes integrated with other pieces in the room. The framing is decorative and prevents glare.

The size of the boxes is limited by the length of standard fluorescent tubes. Using 24-inchers a width of up to 30 inches is practical. Thirty-six-inch tubes will allow for a cabinet 42 inches wide. This can be continued through the 48-inch, 72-inch and 96-inch lengths with an allowance of an additional 3 inches at either end.

If two tubes are used, the depth can be 12 to 16 inches. It should not be more than 18 inches deep unless the opening is sufficiently wide to reach the plants in the back with ease. Figure a maximum of 6 inches between the centers of the tubes. The height should be 18 to 24 inches.

CABINET GARDEN UNDER WINDOW

Mr. Warren F. Cressy has built a number of fine light gardens for his wife Cindy, who is a superb indoor horticulturist. This garden, probably the first he constructed, is very like the one shown in the drawing above, a simple, squarish box. Note how well it fits under the window in the space assigned to it, blending in with the wall and surrounding furniture. Painted white it demonstrates how easily such a light garden can be used in a colonial style room.

Photo by The New York Times

LARGE CABINET GARDEN

This is no more than a large edition of the cabinet garden in the previous illustration. The framing is heavier and the wood is dark. The top has been carefully finished. This light garden actually takes the place normally occupied by a chest of drawers or a table. Its top surface remains an excellent display area. The interior has a shelf suspended in the rear of the garden. Moisture in the trays maintains high humidity in this cabinet.

Photo by The New York Times

CABINET BENEATH THE SILL OF A SUN-ROOM

The principal feature here is the pair of glass-paned doors. When they are closed the humidity within is increased and protection is provided against drafts. The picture also demonstrates how neatly such a garden fits beneath the normal sills of windows and utilizes space which is normally bare. From the home of Mrs. Warren F. Cressy, Jr.

Photo by The New York Times

This garden was built by Jack Golding of Kearny, New Jersey, the famous Begonia grower. The framing is of wood and the top, sides, and bottom are made of sheets of ½-inch plywood. In spite of the short overhang of the frame there is no glare from the tubes because parawedge louvers (see How to Build Light Gardens without Glare, page 40) are suspended below them. The bottom was waterproofed with an Epoxy finish. Plastic crate is used to support the pots.

Use ½-inch plywood for the sides, top, and bottom. In order to fit your box properly to the space you have assigned it you must make a scale drawing in which you will determine which sides are attached to which others (back to all the sides, or back overlapped by two sides and overlapping top and bottom, etc.) and make allowance for the thickness of the board. A half inch all around has to be deducted for the framing which will go on the front. This is all very simple once you lay it out on paper.

The front framing will be 4 inches wide on the bottom and 3 inches wide on top. The two upright pieces will each be the height of the box less 7 inches and the same width as the bottom. If the cabinet is set up high, the framing at the top may be wider but should always be less so than the bottom for appearance' sake. Sand the wood well as this is your show side. Establish your dimensions and the wood can be cut exactly to size at your local lumberyard.

A little house built by Mr. Francis Hall of Brooklyn, N.Y., to display his miniature Geraniums. The chimney is equipped with an exhaust fan which helps maintain the required coolness.   *Photo by author*

Make your box with standard 1-inch nails or wood screws. Then paint the inside with two coats of flat white paint. Epoxy is exceedingly protective against moisture. The frame is attached by means of headless nails or countersunk screws, the holes being filled with plastic wood. Finish the outside to match your walls and furniture.

Determine the position of your lighting fixture and drill a hole in the side or rear of the box to accommodate the wiring. Attach the fixture inside the top in a central position. The tubes should be set apart so that the light is evenly distributed.

If the cabinet is set up high it may be wise to install a parawedge louver under the lights to prevent glare. This device will also make it unnecessary to have very wide framing.

Handy carpenters can achieve beautiful effects with these cabinets. Doors with glass windows or sliding panes of glass on the front will improve humidity control. A deluxe and effective device is to fill the back of the box with a sheet of mirror. This will increase the light effectiveness and improve its distribution.

THE OPEN OR FLOOR GARDEN

Lighting tall foliage plants—Dracaenas, Scheffleras, Aralias, etc—by means of ceiling inset fluorescent tubes or spotlights has been done in institutions and homes for many years. Massive living sculptural effects are accomplished and these indestructibles, with their low light requirements, can be maintained for years with a minimum of care. The introduction of the General Electric Cool Beam spotlights permits bottom or top lighting (the former for visual effects as well as the encouragement of the lower leaves) much closer to the plants than before. The Cool Beam is as hot as any other spotlight, but is so constructed that most of the heat rays are reflected backward and dissipated.

A far more ambitious, attractive, and challenging project is that of floor gardens utilizing both flowering and foliage plants. These can be placed along a wall or in corners as part of the decoration of a room. A whole room can be converted into an indoor garden such as Mr. Jack Golding's, designed by Mr. Richard Kelly, which is described and illustrated on pages 68, 70, and where the light sources cover the whole ceiling. Two other basic types of room garden are (1) gardens which are lighted from fixtures attached to the wall or suspended from the ceiling and (2) those where the light units are set in rigid fixtures directly over the garden and supported from floor level.

An essential requirement of these gardens is a waterproof area, or basin, with a molding sufficiently high (4 to 6 inches) to hold in the soil near the perimeter as well as for framing. Formerly the best way of accomplishing this was to have a tinsmith make a basin of the required size and then edge it with a decorative molding. Now polyurethane paints completely waterproof wood surfaces with a clear or tinted finish.

The positioning of lighting should be decided *after* you have planned your garden. Most practical and attractive is to build up a miniature landscape with

FLOOR GARDEN

This is part of the floor garden of Mrs. Howard (Millicent) Selsam, the noted writer of scientific books for children. The valanced fluorescent light units on the wall are nearly invisible as they are painted the same color. The Selsams built this unit long before anyone else was doing much with light gardening. The movable wooden modules to contain soil and plants were their idea. The principle has many applications in apartment living.

Photo by Eeva

Another view of Mrs. Howard Selsam's floor garden

Photo by Eeva

soil and rock. The soil should be a combination of peat moss, vermiculite, and perlite so balanced that the peat bears no greater relationship to the other components than 1–1–1. This will give excellent aeration, ease of handling with pots, good evaporation and saving on weight.

For rocks use featherrock or tufa or lightweight slags. With these elements your garden can be planned to have heights and depths according to the shape of the space and its relation to the wall of the room. A recycling pump system can be used to simulate streams and waterfalls.

The planting should be in pots, facilitating care and replacement. They can be hidden by rocks or buried in the soil. Tall plants must be set at lower levels and small flowering plants must be placed higher in order to benefit from the lights above. All the flowering plants recommended in our sections on selection and culture can be used in such gardens.

The amount and position of the lighting will depend on the shape and size of the area allocated for gardening as well as the height of the plants used. Narrow gardens along a wall can be accommodated with 48- or 96-inch double tube fixtures attached to shelving extending from the wall and provided with a valance. These should be of wood and painted the color of the wall.

When the area is larger or if it is away from a wall, the lights must be suspended. These will consist of batteries of tubes set in a wooden frame and suspended from the ceiling. Pulleys or Danish lamp pulls are used to permit raising and lowering the lights. This is not merely utilitarian, but is a means of lifting the bulky fixtures up and out of the way when you wish to put the garden on display.

In most such situations planning on maximum illumination is advisable. Because the distances are greater the intensity must also increase. If you underlight, your garden will not thrive. For this reason use Power Twist tubes or those with built-in reflectors or increase the size of the ballasts.

The frame for the fixtures (an oblong shallow box upside down) should be painted reflective white, and the valance must be long enough to reduce glare. Still better is to use parawedge louvers which will eliminate glare completely without substantially reducing the amount of light reaching the plants.

THE SINGLE UNIT FLOOR GARDEN

In some situations—under hanging bookcases, below a series of windows, etc. —where a broad open light garden on the floor would not be unsightly, the construction can be the same as that of a tabletop unit only longer and wider. Use 72- or 96-inch fixtures, at least wide enough to accommodate four tubes. Make a tray or basin of wood or metal at least 4 inches deep. Set rigid standards at either end to support a deep, wide reflector and the fixtures. If the basin is built of light materials it can be movable. Such is the case with the garden illustrated.

ROOM GARDENS

The ultimate in indoor gardening is a room whose whole floor is devoted to gardening and whose ceiling is covered with fluorescent units. At this writing there is only one such garden in a private home, that of Mr. Jack Golding of Kearny, New Jersey. The lighting was designed by Mr. Richard Kelly. This is a major project; in the experimental stage success depends on the employment of a lighting expert-architect who also possesses a knowledge of horticulture. Fortunately, Mr. Kelly has both qualifications and Mr. Golding is both a metal fabricator and outstanding horticulturist.

In this instance 48-inch power twist tubes were used. They are set in a pattern across the ceiling with the centers 6 inches apart. The ballasts were all removed and are housed in the ceiling of the garage which is below the garden room. Means of exhausting the heat from the tubes themselves was installed along with ventilation and humidifying equipment.

Because of the number and position of the light sources it was necessary to create a complete ceiling of parawedge louvers. This completely eliminates glare and the ceiling appears to be black. The intersecting light of so many tubes delivers a relatively high quota of footcandles much farther from the source than in smaller units. In fact, the lower leaves of taller plants are well supplied with light.

The landscaping offers infinite possibilities and challenges.

ROOM GARDEN

This is a corner of the remarkable room Mr. Wilbur Patterson had built for his wife Lynn at Chippewa Falls, Wisconsin. A reinforced ceiling permits the hanging of numerous large basket plants from hooks. The tables are solid and simple and the fixtures are likewise hung from the ceiling. A clever innovation is the use of undertable space. Simple platforms on casters can be moved out for plant care by means of drawer pulls. The lighting fixtures hang from the bottoms of tabletops.

Photo by Dick Jacobs, Chippewa Falls

CELLAR GARDENS

Because they are belowground, cellars, whether utility or recreation, have proved excellent locations for light gardens. Even temperatures and the ease with which they can be humidified and ventilated account for the fact that some of the most successful hobbyists have used cellars.

An example is Mr. Fred Bender of New Rochelle, N.Y., whose Paphiopedilums (Lady Slipper Orchids) are as fine as the best of those grown in greenhouses. His cellar is divided into a recreation room and utility area. In the latter he has enclosed a 9-by-9-foot space with storm windows. There are two levels of staging around three sides of the enclosure, giving the remarkably large usable space of 124 square feet. This compact arrangement accommodates approximately 300 plants, most of which are in 6-inch azalea pots.

Light is provided by 48-inch fixtures with two tubes each, set 6 inches apart. The fixtures are permanently attached to the wooden supporting structure. In addition, there are two batteries, of three 96-inch tubes each, suspended from the ceiling on the long axis above the top bench on either side of the open work space.

On the benches, pans constructed of sheet aluminum are 32 inches by 36 inches, with straight 3-inch sides. Rigid hardware cloth, squared down the sides,

DETAIL OF THE PATTERSON ROOM GARDEN

The photo shows the construction and bracing of the tables, the platforms, and their casters. The same idea can be used with different tables in different places.

Photo by Dick Jacobs, Chippewa Falls

ROOM GARDEN WITH PARAWEDGE LOUVERS

The unfinished light garden room designed by Mr. Richard Kelly, dean of lighting designers, for Mr. Jack Golding of Kearny, New Jersey. The ceiling is wall-to-wall fluorescent tubes and the room is ablaze with light yet the photograph shows clearly that glare is completely eliminated. Ultimately this garden will be an outdoor garden indoors, with paths and beds. At least one wall will be mirrored.

Photo by Jack Golding

Mrs. Robert Gannet of Akron, Ohio, has turned part of her basement into a light garden room quite similar to that of Mr. Bender, described in the text. Concentrating the light units in a small area makes for easier maintenance.

Photo by Robert Gannet

is set into the pans just below the edge and is sufficiently strong to support the many pots.

A humidifier, standing under the bench near the door, consists essentially of a grass mat and a fan. The mat is kept moist by a connection with the house water system, while the fan draws fresh air through and blows it, heavily laden with moisture, into the garden.

Near the house wall, just behind and on a level with the top of the enclosure which has an opening at this point, is a large fan which is activated by a thermostat. The latter is set for a high of 75 degrees F. in summer and 65 degrees F. in winter during the day and ten degrees cooler, respectively, at night. When the fan is activated it opens vanes which are set in the side wall of the house, permitting air to enter. This is then blown through the opening left at the top of the enclosure. As the stream of air is well above the plants, they are never in a direct draft.

Mr. Golding's basement is filled with tables and reflector units like these for growing his Begonias. The two glass aquariums are used for propagating cuttings.

Photo by Jack Golding

Terrariums

I have described Wardian cases as prefabricated glass cases in which plants in their pots are placed as they would be on a shelf. A terrarium is a container of any size which is partly filled with soil into which the plants are set either in or outside pots. It may range in size from a bonbon jar or brandy snifter to a very large fish aquarium.

Terrariums were popular long before fluorescent light, and were used to preserve through the winter attractive little plants gleaned from the forest floor. Wintergreen, Mitchella, little ferns, moss, ground pine, and club moss kept very well in containers, the red berries of the first two plants lending a certain gaiety to the somber greens. A fluorescent light serves no purpose with this type of terrarium which has fallen into disfavor with those who object to removing wild plants from nature. The modern terrarium described here uses only cultivated plants and is designed to suggest a miniature garden or landscape.

Terrariums can provide a highly decorative element wherever they are used in the house. As they maintain high humidity, relatively even temperatures, and ideal soil moisture conditions they are a refuge for plants that do not do well elsewhere in indoor gardens. They provide protection against air pollution. Many tender plants which perform very well in a country house are unhappy in the city. But placed in a terrarium they flourish in spite of pervasive smog. Finally, if you have herbivorous pets or curious children, the terrarium is a safe sanctuary.

The Aquadome Terrarium Coffee Table is from the catalog of the Kenton Collection, 4435 Simonton, Dallas, Texas 75240. It is the first terrarium in production which meets the requirements at the same time of plant growth and modern furniture design. The round cover case is 40 inches in diameter and the bowl, made of ¼ inch thick plexiglas, has a capacity of 40 gallons. This allows space for an unusually large terrarium garden of foliage, succulent, or flowering plants. You can provide sufficient illumination by suspending a growth bulb or Cool Beam Flood lamp, or a large Circleline fluorescent fixture with opaque decorative shade or reflector, above it.

CONTAINERS

Dealers in plastic materials usually have acrylic resin in sheets of various thickness. If you give them the dimensions you need they will cut the sheets exactly and provide adhesive and instructions as to how to use it. You can make small decorative terrariums up to 12 inches high. The sheets are cut with squared sides and must be perfectly smoothed before assembly. Beautiful though these are, the skill of amateurs is rarely adequate and, after a while, the sides warp and spring apart. Containers made with beveled edges last longer but special equipment is needed to miter the edges exactly. Plastic is much more expensive than glass and scratches easily.

Far safer are regular aquariums which are available from tropical fish stores in a large variety of sizes. The standard aquarium has a slate bottom and four glass sides with corners of chromed metal. Recently manufacturers have learned to fuse the glass so that the metal corners are eliminated and the appearance is much improved. The bottom is also glass set in a wood frame.

Because tropical fish lovers like a long case for display, none of the sizes commercially available approaches a cube in dimensions. Capacity is measured in gallons. A 2-gallon tank measures 10 x 6 x 8 inches, 5 gallons 14 x 8 x 10 inches, 10 gallons 20 x 10 x 12 or 24 x 8 x 12 inches, 20 gallons 24 x 12 x 16 inches, and other sizes up to 125 gallons, 72 x 18 x 20 inches. Metal stands are also available.

Consider the size of the area in which you will place your tank as well as the standard length fluorescent tube you will suspend over it.

Aquarium tanks come without cover glasses. For smaller terrariums window-pane glass cut by your local hardware store will do. For larger ones a thicker gauge is required and you will have to have this made by a glazier.

PUT THEM IN POTS

Next I want to recommend something which is anathema to the purists and will bring down upon my head their deadliest assaults. I am tired of trying to make and maintain miniature gardens with plants rooted directly into the soil, and more and more convinced by my experience that there is nothing so satisfactory as planting in pots or some other container. Obviously this is not possible in a dish garden or snifter. But we are speaking here of tanks in which the minimum depth of soil is 1½ inches.

Terrariums, like all miniature gardens, have their beginnings, their prime, and their old age. Only for a relatively short time can they ever be perfect. This is because the plants themselves either grow too big or spread too far. In any event, the symmetry of the planned design is destroyed sooner or later. If the plants are in containers, maintenance is far easier. An unruly plant can be removed without fuss and a perfect new one set in its place. We do not have constantly to remake our garden as long as we have a good stock of substitutes. All that is necessary is to insert fresh material.

A pot is never too big for the garden. If it were, then the plant itself would be overpotted. A tiny plant for a small garden needs only a very small pot. It is as simple as that. And should you want to use bigger plants, you will have to provide an outsize container.

Terrarium planting is always a ticklish matter and only a very deft hand can set a small plant in place without damaging it. Planted in a pot it can be moved around without this risk.

Another advantage is that the plant is in the medium you have prescribed for it. Its roots do not tangle with others. If it needs special fertilizer or insecticide you can use it without affecting every other plant in the garden. If it needs some special attention it can be removed and replaced very easily. Finally, the confinement of the pot will restrain the plant and keep it small for a longer period of time.

Pots, plastic or clay, come in sizes from 1½ inches in diameter up. For the smaller ones you must do some looking around. But this is unnecessary for, like so many rules, ours has an exception. Tiny Sinningias and plants similarly small do not spread and can be planted directly in the soil.

THE SOIL

As you are going to use pots, the growing qualities of the medium are not of paramount importance. Certain plants do crawl out of their pots and root themselves if given a chance. This is the way to keep Koellikerias going, for instance. These new growths are often valuable in themselves.

Since garden soil is very heavy and soilless mixes are light, the latter is preferable. I use a mix which is approximately one part peat and two parts each of perlite and vermiculite. Although the white specks of perlite annoy some people I do not find them distracting and, after a while, the peat will discolor it sufficiently.

Prepare the mix carefully. Be sure the peat is well broken up. Combine the ingredients thoroughly. Then add water a little at a time. As soon as the whole mass, which should be constantly stirred, is moist the watering should stop. If there is any excess pour it away and allow the mix to stand overnight.

DRAINAGE AND STONES

Drainage should not be a necessity if watering is done carefully. But we are liable to mistakes and, anyway, aeration of the soil needs to be aided. So we use perlite, charcoal, or lime chips for the purpose. Actually, pebbles will do.

For the construction of a landscape we want interesting looking stones in different sizes. Tropical fish stores sometimes have these but it is better to collect them casually in the country whenever the opportunity offers. Slags from kiln dumps are superb for the purpose because they are light and easily shaped. Featherrock, which can be bought from builder's supply houses, can be sculptured to any shape or size. Japanese shops carry those smooth rounded pebbles which can simulate a stream bed. A sheet of glass must be cut to size for a cover.

PLANTING

For snifters and similar size containers only very small plants are practical. They must have room for blooming. Calculate the extra height if you are planting material not yet in flower. Sometimes a single specimen is quite sufficient to give a handsome appearance. Larger containers can hold an arrangement of miniatures provided the soil is terraced to create a larger planting area. They can be made higher on one side than the other and arranged in a pleasing way without crowding. Little stones and pebbles will serve to give character to the terracing and set off the individual plants.

Fish tanks are a bigger project requiring careful planning. Gather together the plants you are likely to use and try to figure out where they should go. This is by no means a purely esthetic problem. You want your plants not merely to survive but to bloom, so you must calculate for each one how high it will grow and how near the source of light it must be. Which plants are to be placed lower and which higher? Also take into consideration that those which are set at either end of the terrarium are also under the weaker zone of illumination.

TERRARIUMS

Small plastic or glass terrariums are ideal settings for little flowering plants. A big rubber saucer, plastic dome, and a rock covered with mosses and ferns (plus a few *Sinningia pusilla* planted here and there) are more like the traditional terrarium using local plants from the woods. They can flourish a much greater distance away from the lights than the other plants. The large tank is planted in the modern manner with lots of ups and downs, flowering and foliage plants.

Drawing by Virginie F. Elbert

LANDSCAPING

First lay down about an inch of drainage material. The "scene" is created by building up the slightly moistened soil to suggest terraces, valleys, hills, etc., starting from the drainage material up. Consider the angle of viewing. Leave part of the drainage material uncovered, so that you can build the greatest relative height. The more levels and surfaces, the greater the illusion of a real landscape. The lowest part can be in the center or to the sides and can be continued back straight or angled between the higher parts. A low space in front can suggest the flat land from which the hills rise or a pool. A cleft between mounds can suggest a gorge, a meandering brook, or a valley.

If the terrarium is to be seen from all sides, you can build up to a ridge down the center. If viewed from one side—then a back corner or both back corners can be used as the highest point. From whatever angle the terrarium is viewed the lowest part must be on that side.

SETTING THE POTS

Dig holes for the pots and remove the excess medium. They need not all be set straight up but can be angled into the side of a hill. Once set in place, support and camouflage them with earth and with flat attractive stones creating terraces and valley walls. The natural form of the hills will guide you in placing the stones in a way suggesting a landscape, even to the extent of producing an effect of perspective with smaller stones at the higher and more distant points of a valley.

Do not overcrowd with plants. This is a common mistake. Plants grow and soon use up the air space around them. The individual plants, chosen for their form and color, look more interesting if they stand free. At first the terrarium scene may look bare—but it soon fills up. Also some very tiny plants which do not develop large root systems can be planted directly in the soil and fill the spaces

TERRARIUM IN A FIREPLACE

The terrarium fits perfectly into an unused fireplace in the author's apartment. It is difficult to think of any other solution of this problem which would be nearly as attractive. Normally rather colorful, the terrarium had suffered from a cold spell due to heating malfunction for a day and so was not at its best. But its landscape is clearly along the lines recommended in the text. This was the prototype which has been widely copied.

Photo by The New York Times

between the pots. Examples are *Sinningia pusilla* and *concinna, Phinaea multiflora,* miniature Ficus, Artillery Plant, Kenilworth Ivy, Baby's Tears, and small ivies. If *Sinningia pusilla* is used it will eventually surround itself with moss. In this way you can cover the bare areas.

FINISHING UP

After all your pots have been planted, your lowest levels, over the drainage, can be paved with pebbles. Smooth Japanese pebbles are particularly attractive for the purpose. Then, with a broad soft paintbrush, drifting soil should be brushed out and upward and stones cleared of debris. The plants can be sprayed lightly with clear water to clean the leaves. Do not stop until your garden is perfectly neat.

LIGHTING

Unless you are using a mammoth fish tank you will find a two-tube 24-inch fixture with reflectors will give quite sufficient light. Even in bigger tanks the plants will bloom, for they seem to need less light under ideal conditions. The reflector can be laid directly on the cover glass but it is far better to suspend it an inch or more above it.

MAINTENANCE

If you have watered the medium as recommended, your terrarium should be in good balance. At night some condensation water will collect on the glass which will clear up during the day.

Your terrarium is not a Wardian case because of the proximity of the lighting fixture, which gives off considerable heat. You can reduce this by removing the ballast and setting it a few feet away if you have the space. Otherwise more heat is being generated than is good for the plants on warm days.

Unless you have air conditioning or keep your apartment cooler than most people consider comfortable, the interior of the terrarium will heat up excessively, even in winter. This means that, according to the interior temperature of your apartment or home and the behavior of the plants, you must move your covering glass around to allow air to enter. This destroys the balance but is unavoidable. The soil in the pots will dry out long before the medium around them. In summer it is even advisable to remove the cover completely during warm and humid days. And on real scorchers it is best to turn off the fluorescent tubes. No harm will be done if this happens once or twice a week for a couple of months. On the other hand, an overheated terrarium will develop mold over night with total destruction of the plants.

To water the pots use a wand or tube, giving them the same amounts as you would if they were growing in your open light garden. When the medium becomes too dry, add a glass of water at a time down the side of the glass so that it goes into the drainage. This moisture will work up through the medium. As long as no water at all remains in the drainage the following day you can add glassfuls each day.

When a plant grows too big, pull out the pot. Very often roots will have grown through the bottom holes into the soil. Sometimes, because the mix is excellent for propagation, straggling branches will have rooted themselves. All the better. Just clear them out and repot. Replace the plant with another and do some housecleaning on the rest of your garden.

Unless it is obvious that your plant, though enjoying enough light, still does not grow or bloom, do not fertilize it in a terrarium. If you feel the need is great, use only the lightest of dilute fertilizers. An organic fertilizer will encourage CO_2 production and contribute to plant growth.

FLOWERING PLANTS FOR THE TERRARIUM GARDEN

Allophyton mexicanum (Mexican Foxglove)
Begonias *foliosa, domingensis, fuchsioides, hirtella nana,* etc.
Boea hygroscopica
Chirita micromusa
Columnea 'Chanticleer' and 'Vera Covert.'
Cuphea hyssopifolia
Episcia lilacina 'Fanny Haage' and *E.* 'Shimmer'
Exacum affine
Gesneria citrina, christi, cuneifolia, mornicola, pumila, etc.
Gloxinera 'Cupid's Doll,' 'Pink Petite,' 'Ramadeva,' 'Little Imp,' 'Pink Imp.'
Jewel orchids
Koellikeria erinoides
Lockhartia oerstedtii
Oxalis martiana aureo-reticulata
Phinaea multiflora
Saintpaulia miniatures
Saxifraga sarmentosa
Sinningia 'Doll Baby,' 'White Sprite,' 'Snow Flake,' 'Wood Nymph,' 'Freckles,'
    'Cindy,' 'Poupee.'
Sinningia pusilla and concinna
Streptocarpus cyanandrus, kirkii, rimicola

FOLIAGE PLANTS FOR THE TERRARIUM GARDEN

Acorus gramineus variegatus—Green and white grassy foliage. Requires considerable moisture.

Adiantum bellum—Bermuda Maidenhair Fern—and *Adiantum decorum* are two of several small delicate ferns. Should be rested in summer.

Alternanthera—Joseph's Coat—like small, rather contorted *Coleus*. The three most suitable are *A. bettzickiana, A. bettzickiana aurea nana,* and *A. versicolor,* which is copper colored. There are several others.

Calathea (Maranta) and the closely related *Ctenanthe* and their species include several which are sufficiently small for the terrarium. The precise designs of the variegation make the leaves among the most ornamental available to us. *C. micans* is particularly miniature.

Carex variegata—A little sedge with variegated foliage.

Chamaeranthemum—Tropical creepers with variegated leaves. Best are *C. gaudichaudi, C. igneum,* and *C. venosum.*

Dracaena godseffiana—'Florida Beauty.'

Ficus pumila minima and *Ficus radicans variegata*—A creeper which clings to the ground and forms a solid network of leaves.

Fittonia verschaffelti—Mosaic Plant—The leaves are rather large but the habit is creeping. There are beautiful color variations among the cultivars.

Helxine soleiroli—Baby's Tears—A rapid spreading, almost mossy, standby.

Homalomena wallisii—The green leaves are margined with white and blotched with gold.

Oxalis hedysaroides rubra—Firefern—Beautiful compact Oxalis with red leaves and yellow flowers.

Oxalis martiana aureo-reticulata—The leaves are heartshaped and brilliantly veined with gold. Flowers are deep pink. A gem.

Pellionia pulchra. P. repens, P. daveauana—Interesting trailing oval leaves.

Pilea depressa—Another miniature ground cover.

Polystichum tsus-sinense—A small fern.

Selaginella kraussiana and *uncinata*—These plants deserve more consideration from terrarium enthusiasts. The latter has touches of electric blue amid the green. There are several others worth trying and all are quite easy, and different, foliage plants.

Some others are:

Tiny slow-growing ivies.

Dwarf northern wild ferns—from spore, not plants taken from the wild.

Mosses. They will do best in the dark parts of the terrarium.

Small Peperomias.

Marantas.

Chapter 7

HOUSEPLANT SOILS

To avoid repetitive use of the terms medium and media, the generic word soil is often used here (when it causes no confusion, I hope) although it may stand for a soilless medium.

The old formulas consisting of loam, sand, and humus or leaf mold have been abandoned by indoor gardeners in favor of the so-called soilless mixes. All the constituents are sterilized before packaging, thus eliminating a rather arduous chore for the amateur. A rich organic content has been replaced by relatively inert materials constantly treated with chemical or organic fertilizers, usually in liquid form. The new soils are light, well aerated, providing excellent drainage and do not compact as much with time. Mechanical characteristics and proportions can be shifted around easily to make a full gamut of soils suitable for different kinds of plants. It is much easier to repot or transplant. The components of the mixes are fairly uniform in quality and their characteristics easily understood. Results are especially superior with tropical plants.

Soil Materials

PERLITE

Obsidian, a glassy lava rock, when heated becomes a froth which is precipitated as very light pure white pebbles. This is perlite (also known as Sponge

Rock) which is so widely used in soilless mixes. It is very porous and not only holds water but contributes aeration to the soil. A slight grittiness lends just the right coarseness to an otherwise soft mix.

Perlite can be bought in packages of various sizes. The material should be clean, the pebbles separate. The dust is of no use and should be discarded.

Its extreme lightness causes perlite to rise to the surface of the soil when watering. If the material has been mixed well with the other components, this "top dressing" will represent only a small proportion of the whole in spite of appearances.

Users have complained of nasal irritation from perlite dust. This unpleasantness can be avoided if you open the bag wide and spray lightly with water. Others complain that it does not look natural. Nobody has bothered to color it brown which would eliminate that problem. In practice it absorbs some color from the peat after a while in the pot.

VERMICULITE

Mica occurs as "books" of extremely thin crystalline sheets. When subjected to high heat the pages separate—a process called exfoliation—greatly increasing the bulk, so that the ratio of weight to volume is very low. This material, which we call vermiculite, is also a soil lightener and conditioner like perlite.

Because each of the myriad of platelets will hold a thin film of water by surface tension, vermiculite wets down much more quickly than perlite and does not have the same tendency to float the moment water is poured into a container. Its softness and delicate structure make it a fine medium for propagating cuttings.

Buy standard small mesh material for propagation and juvenile plants and rather larger chunks for mature plants. The books should be square and crisp, with exfoliation very evident—like an accordion, and the color should be silvery. The grade used by builders, and for beds for barbecue pans, is duller in color and consists of large flat chips poorly exfoliated, very soft to the touch. It will break down quickly into clogging fine aggregates. Even suppliers of horticultural materials will sometimes sell a similar grade. It is to be avoided as it breaks down rapidly in the pot and has proved harmful to plants. Since vermiculite is bagged in clear plastic, it is easy to see, and feel, what you are buying.

PEAT

Peat is the product of the partial decomposition of sedge or sphagnum moss. Sedge peat is the coarser and more acid. Sphagnum peat is usually finer in texture and more neutral. The latter is, therefore, preferable for most tropical houseplants. Although the labels of the packages and bales do not always state the derivation of sedge peat, they almost always do when it is sphagnum. Imported fine-grained German peat is reputed to be superior to the domestic product but I have had no difficulty with the domestic.

Since peat is an organic component in soil mixes, the question of relative acidity or alkalinity is raised. This is expressed as the pH factor, and on a scale which runs from 0 (representing high acidity) to 14 (representing high alkalinity), pH 7 would be neutral. Most of our indoor plants prefer a pH between 6.0 and 8.0.

Peat has superseded humus and leaf mold as the organic constituent of houseplant mixes because it is cheaper, lighter, and more reliably uniform in quality. At best it has a mild acid reaction, at worst this may run as low as pH 5, which is not very satisfactory for Gesneriads among others and is why we must add some lime to our mix for neutral pH plants. After a while it becomes progressively more acid through the use of fertilizers and becomes loaded with salts. To offset this tendency frequent leachings with plain water are required. Although some nutrient is slowly released from peat, mostly nitrogenous, additional nutrients are usually necessary, especially those high in phosphorus and potassium, to encourage bloom.

With these limitations peat has proved an excellent material in mixes of every type.

SPHAGNUM MOSS

I recommend the previously mentioned constituents only for general use in potting mixes. Sphagnum moss is an interesting material for the horticulturist and has certain specific uses for which some growers prefer it above all others.

Sphagnum moss grows in immense quantities in acid bogs which are a common feature wherever water is plentiful from South Carolina to the Arctic Circle. People who live in the country usually can collect a sufficient amount of the moss for even the largest indoor light garden needs. The beds are a foot or more thick and the soft, loose material can be pulled up by the armload.

This moss is a tiny plant which makes continuous growth, leaving behind its old stems and leaves in various stages of decomposition, the bottom level being converted into peat. The minuscule leaves contain skeletal cells which are empty and serve only to take in water, which the plant can do to an amount twenty times its own weight. Hence, it has often been described as a vegetable sponge.

The raw sphagnum can be dried and pasteurized. Some growers have found it to be an excellent medium for certain Begonias, Gesneriads, epiphytic Orchids, and many tropical foliage plants. It is also a good propagating medium for large cuttings. A layer of the moss on top of soil acts as a cooling mulch for plants which are sensitive to warmth at the roots.

Sphagnum moss is also dried, milled, and packaged for horticultural use. In this state it is an exceedingly fine, even material, light tan in color and nearly weightless. It is difficult to wet down, and commercial growers prefer not to handle it in large quantities. But in the home, all we need to do is pour it into the lower half of a deep receptacle, a pail, for instance, add some water and stir with a large spoon.

It is an excellent medium for seed germination. Due to some agency, which has not been discovered as yet, sphagnum does not permit the growth of harmful molds which cause damping off. That it can be moldy everybody knows who has worked with it. Almost invariably, after it has been wetted down and standing in the air a few days, a white mold develops on the surface which looks as if it would immediately cause damping off of seedlings. However, no damage ensues. Those who cannot endure this ominous sight need only moisten flats or pots of sphagnum and wait till the mold has disappeared before planting seed.

Sphagnum has a tendency to compact, and, if it becomes dry, will be difficult to moisten after seeding. For this reason I prefer to fill my seed bed with low peat houseplant mix and dust it with sphagnum before spreading the seed.

An advantage of sphagnum is that seedlings and cuttings can be removed without damage to the roots. Another is that there is sufficient nutrient in it to maintain seedlings for a rather long period. This is of value whenever we have sown more seed than we need immediately. Some seedlings can be potted up and the rest left in the flat till we are ready for them.

The relatively neutral pH of sphagnum, between 6 and 7, is particularly suitable for the seedlings of our tropical blooming plants.

SAND

The function of perlite and vermiculite in our household mixes is to replace the sand which was the principal means of altering the mechanical characteristic of a mix in the early days of indoor growing. Sand varies considerably in size of grain and chemical behavior and the packaged sands available are not dependable.

The English, who use sand in their potting mixes, are very particular about quality, and a number of specially mined sands are marketed there. Not so in this country where people must pick up what they can. In any case do avoid seashore sand, crushed sandstone and what is packaged as sandy soil. Coarse builders' sand is often recommended and will do provided you wash it thoroughly several times to leach out impurities.

CHARCOAL

Charcoal chips are often recommended for drainage and as a means of absorbing acids and salts. A good grade can be bought from aquarium supply houses. Recently, however, doubts have been raised as to its usefulness.

Soil Mixes

Even for soilless mixes there is an infinite number of formulas which will work. Experienced amateurs all seem to have their own prescriptions and the situation is compounded by those favored by the horticultural schools of colleges. The Cornell Mix has developed into several specialized recipes. These mixes not only vary the amounts of peat, perlite, and vermiculite but use various quantities of charcoal, superphosphate, lime, etc. Some amateurs find perfection in soilless mixes with worm castings or organic soils added.

It is my belief that the mix consisting of the three basic materials alone is the best proposal for the general grower. The only addition I see as necessary in certain instances is lime for high pH plants. Charcoal has no special value and superphosphate is unnecessary when dilute nutrients are used.

PREPARED MIXES

The only packaged mix with which I have had satisfactory experiences is Black Magic. When used straight it is equivalent to a high peat soilless mix such as 3 parts peat, 2 parts vermiculite, and 1 part perlite. For leaner mixes just add more perlite and vermiculite. In my experience the packaged soilless mixes should always be preferred to those that use natural soil. The latter are generally of poor quality, suitable only for the larger, indestructible foliage plants.

MIXING YOUR OWN

The indoor gardener finds it far more convenient to mix only a quart or two at a time. The ingredients should be well worked together in the dry state and then moistened just enough to be damp all through. A large mixing bowl or basin is a good receptacle. It should be covered and kept close at hand for quick potting.

MEASURING PROPORTIONS

Use a measuring cup or plastic container. As vermiculite and perlite are loose and dry materials, measurement presents no problems. Peat, on the other hand, is packed under pressure in bales and bags. Remove some of the material and break it up carefully with your hands until no lumps remain. Then measure out the fluffy material.

MIX FORMULAS

Here are some formulas, widely used, ranging from rich to lean, that I have found successful.

African Violet Mix

By volume:

3 parts sphagnum peat
2 parts vermiculite
1 part perlite

Rather good for African Violets and most of the flowering plants which need a heavier soil. These include some Begonias, *Cuphea, Punica granatum, Nautilocaly,* and *Drymonia.* In other words, except for the A.V.'s, the larger, fleshier plants.

Tropical Plant Mix

Equal parts by volume of sphagnum peat, vermiculite, and perlite.
This mix covers an even wider range including the small Sinningias, *Columnea, Hypocyrta, Streptocarpus,* and many succulents which do not require the ultimate in lean soils.

Sandy Soil Mix

1 part sphagnum peat
2 parts perlite
2 parts vermiculite

This mix meets the basic requirements of Cacti and the South African succulents as it provides perfect drainage and a low organic content.

Adding Lime

Experts add from a tablespoon to a pint of eggshell per quart of African Violet Mix for the lime loving Gesneriads. The latter figure is probably excessive though it obviously worked for the expert who suggested it. Five tablespoons to a quart is plenty as a starter. After six months you can spread some more eggshell on the surface of the soil.

Black Magic Mixes

Black Magic African Violet Mix is a favorite of many growers of houseplants. Usually eggshell should be added.

VARYING THE MIX

It must be stressed that every experienced grower tends to develop his own mixes. The pages of the specialty magazines are full of formulas. This proves, above anything else, that there is no perfect mix. I have given the simplest combinations because they work. From there you can "improve" according to your conditions and the plants you grow, consulting the experts for formulas which they think are suited to a particular plant. Any mix recommended for general use containing additives is misleading. The mixes I have listed are the *starting point* for indoor light gardeners.

Potting

DECORATIVE POTS

Any plastic or red clay pot will do for growing. But a special one is needed when you want to give a fine plant an artistic setting. Red clay is not unattractive, but the usual tapered shape with a thick rim is far from ideal. Nevertheless it is much better looking than a plastic one.

The average displays at our horticultural exhibits are often a compendium of pretentious gracelessness. One mistake which is often made is to seek out containers which are oddly shaped or overornamented. A basic principle is that for maximum effect a plant must have a simply shaped, neutrally colored background. Mrs. William Hull of Woodbridge, Connecticut, never failed to display her plants to perfection and much of the credit must go to the beautiful pots she used.

Above all other peoples the Chinese and Japanese have a tradition of correct pot and plant relationship. Low or high the shapes are geometrical and soft in outline. The glazes are dark and rich. Black, brown, and deep blue predominate. Japanese pots are imported in many styles and in any size you may wish to use.

Another good source for pots is the craft potteries in this country. The best of these are individually thrown on the wheel. Much of the ware is unglazed—the natural color of the clay. Others have neutral glazing. Some of the designs are fascinating and the style generally follows the rules of oriental potting. Country potters will throw work to your design. The feature of these pots is that they do not compete with the plant for attention.

CLAY OR PLASTIC?

I like the appearance and feel of a clay pot better than plastic. But there is no denying that plastic has many advantages, including economy and moisture retention, and is in no way inferior to clay for growing. Translucent plastic even allows you to control your watering and watch the root system grow. I do use a clay pot when my plant is top heavy, for in plastic it is more likely to tip over.

CROCK

It is a very old tradition to place broken shards or pebbles (called "crock") in the bottom of pots for drainage. It arose from the practice of setting the pots on damp benches in the greenhouse and prevented the medium from becoming soaked.

In the light garden I find this procedure superfluous and a waste of space. We need every inch of it. Furthermore, filling the pot means less watering. Our pots dry out fast enough in the dry house or apartment atmosphere.

SIZES

Depending on the kind of garden he keeps, the indoor grower will use any size pot from the smallest diameter to 12-inch giants. But the average apartment dweller finds that he can do with the sizes from 1½-inch diameter to, at the most, 5 inches. Because most of our blooming plants are rather shallow rooted he will do better with square or azalea type pots rather than tall tapered ones. Square pots are easier to store and will occupy less space on the shelves than round ones. Keep a good reserve supply of 1½-, 3-, and 4-inchers. Five-inchers are rarely used due to the generally smaller plants grown in the light garden.

POTTING

To pot a seedling or rooted cutting, choose a 1½-inch pot and fill with mix to the rim. Just pat it evenly and do not pack. Remove the seedling from the propagating box with as much medium attached to the roots as possible. Hold the seedling with one hand or a pair of tongs and, with the other, poke a hole into the medium in the pot sufficiently large to take the roots without crowding.

Gently set the plant in the hole with the roots just below the surface. Poke the soil around the roots, firm it down and around the plant. The very light mix will go well below the rim and you will have to add extra soil to raise the level sufficiently to support the plant. In doing so keep the soil as light as possible. Place the pot in a saucer and pour in clear water. After the pot has soaked up as much of it as it can hold, any residue should be poured off and the pot is ready for placing under the lights.

When a plant is moved from a small to a larger pot it must be knocked out of the first one with as little damage to the root system as possible. First water the soil thoroughly and allow the plant to stand for a few minutes. Then tap the edge of the pot on a hard surface while supporting the soil with one hand. The entire contents of the pot should drop out easily.

Put a little soil in the new pot and see if your plant will fit so that the division between root and stem will be just below the rim. It is important to remember that in the light garden the soil can be very close to the rim, contrary to the old practice of leaving a rather deep well to hold water. The light mixes drain water immediately and make this superfluous.

Having adjusted the height to your satisfaction, pack soil lightly around the roots and build it up until it supports the plant. Pack inward at the top, toward the stem rather than downward, to give the stem a little stiffening. Watering may be unnecessary.

If the roots are partly bare you must be careful, especially when they are netted and complex, to fill the interstices between them, otherwise you will leave air holes. A drench with a solution of Transplantone may aid the recovery of the plant from the damage it suffers in moving.

Plastic pots have a band at the top which is wider than the body. Unless you are careful, soil will be supported by the top of the root ball and the outward curve of the pot, leaving an empty space all around. So take a stick and poke the soil down close to the walls, filling in with soil as you work along.

Orchid growers use a method which is worth imitating. In packing osmunda and bark into pots they work the material from the outside inward with a potting stick, using leverage on the wall of the pot. It is better with regular soil also to work from the outside inward rather than pack downward. But, since the material is much less resistant than orchid medium, you can do the work with your fingers.

POT-BOUND PLANTS

A plant is badly pot-bound when the roots form a solid cloth near the bottom. If the whole root ball is transferred to a larger pot and is surrounded by fresh medium it will, in this state, be unable to spread out into the extra space. With a very sharp clean knife or a scissors cut the root vertically from halfway down the root ball to the center of the bottom. Do this on the other three sides. Poke your finger up the bottom of the root ball and spread the sections.

When you put soil in the new pot be careful to shove it under the spread roots which will tend to arch.

PLANTS POTTED IN EARTH

It is the experience of many indoor light gardeners that plants which have been potted in earth, even when some of the soilless mix ingredients have been added, must sooner or later be cleaned down to the bare roots. This soil is usually too heavy for the house and the plants do not receive sufficient aeration at the roots. Root or leaf rot are the consequences.

Remove the plant from its pot and gently dunk the root ball in lukewarm water until all the medium has worked itself loose. Partly dry the roots by laying them on paper toweling. In a moist, rather than wet state they can be spread in potting.

Fertilizers and Other Growth Aids

In a previous section I have dealt with soils essentially in terms of their mechanical characteristics and their uses. But soil maintenance and the closely related subject of plant nutrition require a little knowledge of the chemical factors involved. I have reduced the subject here, I trust, to its bare bones and practical essentials.

READING THE LABEL

The principal elements not usually available in soils in sufficient quantity to maintain them over long periods or to encourage rapid growth are nitrogen, phosphorus, and potassium. It is in this order that these elements are listed in the analyses on the labels of packaged organic and chemical fertilizers. The content may be expressed as the elements themselves, but more often the name given to these components is that of the chemical combination, oxide, acid, or salt—for instance, nitrates, phosphates or phosphoric acid, and potash. A formula may read:

> Total Nitrogen 30%
> Available Phosphoric Acid 10%
> Soluble Potash 10%

This means that in an 8-ounce package there will be 4 ounces of active nutrient in the stated proportions. This also means that if the label percentages add up to 25 percent the amount of material in a solution must be doubled compared with the total of 50 percent. When you read that a fertilizer has a content of 30-10-10 this *always* means 30 percent nitrogen, 10 percent phosphoric acid and 10 percent potash, in that order.

NITROGEN

The nitrates are usually the starting point for the nitrogen and protein metabolism in plants. Nitrogen is essential to the green, aboveground growth. It can be derived from the organic content of a soil and is released by water and bacterial action. It constitutes approximately 4 percent of a humus. This means that in 10 ounces of peat there will be approximately one half ounce of nitrogenous material available to the plant. As our soil mixes—really soilless mixes—contain a considerable quantity of peat, they have enough nitrogen to start plants on their way. However, this is soon consumed by the growing plant and must be replaced. Exhaustion of the nitrogenous content proceeds rapidly in the confinement of a pot, accounting for the need of periodic replenishing.

PHOSPHORUS

This element is needed for the development of healthy roots and cells. It has also been found that it is very effective in encouraging the formation of flowers under lights. For this reason, though we may feed juvenile plants heavily on the nitrates, we increase the phosphate—and potash—content of the formulas as our plants approach the flowering stage.

Most soils are low in phosphorus in a form readily available to plants. This is particularly true of soilless mixes. Furthermore it is known that high soil acidity tends to inhibit its release. Calcium added to the soil in the form of lime lowers the acidity and increases the availability of phosphorus. This means that even when high percentage phosphorus fertilizers are used they will be relatively ineffective unless soil acidity is kept low. This is equivalent to saying that we must keep the pH relatively high. Presumably plants which like acid soils and low pH do not need as much phosphorus. Most of our houseplants do.

POTASSIUM

Potassium is essential for starch formation and seems to serve as a catalyst in a number of important chemical reactions. In formulations it usually appears as potash, or potassium carbonate. Here, too, a highly acid soil inhibits the release of this necessary element. Soilless media usually contain a lower proportion of potassium than garden soils. It is also important in flower production.

CALCIUM

Calcium has a considerable effect in encouraging chemical reactions in soils and in the plants themselves. It builds cell walls and counteracts acidity. Nevertheless, it is not a constituent of chemically formulated nutrients.

Many ordinary soils contain enough calcium to serve all purposes. This is not the case with soilless mediums which are low in this element. As we will see, in the discussion of pH below, the addition of calcium to soil mixes is usually necessary. Also it leaches out of a soil very quickly with frequent waterings. However, in those parts of the country where hard water is prevalent, waterings produce the opposite effect and the water must be filtered. Chemical water softeners have a deleterious effect. Filtration through ion exchange resin beds is better.

TRACE ELEMENTS

The so-called trace elements are iron, boron, magnesium, manganese, molybdenum, sulfur, and zinc. Although required in small quantities, they are essential to plant growth and bloom. Organic fertilizers usually contain a sufficient quantity of most of them. Some of our chemical nutrients consist of only the three basic elements described on pages 90–91. In certain instances this may not be sufficient. However, there are any number of packaged chemical nutrients which are enriched with the trace elements, and these are listed on the container.

SIGNS OF CHEMICAL DEFICIENCY

Because the symptoms of deficiency are shared by a number of the elements the specific lack is difficult to recognize. In practice the amateur tries to give a balanced diet and leave it at that. The exceptions are iron and calcium. Lack of them cannot be ignored.

Phosphorus. Excessively dark leaves are a sign but this may be caused by insufficient light. If you know that your light is bright enough and find this effect on the plant, it may be the result of a shortage of phosphorus.
Nitrogen. Simple failure to grow. But this can be due to a soggy medium, lack of light, and root burn from excessive fertilizer. We rarely come across this difficulty because almost all our nutrients contain sufficient nitrogen. If we fertilize at all, our plants are probably receiving enough of this element.
Potassium. Curling under of leaves; yellow tips and margins. I trust the latter symptom more, since there are any number of causes for curled leaves.
Iron. Acid-loving plants need extra amounts of iron. This can be purchased as Iron Chelate or Sequestrene. Most of our acid plants have very green leaves. If the immature leaves turn yellow and the veins stand out green you can be pretty sure that iron is needed. The condition is called "chlorosis."
Boron. Irregular and distorted development of the plant and leaves. Use a fertilizer in which boron is listed as a trace element.
Calcium. Difficult to identify except by the behavior of new growth. It tends to die back.
Magnesium. Whitish foliage. This is a rather rare complaint. Be sure your fertilizer contains magnesium.
Zinc. Mottled and dwarfed leaves. Use a fertilizer in which zinc is listed as a trace element.
Sulfur. Lighter colored veins in leaves—the opposite of the iron reaction. Horticultural sulfur can be purchased in small quantities.
Manganese. Chlorotic mottling of the leaves.

Several of these symptoms can be caused by the attacks of insects. Suspect insects first. A full soil analysis will tell you what your plants lack but this has little meaning for indoor light growers with their soilless mixes. Just be sure that your plants occasionally receive nutrients which contain the trace elements. Also check pH for acidity and for lack of calcium. Few of our plants are acid loving except certain large foliage species. These must be regularly treated with iron.

AMOUNTS OF FERTILIZER

If you use too little nutrient your plant will not grow and bloom well and if you use too much the roots will burn and the plant will die. What is a good middle course?

A good rule to follow is to use one quarter the recommended strength (four times the dilution) when you are feeding once a week and one tenth the strength when fertilizing with every watering. The last figure may be too high, though not dangerous if the plant is growing rapidly. When plants are fertilized indiscriminately it is probably wise to move down to one fifteenth the indicated strength.

If pots stand in saucers and are fertilized regularly salts accumulate in the soil very rapidly. The quantity of nutrient which we pour into the soil is usually much greater than the plant can absorb or use. That is why regular leaching is advisable. A quantity of clear water must pass through and out of the soil carrying along the excess salts. The pot can be dipped in a container and drained, or water can be slowly poured into it in a quantity at least equal to the volume of the pot. With most plants leaching once every two months is sufficient.

pH—ACIDITY OR ALKALINITY OF SOILS

Probably the most important factor for the indoor gardener to know and watch is pH. The pH requirement of many of our houseplants is not known exactly. This is because most of the studies of the factor have been made with plants raised on a commercial scale. Dr. Wherry, of the University of Pennsylvania, made a lifelong study of pH but his list consists principally of crops, wild flowers, and a few common nursery and garden plants, few of which are cultivated indoors.

Trial and error does indicate that the majority of flowering houseplants, if not strongly on the alkaline side, at least are not very partial to an acid condition. And since our soils are not only somewhat acid to start with, but become progressively more so, we are constantly engaged in a battle to keep the pH number around neutral. Nevertheless we must be careful not to overlime our soils for even the Gesneriads will begin to wilt and become chlorotic.

TESTING SOILS

Soil testing kits are available from nursery supply houses and garden centers. The procedure for a good practical test of pH is simple and is described fully in the instructions that come with the kits. A thorough chemical soil analysis is another matter. For this purpose Sudbury provides complete equipment. However the amateur using soilless mixes will learn little at considerable trouble. If a special problem arises he is better advised to send a sample of the soil to the state supported agricultural department of a university.

The simplest test for pH is with litmus paper. Tropical fish stores sell tapes in a plastic container which, when brought into contact with moist soil for a few seconds will change color. Compare the hue of the moist tape with a color chart on the package and you will arrive at an approximate pH number. From the same source simple testing equipment can be purchased for a more accurate reading on your water supply.

INFLUENCING pH

Alkalinity in soil is increased by the addition of lime (calcium), acidity by the addition of aluminum sulfate or citric acid.

Aluminum sulfate may be required for plants such as miniature Roses, Gardenias, Camellias, or Carolina Jasmine, but this is not very likely because our soils usually are sufficiently acid to start with. For the same reason we must often mix in some lime for our other blooming houseplants.

LIMING THE SOIL

The types of lime materials used by the horticulturist are, in ascending order of quick release, limestone screenings, eggshells, pulverized limestone, chalk, shells and marls, and hydrated lime. It stands to reason, therefore, that an amount of hydrated lime will raise the pH more quickly than eggshells but that the effectiveness of the latter will be more long lasting as they will not enter into solution as quickly.

When calculating the amounts of lime to add to houseplant soil we must take into consideration the small quantities normally involved in making a batch, and that the organic components of a mix require more lime to change the pH than the inert materials. The more acid the organic content, the more lime is required to raise the pH to the neutral pH 6 to pH 8 which is best for most houseplants.

The following table gives some indication, necessarily inexact, of the amounts of lime you should add to the basic mixes for the neutral pH plants.

Eggshell, limestone screenings or pulverized limestone to a quart of mix.

African Violet Mix—5 tablespoons
Tropical Plant Mix—3½ tablespoons
Sandy Soil Mix—2 tablespoons

This should raise the pH about 1.0. A teaspoon for a 3-inch pot is more than enough.

Because they are always available I use eggshells saved from baking and breakfast and allowed to stand in a container until dry. Then I pulverize them in a large glass mortar. This only takes a few minutes. When you use a pestle do not pound, but press and twist. If you prefer gadgets a blender will do the job. For each half inch increase in the size of the pot I use an additional teaspoon of shell. But this is done, please note, only for plants that prefer a high pH.

Every couple of months I work a pinch of lime or eggshell into the soil of a 3-inch pot—a fat pinch for a 4-incher. Exact quantities are really not important but I would not recommend larger amounts than those I have given.

TYPES OF FERTILIZERS

Because we use soilless mixes we need not make a test of its chemical characteristics. And we can follow certain guidelines in our fertilizing procedures. Two of the components, vermiculite and perlite, are inert. Only the peat moss is chemically active. The pH of sphagnum peat runs 5.5 to 6.0. We know that this is not ideal for most of our houseplants which have a pH of 6.0 to 8.0. That is why we add lime as described above.

Furthermore we are aware that when we use nitrates which are so essential to plant growth, the acidity of the medium increases with time. Therefore we must also leach out the extra salts by draining water through the pots and by adding more lime from time to time.

We know that the peat moss also contains enough trace elements to start with but that we may have to add more later on. Also the very small amounts of phosphate and potash are soon washed away or consumed. When these two elements are added to the soil they tend to help counteract the acid reaction of the nitrates.

There are two classes of fertilizers most used by indoor gardeners because of effectiveness and convenience. These are the organic fertilizers, from vegetable, animal, or fish derived components and the chemical fertilizers which are compounded from chemical elements in a form known to be acceptable to the plants.

Of the organic fertilizers fish emulsion is very popular. But it runs 5-1-1 which means healthy growth up to a point but no aid in budding and flowering. Liquid Blue Whale is similar in its effect. Sturdy is a unique organic in having a formula of 0-15-14. When we alternate fish emulsion or Liquid Blue Whale with Sturdy we have all the requirements for growth and flowering. We can also switch entirely to Sturdy when a plant is ready to bud and bloom.

The chemical fertilizers come in a great variety of formulas. One manufacturer offers eleven of them. They are all powders which dissolve entirely in water. Those which contain trace elements, listed on the label, are preferable because most of our concern is eliminated on this point.

There is no point in using two chemical formulas at the same time, because they are available in so many combinations. If we want a balanced formula we buy 20-20-20 or 10-10-10, the difference being only a matter of concentration of chemicals. If we need more chemicals for blooming we may choose a 10-30-20 formula or the one recommended for African Violets, 7-6-19. Beyond this general rule I cannot offer specifics, and except for a few commercial plants no one knows just which proportion is the most beneficial in a particular case.

No matter what the advertising claims, do not buy a fertilizer which does not state clearly on its label the proportion of the three basic elements and the trace elements. And, unless you have considerable experience, it is not wise to experiment with agricultural bulk fertilizers.

SOME TYPICAL FERTILIZER FORMULAS

	Nitrogen (Nitrate)	Phosphorus (Phosphate)	Potassium (Potash)	
Fish emulsion	5	1	1	For green growth
Sturdy	0	15	14	Bud and flower
Chemical formulas	20	20	20	Balanced formula
	30	10	10	Green growth. Acid-loving plants. Orchids.
	10	30	20	Bud and flower
	7	6	19	African Violet bloom

There are a number of fertilizer products sold under brand names which are specially formulated for particular groups of plants. Some liquid chemical fertilizers are merely specially packaged dilutions of bulk chemicals. Horticultural nitrates, phosphates, and potash are sold in pound packages at garden supply stores. These can be mixed in the proportion you choose. Of course this is much cheaper but it will lack the trace elements. Since the quantities required for indoor gardening are so small, it is hardly worth the trouble, and the chemicals do not store well in the cartons in which they are packed.

Fertilizer can also be bought in pill and capsule form with the claim that the chemicals give "slow release." That means that they will enter more slowly into the moisture of your soil and, presumably, give out just the right amount of nutrition for the plant's daily needs. This, however, depends upon the rate of release from the pill, not the fluctuating demand of the plant at different periods of growth. You can stop your chemical or organic solution fertilizing at any time but you can't remove the pill once it is planted. Its use is unselective in this and a number of other ways.

Personally I recommend to the beginner a formula which is balanced and contains trace elements. This means a 20-20-20 proportion or any other balance. You can offset fish emulsion with its relatively high nitrate content by Sturdy or a chemical formula with high phosphorus and potassium. In other words, it is not harmful to alternate organic with chemical fertilizers as long as there is a chemical balance. If you can segregate your fertilizing procedure, you can then switch to budding and flowering formulas in the same way.

Remember that all label directions regarding dilution should be at least one tenth if you are fertilizing with every watering. That means that if a tablespoon is recommended in a gallon of water, you should reduce the amount to less than half a teaspoon. When your fertilizing schedule is once a week it is best to cut the amount to one quarter because of the danger of root damage by high concentrations. As long as you are using properly formulated fertilizers regularly there is little chance of underfertilizing. A large part of the dissolved minerals are never absorbed by the plant.

There is another rule that it is well to remember. Plants which are growing rapidly need more fertilizer than those which are slow growers. If a plant stops growing, stop fertilizing and do not resume until growth is well started up again. Do not fertilize a plant with signs of fungal infection or other damage. Do not fertilize as much during a blooming period. If a plant has achieved bloom it has absorbed the right amount of nutriment. Don't stuff it. However, if it is one of those which is everblooming, regular light treatments can continue—lighter than when it was not in bloom.

OTHER CHEMICALS

Hormone Powder

Two products, Rootone and Hormodin are used in encouraging root growth in cuttings. Both are available with a fungicide added. Questions have been raised as to the effectiveness of these products but they do no harm and are a convenient means of sterilizing exposed surfaces. Fermate, dusted on the end of a cutting, is much the same in its action. Mild solutions of a fungicide in cutting boxes prevent damp-off.

Giberellic Acid

Giberellic acid had a vogue for a while as a growth stimulant. It has proved particularly useful in bringing Camellias into flower. The material comes in a pressure spray can and is a good product to have around as a means of reawakeng the activity of a plant which, for some unknown reason, has ceased growing. I find it reacts better on plants with hard leaves than those with soft ones. Its precise effect, favorable or unfavorable, on many houseplants is still unknown. Use with caution and as a last resort.

Phosfon

This growth retardant has been widely used commercially on lilies and chrysanthemums which, under treatment, develop shorter internodes, making them more compact. It can be useful to the indoor light gardener if it works but far too little is still known about it. It is applied as a drench to potting soil as directed. Cycocel is used in the same way and B-Nine is sprayed on leaves and stems. These products seem to be only slightly toxic.

CO_2 IN THE LIGHT GARDEN

CO_2, so necessary for plant growth, constitutes about 300 parts per million of our normal atmosphere. In the old days outdoor hotbeds were fertilized and partly heated with manure. When electric heating cables were introduced it was found that the plants did not do nearly as well. The cause was traced to a lack of CO_2 which had been produced by the decomposition of the organic fertilizer. Further research indicated that if CO_2 is supplied in greater quantities than normal in the atmosphere, plants would grow faster and produce more flowers or fruits.

These investigations caused quite a stir among amateur gardeners, especially those who gardened indoors under lights. People were fizzing their plants with carbonated water which did evaporate CO_2 in small quantities. Others installed equipment in their greenhouses or homes in order to provide a steady supply.

Like so many fads, this one has begun to fade. As far as the light gardener is concerned the reason is simple enough. It is just that he works with compact plants and has space limitations. Rapid and luxurious growth is no advantage to him at all. To pump CO_2 into a terrarium is the acme of absurdity for it is just there that we want the plants to contain themselves and, while blooming, remain as small as possible. Accordingly, whatever its importance in other fields, CO_2 production in the light garden is of no recognizable value at the present time.

The recommended concentration of CO_2 for maximum growth varies between 600 and 2000 parts per million according to one source and 500-550 parts per million according to another. You can buy the gas in tanks from a number of major chemical suppliers who provide you with the necessary controls and tubes plus instructions for releasing the right amount of gas to service your growing area. Naturally the method is only practical for large light gardens—a cellar at least.

Another source of CO_2 is natural gas. If you install a special meter and controls you can deliver, by maintaining a flame, a suggested 1 cubic foot of gas to 1000 cubic feet of greenhouse or cellar per hour. Other methods are a lighted Bunsen burner, or wood alcohol burned in a kerosene or hurricane lamp. One ounce of alcohol consumed per hour will release 400 parts per million to a 1500 cubic foot area.

If you raise the CO_2 supply in the atmosphere, do it only during the hours of illumination and put the plants on a more filling diet of fertilizer than usual.

It is possible that the CO_2 content in the air of a greenhouse using natural soil is higher than in an open light garden. This is because of a higher rate of bacterial action. Somewhat the same effect on a smaller scale can be induced in the light garden by using organic fertilizer solutions which have been allowed to stand for a day or two before use. It is hoped that the peat decomposition will be more rapid, releasing larger quantities of CO_2 around the plant. The effect is similar to using manure in the hotbed.

Chapter 8

VENTILATION AND TEMPERATURE

VENTILATION

Dire warnings are issued by all the experts regarding the dangers of stagnant air, it being asserted that it will breed fungal infection in plants. How then can we account for the fact that our tropical exotics are perfectly happy in a closed terrarium? Recently I have been growing northern wild ferns (spontaneous from spores on slags) and they have flourished in a closed container both winter and summer although accustomed to the fresh air of the out-of-doors.

Therefore I have come to the conclusion that ventilation for most of our houseplants is not a primary consideration. There are two situations which I have found lethal for plants. High temperatures combined with very high humidity encourage gray mold. Cool temperatures and high humidity cause leaf rot. These are comparative terms, of course. One plant will suffer more from either of these conditions than another and in different temperature and humidity ranges. Orchids, for instance, are extremely sensitive. For most of our houseplants the sensitivity is only manifested at the extremes—rather on the cool side than the warm.

Greenhouse growers have to combat the development of heat under glass at

99

very high humidity levels. Hence they maintain a constant moving stream of air. Light gardeners, on the whole, have trouble keeping the humidity up. Heat and dryness are the problem.

One reason why fungus diseases do not often attack plants in a terrarium is that we neither mist nor spray them. Standing water on leaves and in the axils is a chief cause of plant diseases. If you have a state of high humidity do not spray plants which are in *open* gardens but mist them only. If you are accustomed to spraying you must have plenty of moving air to evaporate water in the axils rapidly. A tornado is not required—just avoid stagnation. A small fan will do the trick.

Moving air is, of course, not the same as ventilation, which is the availability of air from an outside source. There is always some air, enough for the plants, I think, if we go in and out of a room a couple of times a day and are careful not to permit it to become excessively hot. In the city it can be a positive advantage to have the windows closed tight to keep out pollution.

Creating ventilation when we want it is simple enough. We can do it with open windows provided we avoid drafts—sudden drops in temperature accompanied by strong air movement. We can use fans and air conditioners.

A common question is whether air conditioners are beneficial. They certainly are in urban environments because they are the only sure means of controlling temperature in summer and they do provide filtered ventilation. Humidity levels must be maintained.

TEMPERATURE

Our principal houseplants (orchids excepted) are happiest in a temperature range between 60 to 65 degrees and 80 to 85 degrees. A drop of 10 degrees at night is beneficial. A day temperature of a minimum of 70 degrees in the city is required for Gesneriads and many other tropicals if they are to bloom. In the country there is more leeway at the bottom end of the scale. If one raises a mixed collection a minimum night temperature of 60 degrees and a maximum of 85 degrees in summer is a good range.

Because we are dealing with a source of light which also produces heat the temperature settings are not those of the room but of the space under the fluorescent lights where the plants are growing. Depending upon the amount of air movement and the season, the temperature close to the lights may be 10 degrees warmer than a foot away. The area directly below the ballast will be the hot spot of your light garden.

Even with air conditioning, temperature change can be very drastic and rapid in terms of the ranges we have discussed. The equipment does not react evenly to seasonal changes and there are times when there will be a sudden drop in temperature along with so much air movement that the effect is of a severe draft. If the air conditioning is controlled by thermostats in the plant area there is less chance of this happening.

Without air conditioning the risks are even greater. A window left incautiously open while you are out for part of a day may, especially during the changes of season, induce a severe drop or rise in the room temperature.

In winter the city dweller has to combat the irregularity of heating in many of the older buildings. One day the place is stifling and the next it is too cool for comfort. Try to keep the humidity high on hot days and air movement to a minimum on cool ones.

During July and August in the city there are days of extreme heat which are lethal to some plants. Streptocarpus and Columnea suddenly wilt, for instance. If you have been on a low watering program the plant is not helped by the excessive dryness of the soil. And if you have watered freely rot may set in. There is no solution except to remove the plants most likely to be affected to a place which has better ventilation even though little light is available. If adverse symptoms appear, drooping leaves in some and sudden drying out in others, you must act immediately. The progress of the damage is very swift. Water just enough so that the soil is constantly slightly moist. Do not fertilize.

If your plants run the risk of cold days in winter be sure to have a plastic drop cloth handy to throw over the unit and shut out the cool air. The heat of the tubes will keep it comfortable inside.

During hot periods water in the trays cools the ambient air by evaporation. Another device is to simply turn off the lights during the heat of the day. No significant harm will be done to the plants.

Air Pollution

When we consider the amount of damage done to human beings by air pollution it is hardly surprising that houseplants should suffer from its effects. We are affected principally in our lungs, eyes, and nasal passages, in fact, wherever tender membranes are exposed to the toxic attack. Similarly the growing tips, the buds, and the flowers of plants are particularly sensitive to a localized effect. Those plants whose pores or surface structures are delicate or specialized may succumb completely.

This scourge is a product of modern industry, its most dramatic manifestations being in urban centers where there are great numbers of factories and incinerators. Visitors from the city to country light gardens are often amazed at the flourishing condition of the plants. This is not necessarily due to superior horticultural skill. We know now that the city light gardener labors under a considerable handicap.

Growers in the New York area were particularly alarmed by the effects of a severe smog in November 1968. The damage to house-grown plants was so great and reported by so many light gardeners that it stirred up a great deal of interest in the subject. But there are other sources of aerial pollution within the home, occasionally from heating units, from our stoves, from the volatile fluids we use for cleaning, from fresh paints, varnishes, and plastic coating liquids. Even pesticides must not be overlooked. The chemicals which destroy the insects may be harmless but the carrier for these poisons is often the real cause of injury to plants.

So we see that the possibility of air pollution is to be found everywhere in modern living. The specific effects, the sensitivity of certain plants and the resistance of others, are little known and have not been systematically studied.

The most sensational effects of air pollution which I have personally observed have been on budding Orchids. It can be more easily noticed and pinpointed with these plants because they bloom sequentially at certain times of the year whereas so many of our Gesneriads and other indoor plants have various seasons and it is not so easy to relate partial failure of blooming to a particular cause. Instances are recorded of whole greenhouses full of Orchids blasting every bud because the smoke from a nearby fall leaf burning was being sucked in by the ventilating fan. Ordinarily we would consider this a very mild form of pollution. The proximity of a much traveled highway produces the same effect when the air becomes saturated with gasoline carbon monoxide exhaust fumes.

City air pollution is compounded of this same carbon monoxide plus sulfur dioxide and other petroleum distillate wastes. But there are also airborne oily dust or soot. When there is high humidity, an oppressive air blanket, called smog, may be formed which has corrosive properties.

How are we to know whether our plants are being affected by air pollution? Principally, I suppose, by the elimination of other possible causes of damage and sometimes by the suddenness of the onslaught. Cause and effect are easily related. A friend using the cleansing fluid "Mr. Clean" noticed that all her plants stopped blooming. When she discontinued its use flowering resumed. Not exactly *quod erat demonstrandum*, but pretty close. Oddly enough, a minute amount of "Mr. Clean" in water is said to benefit plants as do some other detergents.

What can we do about pollution? Not very much, I fear, but, depending on circumstances, any one of the following suggestions may be helpful.

1. Air conditioning screens out some of the particles which poison the air.
2. Good air movement helps. It prevents blasts of smog from settling into a room.
3. Mist your plants daily.
4. Bathe plants which accumulate dust. A mild detergent will do no harm.
5. Enclose your plants in terrariums. This is almost a complete solution.
6. Raise plants which are relatively insensitive to toxic fumes. Plants which react badly are Columneas, Chiritas, Achimenes, and some Streptocarpus.

Chapter 9

HUMIDITY

Creating sufficient humidity in the plant area is the most difficult problem facing the city light gardener. Especially in living areas the air of our homes is relatively dry and the heat of the fluorescent tubes and the ballasts removes any remaining moisture. We can manage, nevertheless, provided only xerophytic plants are grown. Cacti, succulents, and a fairly long list of semidesert plants will do very well. But if we specialize in this way we deprive ourselves of all those beautiful plants on which the popularity of light gardening is founded. It is certainly worth the effort to attempt, at least, to match the moisture-laden atmospheric conditions which are normal in the tropical environment of the majority of houseplants. For the cellar or closed room gardener the solutions are relatively simple but for the apartment dweller there is as yet no perfect answer.

The relative humidity level of the average home is approximately 30 percent and rather less on winter days when the windows are closed and the heat is on. Raise it to 50 percent and plants which were unaccountably unhappy spruce up and gain a robust appearance almost overnight. Leaves flatten out and take on a healthy look, growth increases in rapidity, and buds and flowers appear.

As long as the light is sufficiently strong, even desert plants benefit from high atmospheric humidity. Their fleshy leaves are specially equipped to drain moisture from the air, and much of their intake is at night from the desert dews. Of course our tropical species prefer even more and will do surprisingly well at 75 percent or higher. However, it *is* possible to overdo it.

My plants are in a separate room where, one morning, I left the humidifier on high for too long a time as I found out when I walked in that evening. I immediately noticed that the floor was wet and looking up found that the moisture had collected on the ceiling and that it was literally raining. Some of the plants probably never had it so good since they left their native jungle but peeling ceilings and walls are too great a sacrifice for the sake of giving them pleasure. The humidity was above 85 percent.

Some doubt has been expressed as to the advantage of raising humidity even above 50 percent on the score that it encourages fungi and molds. Certainly there is more risk if, at the same time, water is allowed to collect in axils and pots are soaked through than would be the case at lower humidities. But it is a cardinal rule of houseplant culture that this should not happen and the gain in growth and flower formation is such that it is a risk which must be taken.

It is important to note that to achieve a desirable *relative* humidity, which is the standard measure, much greater amounts of moisture-laden air must be added to normal house atmospheres at, say, 80 than at 60 degrees Fahrenheit. This is not because moisture is being "burned" off by the heat so much as the natural expansion of gases at higher temperatures. To maintain our light gardens at a humidity of 65 percent (or even 50 percent) or better requires special equipment and the assumption of some additional chores.

HYGROMETERS AND HUMIDISTATS

Hygrometers are instruments for measuring relative humidity which may be represented on a column, as temperature is recorded by a thermometer, or by a dial. The amateur who has to guess at the humidity level of his light garden is at a considerable disadvantage. He can see light but he cannot feel humidity so that his judgment of the first may be reasonably close but very wide of the mark on the second.

It is ill advised to acquire one of the little round hygrometers which sits on a table and is merely a toy, or a tube hygrometer with wick which is accurate enough but old-fashioned and a bother. The standard industrial hygrometer contains a sensitive element; it is calibrated at the factory and needs no adjustment or handling after being installed, and it is accurate. Furthermore, a perfectly sound model, which is round or square with a large readable face, is available at little cost. It should be hung on the wall close to the garden, not in it, for it will deteriorate if it is sprayed. A position not far from a fan is the best as the humidity will be registered there both more rapidly and accurately.

A good natural hygrometer is a hank of Spanish Moss. It will remain alive and grow if the humidity is right. Light gardeners find that to achieve this a very high level of humidity must be maintained.

HUMIDISTATS

A humidistat is an accurate hygrometer which acts as an electric switch in the same manner as a thermostat. It is used as the control of a humidifier.

HUMIDIFIERS

Lucky are those indoor light gardeners who can connect their humidifiers to the house water supply. With a continuous flow of water to the unit they are spared the chore of constant refilling of the reservoir and do not have to worry about long hours of operation at maximum output.

One of the simplest machines was developed for use in small greenhouses. It stands on the floor and is about 18 inches square but only a few inches deep, as it contains no reservoir. Water from the house system is trickled over an absorbent sandwich screen and air is drawn through by an exhaust fan which precipitates it through the front opening of the cabinet. The principle is the same as that used in commercial greenhouses where the screens are situated at one end of the greenhouse and the fans at the other.

Room humidifiers have similar frontal dimensions but are much deeper. They usually stand on legs. They contain a reservoir for 8 to 10 gallons of water into which a mesh bag is suspended which draws the water upward by capillary action. A fan is set horizontally above the bag or vertically behind or in front of it and the moist air is driven through the mesh and out the front. These machines are usually equipped with two speed buttons, a level gauge, humidistat (not very reliable), and an automatic shut-off in the event that the reservoir is exhausted.

A less expensive model is the "cool mist" type which usually contains a 2-gallon reservoir. Powered by an electric motor, a plastic disc, with a hollow stem reaching to the water, is spun at high speed. The liquid is drawn up the stem and dispersed as mist by means of blades and slots in the disc.

Because they are uneconomical and inefficient for larger areas "hot vapor" humidifiers are not recommended.

Both the room humidifiers must be filled by hand unless they are attached to the house water line. This can be accomplished by a plastic tube lead-in from the cold water pipe. In the larger unit described, the float, which registers the height of the water on the indicator at the top of the machine, must be replaced by a float valve which shuts off the flow of water when the reservoir is full. The indicator then becomes superfluous. In the smaller unit a float valve must be installed.

With all these units the use of a separate high quality humidistat is advisable. This can be plugged in between the house current and the wiring of the humidifier.

Naturally such improvements can only be installed by those who are handy in such matters. Otherwise an electrician or plumber must be engaged for the purpose.

MISTING

Virtually all successful light gardeners mist their plants regularly. It is as much a part of the daily care as watering and feeding. In fact, one of the purposes *is* nutrition. The benefit to the plants is unquestionable and failure to mist is a common cause of poor growth and flowering.

The mister deposits a thin coat of droplets on the surfaces of the plants. This not only freshens them but, if nutrient is included in solution, constitutes foliar feeding. At the same time humidity is raised within a limited area, and may last for an hour or two. The process seems to take the place of nocturnal dew which is missing indoors.

Two or three times a day is good practice but not later than an hour before the lights are scheduled to go off.

There is a sharp distinction between spraying and misting. The former drenches the plant and water is deposited in the axils and runs down the stem of the plant wetting the soil at the base. This can and does lead to fungal diseases. A properly constructed mister will not deposit more than a fine film on the leaves and these should not coagulate into larger drops that move.

The above distinction eliminates many so-called misters on the market for they are in reality nothing but fine sprayers. Not that small sprayers are not better than nothing at all, simply that they do not do the job in the best way. Flit type guns, household cleanser plastic sprayers, etc., are inexpensive and convenient. To mist correctly, however, requires superior equipment.

The best of the misting-fogging units are electrically driven. The water capacity is not large because the fog is extremely fine, as it should be. Others are pressurized with CO_2 or charged with air. Less efficient but still suitable is the copper trombone sprayer with adjustable head. Fog nozzles for garden hoses may also be used.

The light gardening community would benefit from the invention of a very compact electric fogger which would be fed from a reservoir and operate automatically on several cycles of short duration during the day.

SURFACE EVAPORATION

This is a term which applies to the process by which moist surfaces in the light garden are translated into a localized humidity. In a small garden this can be especially helpful.

The more crowded the pots and plants, provided they are moist, the greater the amount of humidity produced by evaporation. This is a basic source of surface evaporation. But additional humidity is produced when we use trays and fill them part way with water. To prevent pots from becoming waterlogged there must be some material in or over the tray which will raise them above the water level and which, at the same time, will help to increase the evaporation.

Hardware Cloth. This is stiff wire screening, available in hardware stores, which can be laid over the tray and is strong enough to support the pots. If the sides are folded down to the depth of the tray, it can be fitted in, the surface will be flush with the rim of the tray, and it looks neater. A constant water level can be maintained in the tray.

Pebbles. Fill the tray part way, or all the way to the top, with water-absorbent pebbles. For ease of handling these should be light in weight but not so light as to float. Numerous surfaces will contribute to maximum evaporation. Water-repellent stones reduce the evaporation area. Because pebbles are inevitably heavier they are less satisfactory than the two following methods.

Plastic Crate. This is honeycomb molded plastic sheeting, some half inch thick, which is used to diffuse light in fluorescent fixtures. Bought in sheets, it can be cut to size with a saw. It is excellent material for trays, and small pieces are good supports for lifting individual pots to a still higher level. Water in the tray tends to rise along the walls of the honeycomb and a good deal of surface moisture evaporates.

Sand is not recommended for the house both because of its weight and its tendency to become damp all through the mass. It also provides a splendid means for insects to travel from pot to pot.

To prevent insect life from developing in the water in the trays add an eyedropper full of Malathion or a tablespoon of Clorox every couple of months. For algae you can buy algicide pills in most tropical fish stores. Put one in the water at the first sign of discoloration. The addition of Fermate, Panodrench, or Captan in small quantities will keep molds from forming.

FOUNTAINS

Install a small recirculating fountain in floor gardens or in the center of large trays. You can use the water in the tray itself to feed the fountain. It is a space waster, of course, but it does raise the humidity considerably. Small fountains can be bought in most hardware stores and from firms which specialize in pumps.

TENTS

A fitted covering for a single or multiple level light garden may serve a dual purpose. Use it at night to raise the local humidity through concentration of the evaporation from soil, pots, and drainage. As this is necessary only if your day humidity is rather low, there will be no harmful effects from an absence of ventilation. If the tent is opaque it will also shield the plants from lights which may be burning nearby in the room at night.

You can make your tent out of any kind of cloth, though a coated material or plastic is probably best. It will not be airtight, of course, since it will be open at the bottom, but that is all to the good. It could be harmful only on hot evenings in summer.

PLASTIC BAGS

Individual plants requiring especially high and even humidity and protection from drafts, either temporarily or constantly, can be enclosed in clear plastic bags of a size large enough not to crowd them. The bag, which must be airtight, is blown up with pot and plant inside until it forms a firm balloon. Fasten the top with a piece of wire and paper stripping or a rubber band. The balloon must stay inflated else the inside surfaces will gather moisture and leaves will tend to rot on long contact with them.

Be careful to see that the pot and its medium, though moist, are not wet. There should be no standing water in the bag. A good method is to water the plant twelve hours before enclosure.

If at any time the temperature of the room rises above 80 degrees it is advisable to open the bag as otherwise the plant may suffocate.

The chief disadvantage of this method is the amount of space occupied by the inflated bag, but it is one often found useful in reviving plants. Certain orchids react particularly well to this treatment, encouraging roots and leads on inactive pseudobulbs.

You can also use bags as temporary protection for plants which prefer terrarium treatment. In this situation the bags should be left partly open.

CONTROLLING HUMIDITY IN THE HOME

The equipment and methods described above are those which are at present available for humidity control in any of the areas discussed below. The purpose of what follows is to indicate those which are most applicable to particular locations and the special difficulties encountered, if any.

THE CELLAR OR ATTIC GARDEN

The location of the cellar garden may be a belowground level romp room or working area. The garden may be in an enclosure of its own or it may occupy the whole room. Usually it is a rather large affair. Few hobbyists starting out to use such a favorable growing space stop short of the development of a rather extensive garden which may cover several hundred square feet of bench space. In any event the garden must be in some sort of room, and humidity producing equipment must be sufficient for the total area.

A cellar is an ideal place for the light garden, from the standpoint of humidity, because it is rarely completely dry, except in the city, a certain amount of moisture condensing on the cool foundation walls. Air circulation is virtually nonexistent. In fact it is somewhat like a big Wardian case, and far less subject to sudden changes of condition than a greenhouse.

Attics, on the other hand, are notoriously dry and tend to be very hot places in summer. If possible the garden should be enclosed and particularly well insulated.

The two areas, then, are very different except in one important respect: they are isolated from the living rooms of the home, which permits much greater freedom in adapting them to the growing of plants. In both places the humidifiers must be of a rated capacity sufficient for the cubic space, and it must be taken into consideration that the normal attic will draw on the machine more continuously than will a cellar. A cellar installation will make connection with the water line a simple matter. The attic will probably present some difficulties but every effort should be made to hook in with the house system, otherwise the refilling chore will become unmanageable. In both places the maintenance of very high levels of humidity is possible.

THE GARDEN ROOM

A small room, one that is part of the general living area, may be set aside for gardening. Here humidity is easy to control because it is a closed-in space. But it may be difficult to run in a pipe or hose from the house water system.

The only real problem, however, is the effect of humidity on walls and ceilings which are likely to mildew and flake. It is, therefore, advisable *before* installing equipment to paint all surfaces with a waterproofing material. I have found epoxy paint difficult to apply but remarkably durable and moisture resistant—and there are other good brands on the market. Another material which stands up very well is molded press-on brick wallpaper whose plastic coating seems to be impermeable to the concentration of moisture.

A standing reservoir humidifier is usually sufficient. If the room has a window—usually there is at least one—it is both a boon and a nuisance. It will supply extra sunlight to the plants directly around it and good outside ventilation. The sun on a hot summer day, on the other hand, will raise the temperature excessively. There is also a disadvantage to window ventilation in the city—the circulation of pollution-laden air. On the whole it is better to cover up the window and install a fan or air conditioner in one section of the opening.

OPEN GARDENS IN LIVING AREAS

These undoubtedly present the greatest difficulties and a combination of the various devices will be advisable in most instances.

Table models are too small to warrant the use of a humidifier, at least of the types available at present. The principal means of maintaining humidity are: (1) Water in trays, pots and medium; (2) Tents (see above) at night; and (3) Misting with a small gadget which has a short range.

Carts, free standing units, and room dividers may be handled much as above. A standing humidifier directly facing the installation will improve humidity though a good deal will be dissipated. The equipment must be rather small to avoid raising the humidity of the whole room so high as to damage upholstery and books. If the humidistat is set in a protected position within the plant area it will not be affected by general drops in room humidity with the result that the humidifier will be activated only when the garden itself registers a decline below the set level.

The larger plant area requires misting equipment of greater capacity and reach. But then there is the risk of damping down other objects in the room. A sheet of plastic suspended at the back of the unit will catch the moisture and prevent damage. Consider this necessity when you locate and build your garden.

A device of some assistance is the covering of back or side walls with thick plastic sponge. Sprayed or watered daily, these would release considerable humidity. Arranging them so that they will not be unsightly and providing for drainage of excess moisture requires careful planning. The sponge comes in various thicknesses and colors.

SHELVING AGAINST WALLS AND UNDER WINDOWS

The advantage here is the solid backing. However, walls must be protected with plastic sheet unless the unit itself is walled in. A humidifier can be set at one end of the garden or a plastic sheet draped over the front at night. When a humidifier is used at one end of the garden it is advisable to set a fan at the other.

Chapter 10

WATERING

Because our house temperatures normally are higher than those of a green-house and the ballast/tube combination contributes to a further heating, the soil dries out more quickly and we must water more often. The frequent drenchings followed by rapid evaporation is neither better nor worse for the plants but does mean that the grower must be even more careful under lights than in a green-house. It means that moisture-loving plants can tolerate, to a considerable degree, bottom watering, and that those which prefer dampness to wetness must be treated to frequent small doses.

There is no more difficult horticultural art to teach the beginner than water-ing. Each plant requires different treatment, even members of the same species or cultivar. Pot size, root development, size of top growth, packing of soil in the pot, and the exact condition of the mix—all of these make a difference. And no one can judge these mechanical ratios exactly. The normal cultural instructions based on experience often do not apply when it comes to watering because, in addition to the items mentioned above, the general environment plays a role.

In fact nowhere in plant culture is exact observation so essential. It amounts to watching the plant and its reaction to water intake day by day. Plants move by growing, and though the rate is relatively slow it is noticeable. We learn to recognize it by comparison and an effort of memory. That is to say, if we keep our eyes on our plants we will notice the slight changes taking place and be able to measure whether they are slowing up or accelerating, spreading their leaves or shrinking and drooping. You can, with practice, acquire an almost sixth sense for the general condition of a plant—whether it glows with health or is beginning to feel poorly. Indeed, it is most essential to recognize any deterioration immediately so that you can identify cause and effect both favorable and unfavorable, the one so that you can continue a regimen that benefits the plant, the other so that you can change the method quickly.

Here are a few rules to follow:

1. A plant which is in active growth needs more water than one which has ceased to grow. In fact the latter condition is often a sign of overwatering.

2. Plants which naturally grow rapidly usually need more water than those which grow slowly.

3. When a plant has ceased to grow it should be kept just moist. If it is of a kind which habitually goes dormant it should not be watered at all once the leaves have shriveled or, in the case of certain Orchids, pseudobulbs have reached their maturity.

4. Plants whose leaves rise directly from the ground are often subject to crown rot. They should be watered from the bottom followed by occasional leachings or watered carefully and sparingly from the top. Excellent drainage is essential if watering is heavy.

5. If a plant stops blooming, reduce the amount of watering.

6. For most flowering houseplants—never allow them to become bone dry unless tuberous and dormant.

7. Water more in warm weather than in cool.

8. The temperature of the water should be close to that of the room.

In a light garden it is better for the plants to drain into the tray rather than a saucer. Draining leaches out salts and excess water. Accumulations of liquid in the saucer feed back to the plant.

When the light garden is of considerable extent, especially in a cellar, a hose is the quickest means of watering. Attach an extension wand which can be regulated to control the flow.

For smaller gardens Tube Craft's (see source list, page 240) long wand is very useful. The wand, which is of metal, is attached to a length of plastic tubing ending in a metal tube which can be set in a reservoir of water. This, a gallon bottle for instance, must be at a higher level than the shelves. The excellent reach and the slow flow of the water is perfect for watering a large number of pots individually. The reservoir may also contain a nutrient solution for feeding with each watering.

Watering cans with long spouts are the best for reaching around and behind plants. Size is a matter of convenience and your own strength. A good can is made of metal or thick, rather flexible plastic—not the thin brittle type sold in most variety stores. A spray head is unnecessary.

WATERING WHEN ON VACATION

There is really no substitute for leaving the plants with a knowledgeable friend or relative or having him come in and fill your trays once a week so that the plants can have bottom moisture. Suggestions like the packing of wet newspapers in the bathtub are such a nuisance that it would almost be worthwhile to abandon the plants and replace them on return.

The only feasible alternative is the following. Set aside those plants which will tolerate a two to three week drought (for most plants this is about the limit, Cacti, etc., excepted). Raise your plants by means of pebbles or plastic crate almost to the top level of the trays. Fill the trays with water. Make a plastic tent which covers the area. Reduce the light day length to 8–10 hours. Try to keep the temperature as low as possible if it is summer, and not over 70 degrees in winter.

AUTOMATIC WATERING

There is, at the present time, no truly satisfactory automatic watering system for the small light garden. The capillary system has proved satisfactory for larger installations.

GLASS WICKS

Wicks made of fiber glass can be bought cut to specific lengths or by the yard. When potting a plant, the top of the wick should reach nearly to the surface of the soil and dangle a couple of inches through and below the hole at the bottom. A large number of pots can be maintained this way in trays partly filled with water. Even moisture is assured but rather more than some plants can take.

STORAGE UNITS WITH SENSORS

Still another method employs a ceramic sensor to control the water supply. In some models the storage area surrounds the pot, and in others a separate tank is provided. A rubber tube with the sensor at its tip is the means by which liquid is conveyed from the storage chamber to the soil. The sensor is embedded in the soil, and water is released only when the soil is dry. The system is excellent but has the drawback that the amount of stored water is not very large. Most of the units are rather expensive considering the number needed to service a large number of plants.

GLASS OR PLASTIC BULBS

A reservoir of water is contained in a glass bulb with a fine pointed opening. This is inserted into the soil and will moisten it evenly, the supply lasting from a few days to a week, depending on the size of the pot.

CAPILLARY SYSTEMS

For this method, which services any number of pots, a plastic hose is provided which attaches to the house water system. The capillary hoses are very thin tubes with a metal screw tip. The larger hose extends along the bench and, wherever it is nearest to a pot, the metal tip of a capillary hose is screwed into it. The other end of the capillary hose is inserted into the soil of the pot. When the water is turned on, all the pots are moistened at once. Hundreds can be handled in this way. The system works best with uniform plants and pot sizes.

CONSTANT LEVEL SYSTEMS

A number of systems regulate the moisture by flow into trays full of sand—the Humex method from England, for example. A float valve in a reservoir controls the flow, and the sand is kept constantly moist. The weight of the sand filled trays militates against its usefulness for most indoor growers.

RESERVOIR POTS AND TRAYS

Pots and trays with double liners permitting water storage and its slow release to the soil inside are becoming increasingly popular. Thus far these are principally helpful with small plants whose water intake is not very large and for flats or pots of seedlings and cuttings.

The Aquamatic Planter, a small version of the system, works well for me with African Violets but supplies too much water to most of the miniatures such as Sinningia and Koellikeria. It is a good system as long as you are selective in its use. The water supply lasts for weeks.

But the moment it is a matter of larger plants, the present systems do not store sufficient water. A recent system which utilizes sensors in the soil to regulate the flow of water is efficient enough but the supply only lasts for a short time. It will be a while before the automatic watering needs of indoor growers with mixed collections will give complete satisfaction.

VALUE OF AUTOMATIC WATERING

Light gardening is not mass horticulture, at least in the home, and nothing replaces personal attention. To treat a collection of different kinds of Begonias to the same amount of watering would be disastrous. At present the chief use of the systems is as a means of maintaining a water supply to the plants during a vacation lasting up to three weeks. With one or the other of the methods described the plants will survive the ordeal.

THE HOT WATER TAP

Most growers have a horror of using water from the hot water tap. They think that in some way the liquid has been deprived of its virtue or that it has been contaminated. On the contrary, wherever there has been water treatment, the addition of chlorine for instance, the hot water tap is a much safer source and is equivalent to allowing fresh cold water to stand for some time. In the process of heating, the chlorine and other gases are driven off. After the water has cooled it is certainly superior for the treatment of plants.

Chapter 11

PROPAGATION

WHY PROPAGATE?

There are certain, usually large, foliage houseplants which grow very little from year to year so that, for all practical purposes, they are permanent. Such are Beaucarneas, Dracaenas, some Palms and Ferns. Dieffenbachias, on the other hand, will reach the ceiling of a room in a couple of years. That is why we usually have no reason to propagate the first category and why we must start new Dieffenbachias as the old ones approach the limits of their useful size.

Under lights the limitations are still greater. Most of our medium size bloomers soon grow unsightly or too large to handle. If a Columnea is kept in a basket in a greenhouse it may last for several years but in the house will rapidly occupy more space than we can spare.

The other factor, which many neophytes have not grasped, is that all plants have a youth, a maturity, and an old age. The life span varies considerably according to habit of growth. In any event, those plants which we prize for their bloom are not sequoias. Sooner than you may expect their tubers become woody and unproductive or their stems toughen up and no longer produce leaves and flowers as freely. Finally they just seem to fade away.

Having once passed the peak of maturity, plants never look as well again. Starting with a juvenile plant careful culture may bring it to mature perfection. This will last a little while, for weeks or even months, followed by a gradual decline in beauty.

116

If a plant is past its prime, we have the choice of buying a new one or of propagating. When it has been a particularly good plant we will want to perpetuate it rather than take the chance with a replacement. Besides, propagating is simple and it is fun.

There are a number of other reasons which should induce us to put propagation in the house on a permanent basis. Whenever we buy plants from a nursery we should promptly take cuttings so that, if the parent plant succumbs to the shock of transportation and a strange environment, we will have a healthy one coming along for us. Often the plant grown from a cutting does much better than the original one, perhaps because it is started and grown in our light garden environment.

Plants which put out runners, rhizomes, or offset tubers do so because the life expectancy of the parent plant is relatively short. The plant expects the rhizomes to develop new growths, the runners to root themselves, and the tubers to start a new existence before the old tuber dies off. And, because in the light garden the plant has not the space to roam about as in nature, we must perform the service. The tubers must be separated, the rhizomes removed from the roots, and the runners cut off. And each must be encouraged in a new pot or propagating bed to develop an independent life.

One of the greater pleasures of houseplant growing is that of sharing one's treasures with friends. A good supply of young plants is always useful for gifts and exchanges.

POLLINATION

Pollination of flowers for seed has only limited use in the house. Propagating by means of stem or leaf cuttings is far more satisfactory in most instances because most of us do not really need large numbers of the same plant; also, seed takes much longer to grow to maturity. A number of plants which are difficult to grow from cuttings obligingly pollinate themselves. Such is the case with *Sinningia pusilla* and *Gesneria cuneifolia. Chirita lavandulacea* and *micromusa* are examples of plants which must be propagated from seed. *Exacum affine* is another, but seeds are available from most flower seedsmen.

The technique consists of choosing a mature flower and, with a clean, sparsely bristled camel's hair brush, transferring the pollen from the anthers to the stigma of either the same or another flower of the same species. If the corolla is open and the sex organs are prominent, this is easy. When the tube is almost closed you may have to make a circular cut with a small and very sharp scissors at the base of the flower well above the calyx. Anther and stigma are then revealed. If neatly done, the removal of the corolla does not interfere with fertilization.

After that you must watch for the right moment to collect the seed. The pod will swell and finally split. If you can catch it when it is just turning color from green to brown, you can cut it off and place it in a glassine or plastic envelope or bag to dry. When the pod has dried thoroughly the bag should be made airtight for storage. Not all pods split spontaneously in this condition. You may have to do this manually, by crushing it, when you wish to plant.

Those interested in hybridization techniques should consult the special books devoted to the subject.

PROPAGATING SEEDS

In very few instances does the indoor light gardener require a very high percentage of seed germination. Having limited space to work with, the amount of seed provided in a packet is usually far more than is needed. A Gloxinia seed pod produces hundreds of seeds but the grower has room for only a relatively few plants. This makes any complicated procedure unnecessary, such as the use of heating cables, thermostats, and special seed beds. Even when the object is the production of a large number of annual seedlings for outdoor planting, such means are superfluous. After all, the conditions for seed growth are normally far more favorable under lights than out of doors.

MEDIUM

For all kinds of propagating there are dozens of methods, each with their enthusiastic supporters. Far too much fuss is made about the matter as there are a large number of good alternatives. The following is simple and effective.

The best containers for propagating are the same that we use for cuttings —plastic boxes 3 inches high or more. Those used for bread storage, with their rounded covers, are excellent.

Into your container pour an inch to an inch and a half of vermiculite. Level and moisten. Pour off any excess liquid. Onto the surface spread evenly a very thin layer of milled sphagnum moss. Plant your seed on this surface. If it is to lie on top, this is sufficient. If the seed must be buried, cover it with another very thin layer of the moss. When the box is closed the moisture from the vermiculite will permeate the sphagnum.

SOWING

Large seeds are easy to space evenly but gardeners have always been bedeviled by the small ones. Those of some of our houseplants are almost as fine as dust.

One means of dividing the material is to mix it with a medium which is also fine particled. Since I use milled sphagnum I find that it can serve as both top dressing and seeding medium. When the seed is so small do not overestimate the amount you need. Recently I planted a bread box with one pinch of *Gesneria cuneifolia* and ended up with over one thousand seedlings. Take, therefore, a tiny amount and spread it over some milled sphagnum in a glass or ceramic bowl. Stir very thoroughly in the dry state with a spoon and then cover your seed bed with it. If the depth of the sphagnum layer does not appear to be quite sufficient just dust some more over the whole.

With seeds which are slightly larger you may be able to work this trick. Cut a piece of stiff paper to the size of your seed bed. Line it with squares whose intersections are about as far apart as you would like your seeds to be. Punch a hole at each of these intersections and lay the sheet over the soil. Now put a very small amount of seed on a sheet of white paper and spread it well by shaking slightly. Take a darning needle and apply the tip to your tongue and then to a seed. Stab the needle through a hole over your seed bed and withdraw. In each case one, or at most two, seeds will be left behind. Working with a large magnifier helps.

GERMINATING THE SEEDS

Place the propagating box as close to the light tubes as possible and leave it there until seedlings start to appear. During summer it may be advisable to shove the lid aside in the heat of the day. If you notice the medium drying out, spray with clear water. In winter the tubes will keep the seeds sufficiently warm while they are on. But you must take precautions that the temperature does not drop below 70 degrees at night.

Seed varies greatly in germination time. Many an amateur has thrown out viable seed because it did not show aboveground after a month. Consult a chart, such as that in Park's seed catalog, which lists germinating periods or be patient for two months. There are a number of the larger, hard-shelled seed which will take even longer.

HANDLING THE SEEDLINGS

As the seedlings appear aboveground you must watch your propagating box more carefully for signs of excess moisture. Should the surface be clouded by congealed moisture leave the top open for a while.

The first pair of leaflets are actually the cotyledons or halves of the seed itself. It is only when the second pair grow out that seedlings are ready for transplanting. However, unless they are badly crowded, you need not be in a hurry.

When you are prepared to transplant get another propagating box. This time it can be larger in area but no less than 3 inches high. Fill it to a depth of 1½ inches with Tropical Plant Mix just moistened. Do not pack it down. Poke holes where you want the plants to go.

A very useful tool at this stage is a long pair of tongs with the points turned downward. Hold a magnifying glass in one hand (or wear a magnifying visor) and the tongs in the other. Grip the seedling at soil level with the tongs and tug the seedling out by the roots. Because the medium is so light there will be no resistance. Drop the seedling into a hole and work the soil around it with the tongs, making sure that it will stand upright and that all of the root is buried.

When the propagating box is full, place it within 3 inches of the lights. Again watch out for excess moisture. If your medium has been moistened with a solution of Transplantone (Amchem) you may run less risk of trouble.

As soon as the seedlings resume growth you can start to remove the cover part way to harden them off a bit. This is less necessary if they are intended for a terrarium. But for the open garden they will have to get used to lower humidities. At this time you can also spray them once every few days with a solution of chemically balanced nutrient.

POTTING UP

Depending on the normal size of a mature plant, your seedlings will be ready for transfer to pots. A *Sinningia pusilla* will always be tiny, so you can pot when it has only six or eight little leaves for it is probably ready to bloom at that size. Other plants require only half-grown leaves. There is really no rule except an appearance of sturdy health.

Fill small pots with the applicable medium, prepare a hole, and dig out your seedlings with a narrow spoon or a miniature home gardening shovel. Take along as much of the soil as possible so that the plant will not feel totally strange in the new environment. Water lightly after planting with a solution of Transplantone (Amchem). In the first few days set the plants no closer to the lights than a foot. After that you can accustom them to stronger illumination.

SOIL LAYERING

Almost all the trailing plants can be soil layered. Episcias, Columneas, Aeschynanthus, Stapelias, rhizomatous Ferns, Fittonias, Pellionias, etc., will propagate most rapidly and surely by this means.

The first requirement is a package of hairpins. Then fill a small pot with wet sphagnum (natural or milled). Pick a section of trailing stem outside the pot, remove any leaves in the axils at that point, and pin the section well into the sphagnum. If your propagating pot does not reach high enough you will have to put it on a pedestal. Root activity may be more rapid if you treat the section to be buried with hormone powder.

Keep the pot moist and, as soon as growth begins at the tip of the trailer, treat once with a mild nutrient. When the new growth has expanded and begins to assume the appearance of a normal plant, cut the piece of trailer loose from its parent. After a short further stay in the sphagnum it can be potted up in regular mix.

LEAF AND STEM CUTTINGS

Use plastic boxes at least 3 inches high, except for very small cuttings. Fill to a depth of at least 1 inch with small grained vermiculite which has been carefully moistened so that there is no excess whatever. This is my medium for all leaf and stem cuttings, which I find entirely satisfactory.

Leaf Cuttings

Leaves which are fleshy and heavily veined are best for propagation. Those with a thin, soft texture are more difficult; the ones which have shiny, hard surfaces are usually impossible.

Never remove the leaves from the center of a plant whose top growth is in the form of a rosette—an African Violet, for instance. You will probably stunt it permanently. Always use healthy outer leaves.

Although some consider it harmful, I always cut my leaves with a small, very sharp scissors. This is a matter of convenience and accuracy.

The cut should always be made at the base of the petiole, as close to the stem as possible. Trim the petiole to a half inch or less. Brush the petiole with hormone powder for all its length, the cut tip, and about a quarter of an inch at the base of the leaf on the underside only. Do not allow any of the powder to fall on the upper surface of the leaf as it is usually allergic to this treatment.

Poke a small hole into the vermiculite and bury the end of the leaf up to the limit of the hormone dusting in an upright or slightly angled position, the top of the leaf facing up. Allow no more than an inch between medium size leaves. Close the box and set about a foot under the lights. Try to keep the temperature at better than 70 but not over 85 degrees. No further attention is necessary until new growth appears.

Two types of large leaf must be handled somewhat differently. For instance, detach an outer leaf of *Streptocarpus* 'Constant Nymph' (usually at least 10 inches long) and cut into 1½ to 2-inch-long wedges, the point facing toward the base of the leaf with the midvein in the center. Dust with hormone powder on the tip and one third of the underside. Then set in the vermiculite.

Large Begonia leaves are also treated differently. From small leaved ones we usually take stem cuttings. These leaves are both broad and long with the petiole somewhat to the side. Cut the petiole close to the stem, trim to a quarter of an inch, dust the petiole and both sides of the adjacent leaf with hormone powder up to a half inch. Roll the leaf into a funnel and set it upright into the vermiculite.

Some leaves can simply be laid on the vermiculite after the whole of the underside has been dusted and the major veins have been cut. Experts propagate large Begonia leaves in this way but it is a tricky method and the cuts sometimes develop roots without top growth. However, it does work very well with *Chirita sinensis*. Take a leaf and cut the midrib at regular intervals of about a half inch. Dust the bottom with hormone powder, lay the leaf bottom down on the vermiculite, and pass a hairpin through either end to keep it flat. Almost invariably young plants develop through the slits within a short time.

Stem Cuttings

We propagate stem cuttings of branching plants and those which send out surface rhizomes. Examples are *Carissa, Cuphea, Clerodendrum, Euphorbia, Geranium (Pelargonium),* Impatiens, *Jacobinia, Peristrophe, Punica, Aeschynanthus,* and *Columnea.*

In this instance the young growth is preferred. Cut a 2-inch length, clip off an inch of leaves close to the stem, dust length and tip with hormone powder, and set the naked stem section in the vermiculite. From there on treat the propagation box exactly as described above for leaf cuttings. Soft stems propagate more quickly than woody ones.

Where New Growth Appears

Some cuttings will root in a matter of a week or two. Soft stems are usually the quickest; leaves often take many weeks. African Violet leaves, for instance, though very reliable, may take as much as two months before greenery shows.

New growth appears on the upper side of the leaf at soil level. It should be well developed before the cutting is removed from the soil because it is a common occurrence that more than one plantlet grows from the base and these develop successively.

When there is ample top growth the leaf can be dug up and the plantlets and their roots carefully cut apart. Then they can be potted up immediately in the correct mix.

Stem cuttings often show no evidence of rooting. The only test is to give them a slight tug after a couple of weeks. If you do this delicately enough you will notice whether there is resistance or not without damaging the plant. If the sensation is positive, you can pull the cutting out of the fluffy vermiculite without breaking roots. Pot in regular mix. Fewer plants are lost with stem than leaf cuttings.

PROPAGATION BY DIVISION

Division of plants is only possible when there are multiple growths from the soil, which in outdoor agriculture are called suckers. Except when the growths are individually tuberous it always involves damage to the parent plant and therefore requires special precautions.

An example of multiplication by bulb offsets is found in the Oxalis family.

Episcia 'Cleopatra'

Streptocarpus 'Constant Nymph'

Sinningia eumorpha 'Pink'

Episcia 'Moss Agate'

Sinningia 'Freckles'

Sinningia 'Cindy'

Hypocyrta 'Rio'

Aeschynanthus lobbianus

Lantana camara var. *nana compacta*

Gesneria cuneifolia

Koellikeria erinoides

Paphiopedilum 'Maudiae'

Paphiopedilum 'Britta' X 'Clementine Churchill'

Jacobinia carnea

Ceropegia woodii

Exacum affine

Semidwarf *Pelargonium* 'Sneezy'

Malpighia coccigera

Thymophyllum 'Dahlborg Daisy'   *Crassula schmidtii*

Cuphea hyssopifolia

Aechmea fasciata

Punica granatum nana

Clerodendron thomsoniae

The bulbs build a cluster which can be broken up and each one potted up separately. The Gesneriads have scaly rhizomes which can be separated from the root system. These are stored in a plastic bag until they show growth at one of the tips and can then be potted.

On the other hand, you cannot well divide a single rosette of an African Violet. But if it gets side growths you may take a sharp knife and cut vertically at the joint with the mother plant. Sometimes the section comes free with a certain amount of its own root attached. Then it can be potted up without more ado. However, if there is no root growth, the piece is simply a kind of stem cutting and must be propagated in a closed box in the same way.

This is the method of dividing Streptocarpus, Columneas, and Aeschynanthus, to mention a few. The danger to the parent plant is from the wound inflicted by the open cut. To prevent infection the wound should be dusted with hormone powder and the soil *not* replaced around it. Keep the hole open and firm the earth so that it stays exposed to the air. Water for two weeks only from the bottom and as little as possible.

TOP GROWTH CUTTINGS

When an Episcia which has been kept trimmed becomes too tall we can cut off the top few inches and root it. This makes a rather large cutting which does not fit easily into a box. However, we can cut off the bottom leaves along the stem, dust with hormone powder, and bury the stem in a pot of moist vermiculite. Set the pot in a saucer filled with clear water and cover with a plastic bag (clear) supported by a stick. Keep the saucer filled. Place the pot a foot from the lights and in a few weeks you will have a new plant with a still perfect top growth.

The same procedure can be applied to any of the stem plants with rosettes which get out of hand or whose leaves will not root easily.

Chapter 12

PESTICIDES

DANGERS AND PRECAUTIONS

All spray materials, aerosols, and dilute pesticides are harmful to human beings and animals. Most of them are lethal if absorbed in sufficient quantity. Some are less toxic than others but a very large role is played by the sensitivity of the individual who is exposed to them. There is simply no way of determining whether a concentration considered "safe" is, or is not, dangerous to you.

It is a common error to think that the effect of a poison on the system is immediate. Pesticide chemicals work on the organism in a considerable number of ways and probably some of which we are not yet aware. Weeks or months later they may take effect on the blood count, sight, skin, and internal organs. By that time the relationship between cause and effect is no longer obvious and the affected person may continue to use an insecticide, not at all aware that he is increasing the damage each time. Furthermore, we know that some of these chemicals are accumulated in the body so that very small quantities may add up after a period to a destructive amount.

Using pesticides in the house is especially dangerous because of the lack of ventilation and the small enclosed areas. Unless you are prepared to take all the precautions which are necessary it is better to get rid of infected plants than to take any chances with your family or your pets.

Do not believe that quick handling will save you, holding your breath or closing your eyes. Without special covering or filtration of the air, you are exposed. If you are one of those who are particularly allergic to the chemical you are using, the effects can be out of all proportion to the apparent cause.

It is *necessary* to take the following measures when handling pesticides:

1. For aerosol pesticides and fumes from concentrate solutions, wear a Phosdrin mask equipped with a canister and close-fitting goggles.

2. For wettable emulsions and sprays, the less expensive Wilson Agri-Tox respirator can be used safely. However, separate goggles with tension fit are also necessary.

3. For all pesticides: cover hands and lower arms with rubber gloves.

4. Wear clothing which covers the rest of the body even if the weather is very hot. Plastic raincoats are useful for the purpose especially when spraying.

5. Close off the spraying area from the rest of the house and keep children and pets completely away.

HARMLESS AND RELATIVELY SAFE WAYS OF DEALING WITH PESTS

The beginner is likely to be overwhelmed by the variety of insecticides which are recommended for various pests and is justifiably wary of handling most of them. Many modern pesticides and their solvents are lethal for certain plants, and manufacturers' labels give no inkling of these dangers. Coupled with the risk of personal harm in handling, it is no wonder that many growers would rather get rid of the plant than expose themselves to pesticides.

There is no rule that says that only pesticides which are dangerous to humans are most effective on insects. The commercial grower on a large scale needs very wide-spectrum chemicals and very efficient quick killing. The indoor gardener's needs are much more modest. He knows very little about the sensitivity to different pesticidal agents or treatments of the numerous kinds of pests that can invade his garden. And it is known that any number of natural and synthetic products are deadly for particular species of insects.

All the following suggestions may be effective in ridding a plant of its tormentors. Turn to the powerful chemicals as a last resort.

SYSTEMICS AND SOIL PESTICIDES

Many insects spend part of their life cycle in soil. They can be attacked there by using a soil drench. One of the best of these is VC-13 which is effective against most pests. It can be recommended also because, though it contains a poisonous chemical, chlordane, mixing it with water in a container and pouring it into the pot involves far less personal exposure than a spray or plant dip. VC-13 does little damage to most plants. As insects on plants are constantly dropping onto the soil and reproducing there, treatment with this pesticide or a similar one should be a preliminary to the use of other methods.

Even this method, however, has its dangers. The material itself is toxic and should not be used in quantity. Do one pot at a time, allowing an interval of at least a week before soaking another. I give this warning because there have been instances of amateurs flooding all their pots and then sleeping in the room with them. Whether cause and effect is certain or not, the fact is that they were pretty ill after a few days.

Different in their action but alike in the method of handling are the systemics. These are chemicals which are absorbed by the plants and make them a poisonous meal for an insect. Meta-Systox is one of these and there are a number of others. Variable results are achieved, some of them deleterious to the plant. Especially in regard to the plants discussed in this book, no manufacturer of these insecticides can pinpoint the effect on insects and on the plant. They just know it works on some tested plants which are not the ones we are growing. The same precautions should be used as with VC-13 and other soil drench pesticides.

WASHING

Many pests will succumb to a series of washings and soaking on a three-day schedule for about two weeks. Small plants can be completely brushed with the water solution.

1. Wrap the top of the pot with plastic sheet held down with masking tape and flush the leaves and stems with a strong jet of lukewarm water. Use the faucet or a hair rinsing sprayer. Work the plant over thoroughly.

2. Make a strong solution of brown borax soap in a pail of lukewarm water. Add a tablespoon of household ammonia. Wash the plant thoroughly.

ALCOHOL AND BRUSH

When the insects are visible and the plant is of small size you can take a slightly stiff oil-paint brush, dip it in rubbing alcohol, and remove each pest. The progeny of these insects may be invisible, so finish up by brushing lightly over all leaf and stem surfaces.

MANUALLY REMOVING PESTS

Because the above methods are the *only* safe ones I will, at the risk of repetition, describe in more detail how they are done because beginners may have the impression that they are easy ways of avoiding the use of the more powerful insecticides. The fact is that the procedures are *not* easy, and require great patience and care. If you are one of those, like myself, who abhors the use of the very dangerous insecticide chemicals which are so glibly recommended, you will have to go to the necessary trouble. The results are at least as good as far as ridding the plant of its tormentors is concerned, and the methods are far safer for both you and the plant.

When a plant suffers from mealybug or scale, place it in a bright light. Take a narrow, tufted, rather stiff oil-paint brush, place a bottle of rubbing alcohol at your side and go to work. You will see the bugs and the scale easily enough, and, after dipping the brush in the liquid, you can lift or rub them off. What you do not see is the progeny of the mature insects which are wandering out by the dozens from each parent. Therefore, after removing the larger specimens, it is necessary to swab carefully over upper and lower surfaces of every leaf, the petioles and the stems right down to the soil.

Satisfied that you have removed everything visible and washed off the rest, the plant can be put aside for a few days. Then you must do the work all over again. This time there will be fewer insects and they will probably be smaller. Nevertheless the total swabbing *must* be repeated. You will have to go on like that for at least two weeks and, for a month after that, you must examine your plant very carefully every few days. If nothing appears again by the end of the extra month you may be in the clear. If there is a recurrence you will have to persist. In the end you will win out, but it is pretty tedious —a matter of whether you are willing to go to the trouble to save a plant.

When the subject is mites, far smaller and trickier creatures, you are best advised to brush the plant thoroughly with borax soapy water, with or without a small amount of ammonia, and to repeat it every three days for at least two weeks. In between give the plant a daily spray with a real jet of lukewarm water. A hair sprayer is excellent for the purpose. Turn the plant slowly and do the job thoroughly. Mites hate water. After finishing the cure check the plant with a 10-power loupe every few days for at least a month.

Do not give up. The method does work. When you have used it a few times you will become more expert in brushing and washing. Your cleaning will be more thorough, and the cure will be achieved in short order.

If, after all my persuasion, you elect to use chemicals, here are a few descriptions and recommendations.

Recommended Pesticides

PEST STRIPS

Under the labels Vapona or No-Pest Strip, impregnated sheets of plastic, 9½ inches long by 2 inches wide, are sold at gasoline stations, hardware stores, and supermarkets. They are not only effective in ridding the garden of insects, but have proved themselves the most convenient preventive of infestation available. Hanging a strip or two in the garden will keep the pests at bay.

Not long ago a warning was issued by a government agency against the use of Vapona strips. There was evidence that they could be dangerous to the ill or to children if used in a closely confined space. Many took alarm. However, the strips can be used in the normal light garden setup, in a room with open doors or some other form of ventilation.

The strips are sold encased in a rather flimsy pierced cardboard box with a wire hook for hanging. The rated effectiveness is for 1000 cubic feet in a room which remains closed for one hour a day. In actual use it can be hung in a light garden and will do its job in the immediate area. It will kill most small insects in the flying stage.

The chemical is slowly evaporated from the strip, which has an effective life of about two months. The slightly sweet odor is nonirritating and will not be noticed at a distance of two feet.

Whenever a closed container, such as a terrarium, is infested, simply cut a short length of the plastic strip and hang or attach it inside. Leave it there for a few days and you will be rid of the pests.

PYRETHRUM AND ROTENONE

Pyrethrum is made from daisies and rotenone from derris root. Both are relatively harmless to humans when sprayed. Blowing powder around the light garden is not very practical so we generally use an aerosol can. It is effective against a number of the more common pests but not mealybugs or most mites.

NICOTINE SULPHATE

Using Nicotine Sulphate (Black Leaf 40) in full recommended strength and spraying with force, many leaf and stem insects can be eradicated. Although it is relatively safe to handle, it is still a poison and some form of mask should be used when spraying.

MALATHION

In spite of its repulsive odor, Malathion is relatively harmless to humans (as long as normal precautions are taken) and, as a spray or dip, is effective against a variety of insects. The material oxidizes rapidly and loses its potency a few hours after use.

CED-O-FLORA

This new pesticide uses natural oils and is harmless unless taken internally. Fairly effective against a variety of pests and less damaging to plants than some of the other insecticides.

RISKS WITH OILY BASE PESTICIDES

Many pesticides are diluted in an oily base which is destructive to plants. Succulents are particularly sensitive and will shrivel up after one treatment. Always test on leaves before using. This is in addition to the general warning below.

TEST FIRST

Before using any chemical sprays on the leaves and stems of plants (including Malathion) you should first test the reaction.

Wash the plant off well in lukewarm water, if possible under a jet. This will clean off a goodly part of a heavy infestation. As soon as the leaves have dried, apply the solution of the insecticide to the upper and lower surfaces of one leaf with a small brush. Mark the leaf in some way and wait two days. If it still looks healthy after a couple of days, you may go ahead with the treatment. Do not presume that if the chemical is harmless to one cultivar or species it will be equally so for another.

DISCOVERING INFESTATION

Every houseplant gardener should own a 10-power magnifying glass or loupe. It can be purchased from craft shops, optical shops, and jewelers' supply stores. With it you can see mites and leaf nematodes and even the progeny of scale leaving the mother. Without it you will never find the true source of some of the most frequently occurring difficulties with plants.

When a plant suddenly ails, you should look for insects first of all. If it is a matter of drooping, soft, or blackened leaves, the cause is something else. When insects attack, leaves often get "windows," transparent dead cells, or they brown or curl up. But they can be there long before the obvious evidence of their work. Especially in summer keep a sharp lookout for pests on your plants, making a routine of examining them closely from time to time.

COMMON PESTS

Mealybugs Visible oval powdery white creatures. Suspect any plant which shows white in the axils or white dots on the leaves. Small plants can be brushed with rubbing alcohol. Larger plants and heavier infestations may require a Malathion spray or dip. Although they look more or less alike, there are numerous species of mealybugs and they are our most constant visitors.

White Fly Visible white short-distance flyers that turn up mostly in spring and summer. Try a Pest Strip or a Pyrethrum-Rotenone spray. The fly lays its eggs on the bottom of the leaf and hatchings are at intervals so your treatment must last a while. Not a major problem.

Springtails Little insects that run around in the soil. Watch for them floating on the water in your saucer. Easily eradicated with VC-13 in the soil.

Thrips Tiny hoppers and flyers. Same treatment as White Fly plus a VC-13 bath.

Aphids Not common in the house but plentiful when present. Wash as many off as possible and spray, at intervals of a couple of days for at least eight days, with Rotenone-Pyrethrum. They are visible, green or brown, and move around.

Nematodes Two invisible types, soil and leaf, are very dangerous. The soil type makes knots in roots. The leaf type can be seen with a loupe as a transparent, very active, wormlike creature. Isolate pot and plant immediately. Soak pot and plant in Nemadrench. VC-13 may work on the soil type. Do not put your plant back into circulation until you are absolutely sure that it is clean.

Mites Most mites can just barely be seen with a 10-power loupe. There are so many different kinds that you will have to study the subject if you wish to tell them apart. They are extremely persistent and damaging.

Sometimes, if a plant is heavily infested, you can see little white threads clustered in the axils of leaves or along a stem. But your best evidence of their presence is broken pieces of web on the undersides of leaves. Very often you must examine many leaves before you find an active mite but the threads will tell you they are there.

There are Cyclamen mites, false spider mites, and spider mites. It makes no difference in the house. Eradication is certain only after a number of treatments and constant checking of the condition of leaves and growth.

Since mites do not like water, treat them to repeated sprays. The one specific chemical which combats them is Kelthane. This is not pleasant stuff to handle. Take all precautions in spraying or dipping. Be sure also to drench the pot and soil.

Pest Strips have some effectiveness against these scourges in the flying stage of their life cycle. Ced-o-Flora is also worth trying before you turn to Kelthane.

Scale Visible, hard-shelled, domed, shiny, brown or black insect clamped tightly to green stems and the undersides of leaves. Brush off with rubbing alcohol and spray with Ced-o-Flora. Use VC-13 in the soil. A number of treatments may be necessary.

Snails Not much of a problem for indoor gardeners, usually appearing only in terrariums where stones or plants from the country have been introduced. They are occasionally found on nursery plants. Treat the soil with Natriphene or put out a low dish with beer and Metaldehyde bait.

DISEASES

Rotting of crown or root is commonly caused by overwatering, especially on cool days. If the crown goes limp, check the stem. The damage will appear there first. If there is any healthy part of the plant left, take cuttings and propagate. The rest of the plant and the medium should be thrown out.

Powdery mildew occurs when humidity is excessively high and there is a lack of ventilation. It appears as a gray powder on stems and leaves or as a solid webbing. Damage to the plant is very rapid. Dust with Fermate or sulfur and you may save the plant.

A common occurrence is the loss of buds just ready to bloom, called bud blast. This can happen if the weather is too cool, because of overwatering, or just polluted air. There is nothing to be done except to study your plant and try to counter the conditions which seem to have caused the loss. Just a little too much water will cause all the flowers to fall from a Columnea.

Some Pesticides and Fungicides

Acti-dione—Fungicide for powdery mildew of roses.

Benlate—Black spot and powdery mildew. Especially effective on Begonias.

Captan 50 percent—Old remedy for rust, black spot, etc. Effective.

Diazinon—Pesticide for aphids and mites. Effective with orchids.

Fermate—Excellent general fungicide.

Isotox Garden Spray—A mixture of pesticides useful as a general soil drench or spray.

Kelthane—Most effective miticide.

Malathion 50 percent spray—Good all-around insecticide.

Panodrench—Best for damping off of seedlings.

Pentac—For rose mites.

Vapona—Available in impregnated strips and liquid to be used in a vaporizer. Very effective insecticide.

Chapter 13

BUYING PLANTS
AT THE NURSERY

BLOOM

Whenever possible buy a plant in bloom. This is a good idea even if it is the only one showing color in a large selection. At least you will have the certainty that it is capable of flowering. It is also sometimes true that the first plant to flower is also the most vigorous one. Should you bring a green plant home and discover weeks later that it does not have the flower you intended to buy you will have to accept the disappointment or go to considerable trouble to get a replacement.

The importance of this advice will be understood if you remember that the flowering of plants from seed may vary considerably. Orchids with the same species name may have flowers ranging from 1 to 4 inches in size and, unless you are very experienced, you would never be able to tell the difference from the appearance of the green plant.

Carefully compare the flowers for texture, brilliance, pure color and substance. Choose the plants which have the clearest markings and zonings.

The number of flowers in bloom is not important but rather the total number of buds and open flowers. In fact, evidence of gradual blooming over a longer period is preferable.

132

PEDICELS AND PEDUNCLES

In most plants a sturdy pedicel or peduncle, one which bears the flowers stiffly at the proper distance above, and the most attractive angle in relation to foliage is a good sign of the quality of the strain. When the flowers are borne on weak supports they bend or fall over in an unsightly way and will rarely last long. This is a characteristic of many carelessly bred cultivars.

CALYX

Observe in Gesneriads, and other families whose flowers have a clasping calyx, the firmness and tightness of its grip on the corolla. If the calyx is observed to spread even on newly opened flowers, the chances are that the corolla will be dropped prematurely. This, again, can be a quality of the strain but sometimes will vary from plant to plant.

HABIT (growth pattern of a plant—general appearance)

In any group of plants there will be a difference in habit. Some will have a tendency to sucker more than others, some to branch more. Unless the plant has been trimmed, its shape will be prophetic of its future development. Be sure that you like the *way* it is growing—that it is decorative to your eyes. Strength of stems and side branches are symptomatic of healthy growth. You will also note that some tend to grow taller, others to be more compact. Remember that, for light gardens, compact growth is the best in most instances. When examining plants with a more vertical growth hold them up to near eye level; do not look down on them or you will have a false perspective view of their shape.

FOLIAGE

Leaves give clear indications of plant condition. It is a matter of texture, color, and sheen. Plants which are chlorotic or have an otherwise unhealthy look are usually withdrawn from sale. But there are often differences to be noted in the bearing of the leaves, their flat open look, the richness of coloring, and whether they sparkle or not. Leaves should be firm and crisp. If there are zones or veins in contrasting colors look for those with the sharpest definition.

ROOT GROWTH

It is not easy to tell whether a plant is sufficiently rooted without removing it from its pot. In many species a single piece of stem is open to suspicion unless it has branched somewhat. It is wise in such a case to check with the nurseryman and receive assurances on this point. Good top growth and branching low on the stem usually indicate a healthy root.

Turn the pot over and examine the holes for potbinding. If root shows through, the situation may not be acute but it is open to suspicion. A certain amount of potbinding will do no harm, but if the roots have formed a solid net along the walls of the pot you can anticipate trouble. Check this with the nurseryman, too.

INFESTATION

The general appearance of the benches at a nursery will tell you a good deal about whether or not to fear infestation. Neat, clean houses are certainly less likely to be subject to the prevalence of insects. There is less danger too if soilless medium has been used.

Examine leaves and axils closely. Little black specks or a white powdery effect along the veins on the underside can be mites. Juvenile mealybugs are tiny but they do move when touched with something pointed. Gum or sap is another indication. Curling of the leaves, "windows" (transparent cells), and holes speak of insect damage. Holes are frequently caused by slugs. Watch also for a dropping of lower leaves and if any of them are in the pot, examine them closely.

When in serious doubt about a desirable plant ask the nurseryman to knock it out of the pot or water it or both. Water will bring slugs and other creatures to the surface. Some nurseries still do not sterilize the ordinary soil they use. Almost invariably there will be some life there, larger than microscopic, which is not always harmful but not exactly the sort of thing you will want to bring into the house.

Pots are usually standing on moist benches. Tip the pot and some of the smaller insects will be seen crawling around on the bottom.

When you get your plants home douse the soil with a soil insecticide and then enclose the whole plant in a plastic bag for a few days. If there is any infestation it will become apparent and you will be able to deal with it. Don't ever let it join your other plants for a period of two weeks at least. Even with the greatest care in choosing you may bring home a plant which within a few days is loaded with mites, spiders, or mealybugs. It has happened to me on numerous occasions.

The Clone

Technically speaking a clone is a plant produced by vegetative propagation and therefore a mirror image of its parent, which is not true of plants raised from seed. Now, suppose we fertilize the flower of a species. The seed pod produces, let us say, a hundred seeds and a hundred plants. When mature, the chances are good that all the plants will grow in much the same way, have the same leaves and flowers. But if we line them up and compare them we find that some are weak, some average, and a few, perhaps only one, has superior characteristics.

Supposing that there are a few of these better plants and that they are distributed to as many growers. In each case vegetative propagation of the parent will produce mirror images. But even these few plants will not be exactly the same, and their offspring will differ from each other just as did the parents. It may take several generations of culture before the growers recognize, among the many possibilities, the strengths or weaknesses of their particular plants.

All of these clones may be generally satisfactory or, in the long run, the opposite. Or one may, after all, prove more sturdy, more insect resistant, less liable to fungal rot, more floriferous, etc. If you have received your plant from one of the other clones you may have considerable trouble with it. The "good" clone may be entirely satisfactory. That is the clone we are always looking for.

Most of the tropical indoor light gardening plants are propagated vegetatively. Nevertheless, we do not necessarily acquire the best available plant. Grower A has chosen one plant and multiplied it for his stock. B has chosen a different plant. Although both may be equally conscientious and give the same care to their cultivation, your results if you acquire your plant from grower A may be very different from those of B's plant.

The point of all this is that your experience with a particular plant known to be especially suitable for light gardens is not a final criterion. You may think that it is impossible to grow it, or that your conditions are unsuitable, or that you have missed some essential of culture—in which case you may pester other amateurs for additional cultural information. And, all the time, what is really at fault is a clone which is either inferior in itself or does not adjust well to your conditions. Acquiring a plant from another grower, if the parentage is different, may give you entirely different results.

Orchid growers are very conscious of the importance of clones. A particular clone may be so superior that its divisions are much sought after as exhibition material. Orchidists have kept very careful records for over a hundred years and can trace the lineage of their cultivars and their clones. Certain clones are known and cherished, each generation being considered more valuable than other plants of the same cross.

Other plant enthusiasts have not been so concerned with the problem and, as a result, we rarely know whether the parent is a superior clone or not. So don't give up with the first plant of a species which fails to behave itself. The next one may act quite differently.

Acclimatizing Plants

As most of our light gardening plants are shipped to us from or bought at a nursery it is important to understand the effect of the transfer to a new home and how to deal with it. You must first of all understand the drastic nature of the change that takes place. Within the space of a few hours the plant moves from one microclimate to another—from sun to artificial light, from high humidity to a rather low one, from short to long days, from superior to poor ventilation, and so on. But that is not all. During its growth in the nursery it has been subjected to a particular schedule of watering and feeding. In most instances there will be a change of the nutrient itself and the degree of concentration.

It is rather to be expected, therefore, that the first weeks in its new home are the most difficult and that a very large percentage of plants eventually pine away for reasons which are inexplicable to the owner. Usually the nursery is not at fault. Of course if the plant arrives through the mails in bad shape there is nothing much one can do about it. But nowadays packing is normally careful and full responsibility for the plant rests with the new owner.

As soon as a new arrival is unpacked, if at all possible, a leaf or stem cutting should be made and planted. It is a common experience that it will do better than the parent and it provides, in any event, a substitute.

Next, remove all flowers and seed pods and trim off excessive growth. Don't expect it to put forth maximum effort during the coming weeks. The less there is to support the better it will do.

In respect to culture, treat the plant as if it were somewhat debilitated, which it will become for a while through natural causes, watering sparingly and feeding not at all. Introduce it to the lights gradually. Give it a spot toward the sides of the tubes and remove it from the garden for a few weeks after 10 hours of exposure.

At the end of three weeks the plant should start to grow. When this takes place it is time to repot. Unless severely potbound use the same size and switch to your own medium with which you have been having satisfactory results. From here on you should have no difficulty. After repotting, as growth continues, you can start your normal fertilizing program.

Chapter 14

THE MIRACLE
BLOOMING PLANTS

The phenomenon of light gardening is itself something of a miracle. And it is equally a miracle that it has the ability to change the growth habits of certain plants so drastically that they no longer obey what we have always believed were the natural laws. Who would have guessed that plants could be bloomed with exposure to continuous light? Where in nature do you find plants which bloom all the year round? Yet that is what those which I have dubbed Miracle Blooming Plants actually do. They also happen to be the easiest light gardening plants to grow. I can perform no better service to the neophyte than to introduce him to these wonderful plants, segregating them from the more difficult and challenging ones.

In a light garden, unless we insist on it, there are no seasons and no cloudy days. There is, for instance, no alternation of rain and drought, of heat and cold. Subjected to an almost unchanging daily environment, certain plants, in their blooming, become fixed in a routine. In nature some signal—a seasonal change—causes them to grow more rapidly and to put out buds and flowers. Another signal causes them to rest. But under lights nothing happens to change their ways and, once in bloom, they continue on and on.

What the exact process is in each case we do not know nor why some

137

plants react one way and some another. There are those which seem to recognize the lapse of time and go through a cycle in spite of the regularity of our light day. The related plants, *Sinningia speciosa,* the florist Gloxinia, and *Sinningia pusilla* are tuberous. The tuber serves to carry them over the dry season. Belonging to the same genus, they are as closely related as plants can be. Yet the Gloxinia goes dormant after blooming and *S. pusilla* never stops. The essential difference in habit is that the Gloxinia puts out one or several growths simultaneously from its tuber. Each of these forms crowns and clusters of flowers. Once these have died off the plant has nowhere else to grow. *S. pusilla,* on the other hand, develops flowers consecutively and is always ready to start new growths from the tuber. Such details of habit may make the difference.

Up to now just ten genera have been found to contain miracle plants. The number of species and cultivars which behave in the same way is considerably larger. A light garden consisting entirely of Miracle Blooming Plants is full of color and variety. The ones I list and describe are those with which I am familiar. This is not to say that there are not many others. Expert light gardeners may have tried different plants and come up with the same results. But, if they did, they have not spread the word. The list has grown year by year and we will undoubtedly add many more in the not too distant future.

The claim to everblooming characteristics has been attributed to many new introductions. Some of these have been fine plants and have settled into the general repertoire of light gardening. But the vast majority have proved, on continuous testing, to be either more difficult than claimed or just less persistent bloomers.

Of course, none of these plants live forever. As I have pointed out earlier, they run their course. They do vary in their life span but each one is good for months on end of vigorous bloom.

AFRICAN VIOLETS

Although discovered in the 1890s *Saintpaulia* (*Gesneriaceae,* South Africa) only became popular in the United States from 1936 on. Commercial fluorescent tubes appeared on the market in 1938. Hence we can say that the ideal houseplant and the means to raise it *anywhere* in the home have grown up together.

Since it is *the* miracle houseplant of our time, it could not be left out of this section. Yet so much has been written about it—whole shelves of articles and books—that there is nothing that can be added in a short discussion. Nevertheless it can be of some value, along with standard instructions for culture, to mention what overhybridization has done to the genus, not merely to express a personal opinion, but as a guide to those who are acquiring plants for the first time.

Due to Saintpaulia's ease of culture, propagation, and hybridization, any amateur has been able to get into the act of creating new plants. Every year there are thousands of crosses and hundreds of new commercial introductions. Although over the years remarkable progress was made in developing larger and more colorful flowers than the species, the end result has been such a hodgepodge of plants varying little from certain basic forms that the choice of particular plants is a real hurdle for the beginner. There are shapes and colors to suit the best and worst taste, especially the latter.

There are so many choices that no difficulty is experienced in finding plants with a good habit, clean single or double shapes, and beautiful coloring. At the nursery you will probably pick out a large plant which just happens to be in perfect bloom. But you have no means of knowing whether it will do well under fluorescent light, whether its flowering is continuous, if it is sturdy, nonsuckering and resistant to disease. A major reason for the complaints of many city growers that they are unsuccessful with this easy plant is that they have acquired ones which have had faulty breeding.

The lesson of the above is that you should never give up on African Violets. No other plant will, in the long run, bring you so much pleasure.

Choosing Plants

A reasonably foolproof way of going about acquiring your first African Violets is to choose plants which have the Rhapsodie or Englert labels. These are carefully bred singles and doubles in a variety of colors. They are conservative plants, compact and floriferous. All of them have the characteristic of blooming quite upright in the center of the rosette.

There are many other hybrids which are more spectacular—I particularly admire the huge star-shaped blooms—but there I must leave you on your own with the following general suggestions and rules.

Double flowers last longer than single. Look for straight peduncles bearing a number of buds and avoid the stragglers. The leaves should lie flat and grow symmetrically. Whether a plant has a single crown or not is only important to judges but avoid one which has a number of suckers. If the nurseryman has removed them you will see the scars on the central stem. Notice whether the flowers on a plant are evenly colored. Choose young plants which have started to bloom—not full-grown ones.

When you have decided what color you want, whether single or double, speak to the nurseryman. Inform him that you want a plant that will grow easily and well under lights, is floriferous and disease resistant. Tell him you do not want a novelty but a tried and true plant which will be trouble free. Chances are that he is unhappy about pushing new and unreliable plants and will pick out a good one for you.

Species

Recently there has been a revival of interest in *Saintpaulia* species. It may be caused by a surfeit of the artificial shapes of some of the latest hybrids. Certainly the original plants have great charm and a few are no more difficult to grow than the cultivars. Worth trying are *S. grotei, ionantha, tongwensis, confusa,* and *orbicularis* as starters.

Miniatures

For a while all the rage was plants with 4-inch leaves on superlong stems which were grown to monstrous size. Now the miniatures are proliferating. Hybridizers have had their problems eliminating a tendency to sucker and keeping the flowers blooming. They make lovely terrarium subjects.

Culture

How amateurs specializing in African Violets can go on year after year rehashing all the details of culture is a marvel of persistence. Unless you are preparing a plant for judging there is no need to become involved in complicated procedures.

Use African Violet Mix with the addition of a teaspoonful of ground eggshell to a 3-inch pot. Keep moist, not wet, and fertilize with a high-phosphate-potash formula. Contrary to the myth African Violets require a fair amount of light. In the country the sun may be too strong in a west window but in the smog zone that is what it needs. Keep them within 10 inches under the lights. Some have even found that their plants will not bloom without the addition of incandescent bulbs but there are plenty of growers who find this unnecessary.

For blooming do not expose the plants to temperatures below 60 degrees. A minimum of 65 is safer. Water should be at room temperature. Do not soak the leaves but they do like a misting. Allow all but the bottom quarter of the pot to dry out before watering. Do not allow to stand in water. You will have more flowering if you remove the first buds of a young plant. Do not remove leaves from the center of the rosette. Do remove suckers, which you can use as cuttings for propagation. Do not allow to become pot-bound. Replenish the lime every three months.

After some time the plant will develop a thick stem. There are two ways of dealing with it. Unpot, clip off most of the root, and set the plant deeper in the old or a larger new pot. Or cut off the top of the plant allowing an inch of stem, remove some bottom leaves, dust with hormone powder or sulfur, and plant in moist vermiculite under a plastic bag until new growth starts. Plants started from leaves generally perform better than the rooted tops of the old ones.

BEGONIA SEMPERFLORENS

The everblooming bedding Begonias are among the most reliable of house-plants under lights. Here again, as with Saintpaulias, the plants are so popular and so easy to hybridize and select that growers all tend to give their own names to those they sell if they can find the slightest justification in some slightest variation of flower or leaf. The only moderately safe rule to follow is to collect dwarf forms. The singles produce flowers more prolifically and constantly than the doubles. The latter are ugly little twists of petals but do have the advantage of stronger coloring and lending the plant a more orna-mental appearance. Choice then becomes largely a matter of taste. Most of the cultivars will grow and bloom very easily and also propagate without difficulty.

The advantage of the dwarf types is that they remain fairly compact. Others tend to stretch, and though they can be pruned, scars are left behind and it is difficult to maintain a neat look. They are such watery-looking shapeless plants that their only recommendation is constant bloom and ease of culture. But that is a great deal. They are dependable.

The flowers of Begonias are of two types, male and female, growing together on the same peduncle. Pinching the female flowers increases the size of the more shapely male flowers and encourages more vigorous growth. In these little plants it is a bit of a nuisance and most people do not bother but the gain is considerable and should be worth the trouble.

These Begonias prefer an African Violet Mix with an extra part of sphagnum peat but will also do well in pure fine sphagnum peat. They should be packed lightly into the pot and kept constantly watered. If you have received a plant in a sandy mixture, wash off the roots with lukewarm water and replant. Sixty percent humidity and temperatures above 65 degrees encourage bloom. Below that it is advisable to cut down on watering temporarily as growth will slow up.

As plants go, these are not long lasting. A year is a long time to keep them in good condition. But it is only necessary to cut off a length of young growth, remove two leaves, powder with rooting hormone, and set in any light sterile mixture.

These Begonias attract more than the usual complement of insects to feed on their juicy leaves and stems. For most problems wash the plant well in a strong solution of yellow soap. For mites douse pot and all in a low solution of a miticide and if you are uncertain about the visitor try Malathion.

I have not mentioned fertilizer. As a matter of fact Begonias need very little. Occasional treatment with a balanced chemical solution will do. For best bloom they should be rather close to the lights but not so close as to scorch them. About four inches will bloom most of them.

The green-leaved varieties are both double and single. The red-leaved, which require somewhat more illumination are almost all double. Calla Lily Begonias have variegated foliage and look even worse when they are normal (in my opinion) than the others when they have been pruned excessively. They too require more light and are also rather less sturdy than the standard types. Pick the bushy ones and the dwarfs for the others can grow pretty big.

The reader will guess that I am not too partial to this group and be right. It is a Miracle Plant, to be sure, but a last resort. If you can't raise them the others will be too difficult.

COLUMNEA 'CHANTICLEER'

Columnea, the Goldfish Plant, is one of the most spectacular of all exotics. Grown in baskets, its long stems trailing down as much as 6 feet in fine specimens, the 3-inch-long winged flowers in profusion, it is a magnificent sight. At Cornell a number of hybrids were developed which were more adaptable to greenhouse conditions and had a longer flowering season. Light gardeners were disappointed to find that the habit was quite unmanageable. But hybridizers have been working on the plant to make it grow more upright and compact. First success was achieved with *Columnea* 'V. Covert' which is small growing and more sturdy stemmed at the sacrifice of large flowers. Many plants were introduced which claimed to be everblooming. In the greenhouse this might be the case but in the house under lights the majority have been seasonal.

Within a short span of time three Columneas have been introduced which are a distinct improvement. *C.* 'Early Bird' is large flowered, bright red with yellow stripes in the corolla. *C.* 'Mary Ann' is dark and smaller. *C.* 'Chanticleer' is orange and has medium-size flowers. The last is really everblooming, is strong stemmed, stays neat when pruned, and is very floriferous. Mrs. Warren F. Cressy, Jr., brought it to my attention and my experience confirms her enthusiasm.

Columnea, being epiphytic, is used to growing in a very spongy, well aerated medium. Like other such plants it detests still water at its roots. This is the essential feature and difficulty of its culture.

Use Tropical Plant Mix with eggshell added and pack it lightly around the plant. Water only after the medium is thoroughly dry. It should not stand in a saucer. Place it about four inches under the lights. If it trails a bit the lower branches will still flower at this distance. Mist once or twice daily. Fertilize only once a month with a balanced nutrient. Keep the temperature above 65 degrees.

That is all there is to it. But be careful about that watering. The moment it becomes excessive buds will blast and root or stem rot may set in. Water only when you have decided that neglect has gone far enough and you can't stand the strain. It is even advisable, when the plant is budding, to water not all the way through but only a small quantity from the top. Yellowing leaves will warn you if the Spartan tactics have gone too far. This symptom is not one to cause serious damage and is immediately curable. Overwatering is not.

Provided these simple instructions are carried out there is no reason why the three Columneas listed will not prove miracle plants, blooming continuously.

Trim your plants whenever they begin to wander too far from the lights —that is when tip buds won't bloom. Strip the lower part of the cutting of its leaves, dust with hormone powder, and set in moist vermiculite. Cuttings bearing buds will come into flower if potted up in a very light mix, kept in a clear plastic bag for a while and set quite close to the lights.

CUPHEA HYSSOPIFOLIA

I was familiar with *Cuphea platycentra*, the Cigar Plant, long before I discovered *C. hyssopifolia* (*Lythraceae*, Central America). The former has a long red tube flower with a black tip and can be grown under lights with difficulty because of its lankiness. It has been the most popular of the Cupheas with indoor growers.

C. hyssopifolia, at first sight, is far less attractive. It is a little shrub, with oval opposite leaves in great profusion, and little purple pink flowers which are almost perfect replicas of *Lythrum salicaria*, the popular garden ornamental and immigrant wild flower of our marshes. When I brought one home and kept it in my light garden for a while I began to appreciate its high merit as a house plant.

It is a perfect example of how a plant which appears small in a greenhouse can look adequately large in the home. It blooms constantly, summer and winter, has a delightfully neat habit, and is extremely adaptable. It will grow in soilless house plant mixture, enjoys plenty of moisture, and it can flower a foot away from the lights. It will bloom when only an inch long, grows slowly, prunes well, and can be made into a little shapely shrub which will fit even in a terrarium. It does well with any kind of balanced fertilizer. Indifferent to warm and cool temperatures that are usual in a house it will bloom just as well with 12 hours light as with 16.

Cuttings root very rapidly in moist vermiculite and continue blooming all the time. A most versatile and reliable plant.

EPISCIAS MOSS AGATE AND CYGNET

Episcias (*Gesneriaceae*, Central America) are such beautiful foliage plants that for many the flowers are superfluous. The latter are tubular with a flat wide spread of lobe and mostly an inch or less in diameter. Yet the white, pink, orange, or red coloring is so brilliant, the contrast with the leaves so striking, that a very few will light up a large plant. If you visit a commercial nursery you will find many cultivars in bloom. Bring them home to a light garden and you will discover that flowering them continuously is by no means easy. Of all the hybrids three have met our needs. *E.* 'Acajou,' a very early cultivar, was for a long time the easiest. Since then it has been replaced by larger leaved and flowered plants of the same type and Episcias 'Moss Agate' and 'Cygnet' have taken the overall lead in reliability.

Episcia 'Moss Agate' bears 4- to 5-inch heavily quilted bright green leaves. The flowers, large for an *Episcia,* are a brilliant red orange, the lobes of the corolla fringed. *Episcia* 'Cygnet' is a cross of the white flowering species *E. dianthiflora* and *E. punctata. E. dianthiflora* is a prettier plant but requires very high humidity. The leaves are scalloped and a velvety dusty gray green. The flowers are large for an *Episcia,* white, and heavily fringed with purple dots at the base of the lobes and in the wide throat. Both of these plants are everblooming if given the necessary care.

Every once in a while a grower claims that plants such as Episcias will withstand temperatures of 60 degrees or less without damage—in fact keep blooming. That may be so in exceptional cases but the light gardener who wishes to have continuous bloom cannot take the chance. These are plants from the warm tropics and relatively low altitudes. They like it warm and a 65-degree minimum, if you can maintain it, is always the best. The rule applies to most of the Gesneriads we grow in the house.

The soil should be African Violet Mix. Episcias are good feeders and can take both balanced nutrient and an occasional treat of fish emulsion or high-phosphate potash. They like plenty of water and consume it in quantity. However, if watering is heavy and the temperature goes below 65, root stem rot often sets in. It is a good idea not to permit them to stand in water. High humidity and misting help blooming.

Episcia 'Moss Agate' develops a strong central stem if suckers are removed. The problem with suckers is that the size of the plant increases very rapidly and the room in the pot becomes insufficient, whereas, if the plant is trimmed, the roots will be able to support the central stem growth.

Episcia 'Cygnet' has an even worse suckering habit and one that is not attractive. But if the plant is trimmed back rigorously, it develops a fine mound of foliage and is more floriferous.

Light requirement is a position 4 to 6 inches under the lights. Don't expect a plant to be at or near its peak in less than six months. Suckers root easily in moist vermiculite.

EUPHORBIA SPLENDENS VAR. BOJERI

Euphorbia splendens (Euphorbiaceae, Madagascar), Crown of Thorns is a desert plant with canes like a briar, long sharp spines, and red flowers which are two opposite kidney-shaped bracts, like the red leaves which surround *Poinsettia.* Most of the year the canes are bare but seasonally they will break into leafage and bloom. Var. *bojeri* is a dwarf form which is better suited to the house and which reacts in a remarkable way to fluorescent light culture.

Most desert plants require a long rest period without water but this *Euphorbia* is an exception. They also are accustomed to very bright sunshine and will not bloom in the low footcandle light of our tubes. Euphorbia here also breaks the rule. In fact the essential feature of culture is maintaining constant moisture, actually soaking it more than is usual with most Gesneriads. When treated in this way the plant will stay constantly green and will bloom all the time and in profusion.

The small leaves, wider toward the ends, are attractive and the flowers, depending on the clone, range from pink to brick red, lasting at least a week. Usually there are two on a peduncle. And in order to bring it into bud the plant need not be closer than about six inches from the lights.

Ordinary tropical mix can be used and the plant does not suffer from average amounts of balanced mix or fish emulsion. But never dry it out. It will immediately drop its leaves, go into dormancy and if watered then will rot away.

Even though small in comparison with its very large relative, var. *bojeri* grows quite rapidly. Fortunately it can be trimmed and trained beautifully. The cuts exude a milky gum in such quantity that it will drip away, but the plant does not seem to mind and will branch nicely.

Cuttings are taken in this way and the cut ends lightly burned with a match to stop the bleeding. Planted in moist vermiculite after dusting with hormone they root with remarkable ease and soon are blooming.

Hybrids known as *Euphorbia x keyesii* (*E. lophogona x E. splendens*) have also been introduced as houseplants. Coarser of leaf, they produce larger flowers in greater numbers but they are not as attractive as *bojeri* and not as consistent.

Euphorbia bojeri is another example of how fluorescent light culture can change the habits of certain plants in ways which make them superior to anything grown in greenhouses.

EXACUM AFFINE

We are only beginning to be aware of the treasure of fine plants for the indoor grower to be found among annuals and biennials. The assumption has been that these will bloom for a short season and then die off. But this is not necessarily the case as fluorescent lighting seems to prolong their useful life beyond our expectations. Already a number are becoming established favorites and among them *Exacum* represents close to the ideal of what we are all seeking.

It is a biennial from Socotra, an island in the Indian Ocean from which comes *Begonia socotrana*, parent of the Hiemalis and Cheimanthas tuberous Begonias. It is nearly perennial in the light garden and a continuous, easy bloomer.

Exacum has fleshy stems, is much branched, bears smallish shiny leaves.

Flowering often starts when it is only an inch or two high. The blossoms are ½ inch in diameter, five-petaled, short-pediceled. The color is a lavender blue of considerable brightness, and from the mouth of the tube issues a cluster of brilliantly yellow curved stamens. When fully active it is literally covered with flowers.

Lightly packed African Violet soil, a position 4 inches under the lights, and regular balanced fertilizer will satisfy it. Its only sensitivities seem to be to temperature and watering. In regard to temperature, 60 to 85 degrees seems to be the proper range. Excessive heat will do some damage. In spite of its fleshy appearance it is not partial to a very wet soil. But keep moist at all times.

Start in a 3-inch or smaller pot and move to larger ones as it grows. Naturally a plant that flowers so much needs cleaning, and trimming will make it bushier. But as it continues to grow there comes a time when the stems become rather thick and the cut ends unsightly. This is usually after at least six months of constant bloom. Then it is advisable to start new plants.

Seeds are available from a number of firms and it is easy to collect your own by pollinating once you have a plant in bloom. The little stigma curves out quite close to the stamens and it is only necessary to establish contact with the use of a tweezers to secure a good crop. Germination is in about two weeks.

A white form called 'Blithe Spirit' behaves equally well. Dwarf varieties are not recommended. They bloom profusely at first and then seem to wear themselves out.

GESNERIA CUNEIFOLIA

This species is one of the wonderful Gesneriad miniatures which do so well in the terrarium. On the shelves it is touch and go but enclosed it is one of the easiest plants to grow and bloom.

The leaves are dark green, shaped like long spoons, and hard surfaced. They grow in rosettes around a stem which moves slowly upward. The flowers appear on slim pedicels and, according to the clone, are orange, burnt orange, or quite red and about an inch long, tubular, slightly flared and lobed at the tip.

I pot *Gesneria* in African Violet Mix with lime, keep it constantly wet, feed it very little, and set it anywhere from 6 to 12 inches under the lights in high humidity. Temperature should never go below 65. And it must not be dry for a single day else it will collapse completely. It never drowns.

Although fibrous rooted, *Gesneria cuneifolia* forms new crowns from the base and these can be separated and propagated or, if they have some root attached, potted up. A healthy plant may eventually reach a height of 8 inches and displays the phenomenon of constant bloom even from axils that have lost their leaves. This is very unusual in the Gesneriads. At this point, however, it will be rather unsightly, in spite of the color, and the top must be cut off and an attempt made at propagation.

The leaves root only with the greatest difficulty. Stem cuttings are slow too. But the flowers pollinate themselves and produce quantities of seed which is as fine as dust. These germinate easily and are not difficult to bring to maturity.

When planning to collect seed, leave the calyces on the plant and watch till they turn brown. Cut them off and place in a glassine envelope until thoroughly dried. Crush the ovaries directly into your seed propagating box, spreading as best you can. When the tiny seedlings appear and have two leaves pick them out with tweezers and move to another box with Tropical Plant Mix. Set them about a half inch apart. Keep the box covered until you see that they are ready for regular pots. Then change to African Violet Mix.

There are two variations of *Gesneria cuneifolia*, one called El Yunque and the other Quebradillas. Both are from Puerto Rico and are smaller flowered. As bloomers they are equally satisfactory.

LANTANA

Lantana (*Lantana camara* and hybrids, *Verbenaceae*, tropical America) is popular as a porch basket plant. With age it becomes woody and can be trained as a tree with a slim stem and a round mass of foliage at the top covered with bloom. The individual flowers are small but form an umbel which is showy. An unusual feature is the way the flowers in the concentric rows vary in color. The range is from white through yellow to deep red.

Nana compacta, a dwarf form, makes an excellent houseplant under lights. Not only is it easy and floriferous, it can be pruned as a shrub and, in this state, will last for years. Its popularity as a light garden plant will grow, I am sure, when people come to know better how relatively foolproof it is. It has just one minor problem. White flies love it. However, they are among the easiest insects to get rid of in the house.

Seed is slow in germinating. More than a month may pass before there is a sign of life. Hence it is better to purchase a young plant of this long-lived cultivar.

Culture is remarkably easy. It will thrive in any one of the mixes and will withstand cool temperatures. It is one of the few blooming houseplants which is not fussy about humidity. If it is heavily watered it will tend to grow very fast and become leggy. If kept quite dry it will slow up. Flowering will be more regular on a smaller plant if watering is moderate. It needs hardly any fertilizer. High nitrogen formulas suit it and a treatment once a month is ample. It does like the maximum light you can give it. The top of the plant should be within 3 inches of the tubes.

Color combinations vary so much that it is advisable to see a plant in bloom when purchasing. Cuttings are taken from young growth and will root easily in moist vermiculite.

OXALIS REGNELLII

No matter how often I insist on the special virtues of *Oxalis regnellii* my amateur growing friends are always offering me other species and cultivars which they claim have been blooming continuously for them. Other species and cultivars have quite a long blooming season. But what my friends do not know as yet is that their plants will certainly go dormant. I have tried most of the popular ones and have found this to be the case.

These are all tuberous plants—not all *Oxalis,* of course, but those which most people know and grow. Each plant is really a collection of pips which multiply rapidly. As in most water-storing plants *Oxalis* has these for a reason —to outlive a dry or cold season. Hence they do eventually die down, must be stored away, and a few months later they will sprout again.

Oxalis regnellii is the exception. As long as it is kept very wet and in light it will continue to grow and bloom. If I am asked which plant I would recommend as the easiest and most reliable for a beginner, I invariably answer with this *Oxalis.*

It is a very pretty but not spectacular plant. The long petioles of the leaves bear the usual three segments. But instead of being rounded, they are exactly triangular. In a way, therefore, it is unique. The flowers, on equally long peduncles, are simply white. But each one bears several in succession.

The production of leaves and flowers is continuous and profuse. And, if the light is good, the leaves and flowers stand up better than in most *Oxalis* which tend to sprawl. Such a productive plant needs constant tidying. All that is necessary is to pull out the dead stems.

Use Tropical Plant Mix packed rather firmly, and fertilize no more than once a month with 20-20-20 formula. Keep the tips of the leaves within 4 inches of the lights. Bloom will continue at 60 degrees or even less and there is no danger of wilt from overwatering. Just don't forget to keep the moisture constant.

When you want to propagate, you need only separate some pips and pot each one up separately. The leaves and flower stems may die down but, if you keep the soil moist, new growth will soon appear.

One point worth noting: when pips have become crowded in the pot some of them will develop a sort of tuberous stem which is quite thick, presumably as a means of escaping from the pack. These stems can be broken off, dusted with hormone, and treated like a tuber.

If *Oxalis regnellii* goes dormant it is evidence that you have been truly neglectful.

DWARF POMEGRANATE

No other indoor garden plant arouses as much delight at first acquaintance as the dwarf Pomegranate. A little tree with the greenest of tiny oval foliage, which blossoms very much like a Fuchsia and then bears real, though small, round glowing red pomegranate fruits is something to cause wonder. It is an old and popular European ornamental which is much grown in pots out-of-doors in the Mediterranean countries. We have found that it grows equally well under lights.

Start with a well grown plant and accustom it to African Violet Mix. Keep it moist at all times, fertilize regularly with balanced formula and fish emulsion, and keep it fairly close to the lights. It does like good humidity but can do without it. If the leaves drop, mites may be the cause.

The flowers are over an inch long and the corolla, which is tomato red, is sheathed in an orange calyx which is tubular and quite hard. If you want fruit simply blow hard into the flower. This will pollinate it. More than one pomegranate is not advisable as it saps the strength of the plant though it is only 2 inches in diameter. When it is ripe the leathery skin splits. Remove it, work the seeds out, and dry them. They are viable but take a long time to germinate.

Easier is to take a stem cutting. The young growth roots readily in moist vermiculite.

This is a plant which is particularly adaptable to bonsaiing. If you understand the art you can make an exquisite show plant which is always green, always blooming, and produces fruit when you want it. *Punica granatum nana* is its varietal name.

SINNINGIA PUSILLA AND HYBRIDS

Sinningia pusilla (*Gesneriaceae*, South America), a true miniature, is a close relative of the huge flowered *Sinningia speciosa,* better known as the florist Gloxinia. It has the form of the Slipper Gloxinia of which the florist type is a mutation. But the tube is narrower, the flare of the lobes somewhat wider, and the whole is less than a half inch long. The color is a watery blue. Borne on slender pedicels well above the flat rosette of small, dark green, hairy foliage, it is a charmer. S. 'White Sprite' is a pure white sport.

Its limitation is that it must be grown in terrarium conditions because of its requirement of high humidity. But then it will bloom unceasingly and produce seeds which are scattered all about, resulting in more plants which are very welcome as they take up so little room.

Give them Tropical Plant Mix and the even moisture of the terrarium or any transparent container, fertilize rarely and keep them no more than a foot from the lights. Sixty-five degrees or higher is best. If the soil is wet the plants will rot.

Leaves can be used for propagation but the easiest way is to keep a couple of plants in a small container. As long as they bloom you are bound to have young plants coming up all over the place.

If your S. *pusilla* dies down or its leaves rot, dig up the little tuber, dry it out well, dust with Fermate or some other fungicide, and plant it with the top just level with the soil, taking care this time that the latter is not wet. In no time it will sprout again.

It is the greatest good luck for light gardeners that S. *pusilla* and S. *concinna,* an equally small and pretty but more delicate plant, can be crossed with other, much larger species in the genus and that everblooming characteristics are carried over to the progeny. Thus a number of beautiful small and larger plants with interesting coloring have been developed. Only the following can be classified as Miracle Plants at the present time. All are better grown in a terrarium.

S. 'Dollbaby' (Katzenberger) (*Sinningia pusilla x S. eumorpha*) was a fantastic breakthrough. The leaves are over an inch long and the flower, purplish blue and white, may reach up to 2 inches. The tetraploid (Lyon) is fertile but leaf propagation is advisable. Treatment is the same as for S. *pusilla* and bloom is just as continuous.

S. 'Cindy' (Talpey) (*S. concinna x S. eumorpha*) is of more recent vintage. The size of the plant is about the same as 'Dollbaby' and the flowers even more beautiful because they are zoned in blue purple and white with purple spots symmetrically arranged in the throat. It is a much sturdier plant than S. *concinna* and everblooming. Propagate it from leaves. It is rather disconcerting to find a tuber as big as an unshelled peanut under the leaf after a while, without any top growth. Pot up the tuber in just moist (nearly dry) Tropical Plant Mix, cover the pot with a transparent plastic bag, and set in a warm place, for instance, on top of the reflector of a light garden just over the ballast. After a while it will sprout. A magnificent plant in bloom.

S. 'Snowflake' (Clayberg) (*S. pusilla x S.* 'White Sprite') This is a fringed version of 'White Sprite' and behaves like any other pusilla.

STREPTOCARPUS 'CONSTANT NYMPH'

Although it has all the other characteristics of a Miracle Plant *Streptocarpus* 'Constant Nymph' almost misses because it grows so fast and so big. But it compensates with breathtaking beauty.

It is a stemless, fibrous rooted Gesneriad with leaves over a foot long which spray out directly from the ground. That keeps it comparatively low for its breadth. Several flowers are borne on long peduncles—handsome large blue trumpets. As each dies off others raise their heads so that there is continuous bloom all year round.

'Constant Nymph' can be started in a 3-inch pot but will soon outgrow it. Give it the most ordinary African Violet treatment, the mix, the fertilizer, and the misting. It does like plenty of water and can stand some in the saucer.

After your plant has grown into a 5-inch pot you may want to call a halt. The best way is to divide it by the method described under the heading of

Propagation by Division (p. 122). The seeds are very tiny and it takes time to bring the plant to bloom. Better to take leaf cuttings. This is done by cutting off one of the long ones, cutting again into sections about three inches long with the midrib forming a point, and planting in moist vermiculite. The young plants grow at the front of the leaf more quickly than with African Violets.

Keep the tops of the leaves about eight inches from the lights. The graceful flowers will reach upward.

Recently introduced white and varicolored variations of 'Constant Nymph' are large flowered and as satisfactory as the original.

The plants described in the previous pages are those which at present I would recommend to beginners in the art of fluorescent light gardening. They have the advantage of combining ease of culture with continuous bloom. And there is nothing which will encourage a newcomer to the method so much as success with his first experiments.

Over a number of years I have struggled to find the best plants for this purpose. From time to time plants have been added and others removed from the list. Partly this came about because I was deluded by some temporarily satisfactory result, partly because new ones appeared which were superior to one or more that I had previously favored.

The Miracle Plants have been tried by members of the Indoor Light Gardening Society and they, too, have found them a great help in getting started or in keeping some plants constantly in bloom in their mixed gardens. So try these out first. Nothing will also be more certain to disappoint than to acquire lighting equipment and then buy a miscellaneous group of plants, purely because they are momentarily attractive, and try to grow them in an unsuitable environment.

The next section deals with large families of plants, useful to the light gardener. And the following one will include a single or a few plants from a number of different families which are widening our horizon.

Chapter 15

PLANT FAMILIES
FOR THE LIGHT GARDEN

    This section deals with the plants of families which have contributed the greatest number of individuals to light gardening. In the previous section I have segregated out those, both from these families and others, which are of particular use to the beginner. It is equally helpful to keep the plants of the following families together rather than intersperse them alphabetically through the miscellaneous list. Because they belong to a family they have similar characteristics and therefore a culture which does not vary drastically from plant to plant. The number of Gesneriads and Orchids is so large that the reader would be obliged to refer to the index whenever he wanted to find a plant of one of these families. And descriptions and cultural directions would not only occupy more space but be irritatingly repetitive. The headings give family names and, where pertinent, areas of origin and common names.

BEGONIAS

    This section does not attempt to cover the full range of Begonias, even of those which are profuse bloomers. For detailed information the reader should consult the many books devoted exclusively to this subject.

I doubt whether any other family, at the present time, provides so many species and cultivars capable of being raised under fluorescent lights. In the huge repertoire there is an almost infinite variety of leaf form and, though some of the plants run to rampant growth and others are extremely sensitive, there is hardly a single one in cultivation that cannot be managed by a grower with some experience.

As flowering plants many kinds leave much to be desired. The colors are often watery and the effect of two petals in rather lax clusters offers so little variety that only the fanatic dissolves in enchantment with them. Nevertheless everyone will find some types that please him, and it is more the general appearance of the plants which counts. At least the remarkable leaves are always there, the flowers counting as a bonus.

Even Begonia fanciers are not very enthusiastic about the flowers. They seem, indeed, to be chiefly an evidence of superior culture in their eyes. In fact the Hiemalis Begonias which are beautiful flowering plants and have the additional charm for light gardeners of blooming in winter are rather neglected by your true Begonia hobbyist. For the light garden, on the other hand, they are a challenging choice.

One group, the Rex Begonias, we will not discuss at all. Justly famous for their silver or varicolored leaves, they are the least floriferous of the family and do not fit into the framework of this book.

The Begonia family is unusual in possessing one huge genus found in various parts of the tropical world and three minor genera which are not in cultivation. However, the genus is enormously varied and it has been necessary to divide or classify it according to features of the root, leaf, and flower. In the different categories the culture is quite different. However, it can be said that almost all Begonias perform well with relatively little light, a characteristic which has made them favorites for the light gardener. Many of them, furthermore, are notoriously choosy about the amount and frequency of watering. It is the aspect of their culture on which any would-be grower must concentrate from the first.

Semperflorens or Wax Begonias

In respect to both ease of culture and continuous bloom these are miracle plants and are therefore to be found under that heading on page 141.

Belva Kusler Hybrids

This Midwestern lady has produced over the years two dozen or more truly outstanding, thoroughly tested hybrids which are superior in vigor and ease of culture to the parental species. Some are too big for the average light garden though perfectly suitable to cellar growing. Most are of the hirsute or cane types. Six of the more compact plants are:

'Crispie.' Crinkly bronze leaves, white flowers.

'Gwen Lowell.' Bushy. Hairy bronze leaves, lighter veined. White flowers.
'Jill Adair.' Smooth green leaves, white flowers.
'Lenore Olivier.' Dark green leaves, pink flowers.
'Miyo Berger.' Black leaves, ruffled, with silver pink markings. Pink flowers.
'Victoria Kartack.' Small satiny leaves. Bushy. Pink flowers.

Angel Wing or Cane Type

The Angel Wings are notable for bearing their leaves vertically. The leaf has a rounded upper lobe and a long, pointed, often silver-speckled lower part. They grow mostly on erect stems which can be very long. The flowers are in pendent trusses. Among the easiest Begonias to grow under any conditions, they like plenty of water, African Violet Mix, high humidity, and balanced fertilizer. Most of them will grow freely in coarse sphagnum moss. For the light gardener they present the problem of length and they will bloom only if exposed to maximum light. Some with a more compact habit are the following:

B. 'Dancing Girl.' A fairly compact plant with unevenly shaped leaves variously marked with swirls and dots of silver. Very easy to grow.
B. *dichroa.* A low grower with bright green leaves, orange flowers.
B. *di-erna.* Silver-spotted leaves and coral flowers. Extremely vigorous.
B. 'Elaine.' Dark green leaves, red beneath. Pink flowers.
B. *lobulata variegata.* Serrate leaves, silver spotted. A warm grower.
B. 'Mme de Lesseps.' Pointed leaves. Large white flowers. Very vigorous and easy to grow.
B. 'Orange Dainty.' Small green leaves and orange flowers in sprays.
B. 'Pinafore.' Silver-spotted leaves, salmon flowers.
B. 'Red Compta.' Coppery leaves, pink flowers. Dwarf.
B. 'Rosie Murphyski.' Despite the name a fine Begonia. A dwarf with silver-spotted leaves, pink flowers.
B. 'Sylvia.' Ruffled leaves, pink flowers.
B. 'Tom's Fantasy.' Reddish leaves with silver spots, coral flowers. Dwarf.

Hirsute Begonias

Though they have hairy leaves, the botanical feature is the hairiness of the calyx, about midway in culture between the Angel Wing and the more difficult rhizomatous types. Most will endure plenty of water but a high humidity (70 percent or better) makes them really flourish.

B. *laetivirides.* A dwarf with furry white leaves and white flowers.
B. 'Marguerite.' Small narrow leaves, pink flowers.
B. *schmidtiana.* Hairy leaves, white flowers. Dwarf.
B. *scharffiana.* Pink flowers. Compact.
B. 'Elsie Frey.' Glossy dark leaves, pink flowers. Winter flowering.

Rhizomatous Begonias

It is with the rhizomatous Begonias that we encounter most of our watering troubles. When you see them at the nursery lined up in their pots, each one as healthy looking as the other, it would seem as if nothing could be easier than to keep them going—at least the foliage. But they react badly to the change of residence, will sulk and drop their leaves when you water them, will stop growing and, if you are not very careful, die off completely.

For many of these Begonias a condition of soil humidity rather than moisture might be the better term. The rhizome crawls along the top of the ground and often decides to crawl over the rim and out of the pot. In its fleshy interior it seems to store sufficient moisture to keep the plant in condition for several weeks. The leaves rise directly from the surface of the rhizome. Any excess moisture at all in the area will sometimes make the young shoots rot out.

The solution is a highly porous Tropical Plant Mix, no packing, and a light watering only when the top is bone dry and a finger dug into the soil feels only the slightest moisture. Instead of pot watering keep the humidity at 65 percent or higher and mist regularly. Without the humidity the leaves will curl and turn brown along the edges. Fertilize only once a month.

The best dwarf plants are found in this group for the natural growth is rather horizontal and the leaves of many are not large. They will get along with very little light but if you are looking for bloom you must move them close to the lamps, always observing how the leaves react. The plants will endure a wide range of temperatures.

Loss of leaves is not always the effect of bad culture. If you have followed a strict discipline in regard to watering and the leaves gradually dry up, especially in winter, it is merely a sign of semidormancy and as long as the rhizome does not shrivel you need not be concerned. Place the pot where it will get some reflected light and do not water at all. Just mist rather heavily once or twice a day until new growth starts.

All rules have their exceptions in horticulture. I have found that a Begonia cultivar, which showed an absolute abhorrence of water for a long while, suddenly became more tolerant and grew more rapidly. This is to be watched for. But let the plant tell you by its greater vigor that it is ready, and raise the liquid dosage slowly. Never, on the other hand, really soak the plant.

The following are only a few from a very large selection. Incidentally every Begonia expert will disapprove of any list according to his own success or preferences. And it is not claimed that those I name are necessarily superior. It represents only an attempt to find the more compact species and cultivars which have been on the easy side in cultivation.

B. 'Aquamarine.' Small silvery leaves, light pink flowers.

B. 'Baby Perfectifolia.' Small green leaves with a chocolate border, light pink flowers. Miniature.

B. 'Black Falcon.' Star-shaped leaves, pink flowers.

B. 'Black Knight.' Brown star leaves, coral flowers. Dwarf.

B. 'Bow Arriola.' Bronzy leaves, pink flowers.

B. 'Bow Joe.' Brown star-shaped leaves, pink flowers.

B. 'Bow Nigra.' Black star leaves, small pink flowers.

B. *bowerae*. Eyelash Begonia. Leaves stitched black on edge, pink flowers. *Forma nigramarga* has green leaves with black markings. Eyelash edge, pink flowers.

B. 'Chantilly Lace.' Round leaves stitched with black, pink flowers.

B. 'China Doll.' Star leaves, pink flowers. Miniature.

B. 'Cleopatra.' Star leaves, brown and chartreuse. Pink flowers.

B. *fuscomaculata*. Chocolate colored leaves, pink flowers.

B. *gilsoni*. Smooth, pointed leaves, pink flowers.

B. 'Norah Bedson.' Round leaves, bright green, marbled brown, pink flowers. Dwarf.

B. 'Persian Brocade.' Star-shaped, emerald leaves, black-edged. Compact.

B. *rotundifolia*. Little round leaves, white flowers (for a change).

B. *tenuifolia*. Thick leaves, pink flowers.

B. 'Zaida.' Dark brown leaves, coral flowers. Dwarf.

Small-leaved Spreading Begonias

This is a designation which has come into fairly recent usage to cover a large number of plants which do not fit easily into the other categories. From our point of view they have the advantage of being smallish plants or miniatures. As a group they are somewhat less sensitive to watering than the rhizomatous plants.

B. *bartonea*. Pleated brownish leaves, dusted silver. Pink flowers all year.

B. 'Bayern.' Miniature angel wing, pink flowers.

B. 'China Boy.' Green leaves with red veins and pink flowers.

B. *cubensis*. Crinkled leaves and white flowers. The Holly Leaf Begonia.

B. 'Digswelliana.' Serrate leaves, red flowers. Dwarf.

B. *domingensis*. Crinkled leaves, pink flowers.

B. *foloiosa*. Fern Begonia. Oval leaves, white flowers.

B. *fuchsioides* and *fuchsioides rosea*. Tiny glossy leaves, red and pink flowers respectively.

B. *hirtella nana*. Pleated leaves, white flowers.

B. 'Medora.' Green leaves with silver spots and white flowers.

B. *incarnata*. Toothed green leaves, pink flowers.

B. 'Preussen.' Bronze leaves, pink flowers.

B. 'Sachsen.' Coppery leaves, pink flowers.

B. 'Veitch's Carmine.' Pointed leaves, red flowers.

B. 'Winter Jewel.' Green leaves, pink flowers in winter.

Tuberous Begonias

The ones we list here should not be confused with the huge flowered outdoor growing plants which are so popular. Ours are definitely indoor plants which can be raised under lights. There are two strains, both offspring on one side of *B. socotrana* from the island of Socotra in the Indian Ocean. The one, called the Cheimanthas, is from a cross with *B. dregei* which produced the Christmas Begonias and is usually now included in catalogs under the heading of tuberous or semituberous Begonias. The other, the Hiemalis, derives from crosses with various Andean species. The Cheimanthas are a more vigorous breed but the Hiemalis produce some of the handsomest flowers in the family.

The culture of both strains presents difficulties for the light gardener. The whole group is subject to a fungal infection which has at times been the despair of growers. Anyone planning to grow a number of these plants should have on hand a stock of the fungicide Benlate, made by DuPont. The spray is very efficient as a control. Many of them also prefer cool temperatures and should be well dried out between waterings.

Soil. Growers recommend a mix of equal parts peat moss, sand, and humus soil, fortified with leaf mold or well rotted cow manure. The same results can be achieved with African Violet Mix and the use of organic fertilizers either in the soil or when watering. The mix must be light, the drainage perfect.

Humidity and watering. The humidity should be better than 50 percent. Regular misting will help. The watering should be the same as for rhizomatous Begonias except that they can be given more liquid when in active growth. Clay pots suit them better than plastic ones because they will evaporate some excess moisture and contribute to coolness of the roots.

Light. Since we grow these Begonias for flowers, not foliage, we should give them good light—as much as a Gloxinia requires. If your Hiemalis do not bloom, try a short day of 10 hours.

Temperature. Air conditioning will keep temperatures at a maximum of 75 degrees Fahrenheit. Without air conditioning, you must depend on air circulation. A light mulch of sphagnum moss helps cool the roots.

Propagation. These Begonias should be renewed each year and those which bloom in winter must be carried over the summer in a dormant condition with just slightly moist soil. When new growth starts up take your cuttings, which can then be grown, after dusting with a root stimulant, in a sphagnum-vermiculite mix.

Flowers. The Christmas Begonias—Cheimanthas and related plants—flower much like other species and cultivars, although more freely. The Hiemalis, on the other hand, are real beauties, with large single or double flowers in fine shades of whites to reds and delicate zonings. A Hiemalis in full bloom is one of the handsomest plants it is possible to grow under lights.

Cheimanthas

B. 'Gloire de Lorraine,' 'Gloire de Sceaux.' Vigorous plants with roundish crinkled leaves. Prolific winter bloomers.

B. 'Marjorie Gibbs.' The Christmas Begonia. Pink flowers in winter.

B. richardsoniana. Little leaves on red stems, white flowers. Branching but small.

B. 'Richard Robinson.' Maple leaves spotted with silver, white flowers. Winter.

B. weltoniensis. Red veined green leaves and pink flowers. A beauty.

Hiemalis (all winter flowering)

B. 'Baardse Glory' and 'Baardse Wonder.' Rose and red flowers respectively.

B. 'Emily Clibran.' Most famous of the strain. Double salmon-pink flowers. A prolific bloomer and a fantastic sight when well grown.

B. 'Emita.' Light salmon single flowers.

B. 'Exquisite.' The description is apt. Dogwood pink. The leaves are reddish, the flowers very large and cup-shaped.

B. 'Fairy.' Both double and single flowers in pink with a yellow eye. Flowers longer than most of the others.

B. 'Man's Favorite.' Ivory white and very large.

B. 'Pink Perfection.' Double pink. Floriferous but rather trailing.

B. 'Princess Irene.' Bright yellow double.

B. 'Rose Queen.' Vigorous. Rose-red double.

B. 'Snowdrop.' Double white.

B. 'The President.' Huge red flowers. A good grower.

BROMELIADS

Bromeliads make a sufficiently spectacular show in florist shops which often carry a few because they need little attention and make handsome gift plants. They have also been very successfully grown under lights—almost as well as in Florida. Yet it has been as difficult to induce average light gardeners to try this family as to bring them to appreciate the possibilities in orchids. Except for the rather spreading habit of the more colorful species, they make almost ideal light garden subjects. Perhaps the fact that mature plants are rather expensive has been the chief deterrent. In compensation they are very long lasting and difficult to kill.

This is a New World family which is to be found everywhere in the American tropics, growing usually on trees. The root system contributes little to nourishment, serving principally for attachment. The leaves, however, are equipped with feeding cells and many of the plants have "vases" formed by these same leaves, which collect and hold water and into which organic debris and insects fall and supply the very small amounts of food they require.

In most Bromeliad species the flowers, which are three-petaled, are in-

significant. Color is supplied by an inflorescence whose bracts retain their brilliance long after blooming, or by the flushing of the leaves with brilliant tints
in the area of bloom. These color effects, in many species, last a long time. In
addition some species produce handsome colorful berries—orange, blue, or
white for instance—which also last very well.

Bromeliads grow very slowly in the house, therefore nobody is advised to
start with seed. Since the root system is small, large pots are unnecessary.
Since many of the plants are top-heavy, clay azalea pots give more stability
and plastic should only be used for small specimens. Most plants can be
accommodated in a 5-inch or smaller pot.

Almost anything will do as a medium—chopped osmunda, leaf mold,
German peat, orchid mixes, even gravel. Drainage should be good as retained
moisture can encourage rot.

Long hours (14–16) of fluorescent light encourage coloration of leaf and
inflorescence. Certain species, for instance, even when not in bloom, have
reddish leaves when exposed to strong light but are quite green if the light is
inadequate. It has also been proved that for these plants windowsill light is not
nearly as effective as fluorescent. Bromeliad growers report that Optima tubes
are, in this instance, necessary to make the plants bloom. The normal commercial tubes and Gro-Lux have not been as efficient.

Humidity should be 50 percent or more and the plants benefit from frequent
mistings. Vases should always have some water in them. Fertilizer solutions
need to be cut drastically. A balanced solution of 20-20-20, for instance, needs
cutting to one-eighth the labeled recommendation. Water the roots only after
the soil is dry.

It has been found that ethylene gas will induce flowering in mature
Bromeliad growths. The same effect can be achieved in the house by encasing
the plant in plastic for five days along with an apple which produces the gas.
A blooming stalk will appear within six to eight weeks.

Most Bromeliads produce more than one offshoot each year and this should
be separated from the parent by a clean cut at the joint and potted up. As
flowering takes place only from new growth the old plant can be discarded.
The exceptions are those species which develop a single growth from the center
of the old plant. The older leaves dry out gradually leaving the new ones room
to develop.

In short, Bromeliads are among the easiest of plants for the indoor gardener
to grow. The only major requirement which is something of a chore is the need
for almost continuous misting to achieve superior plant growth. When the
inflorescence begins to grow move your plant close to the center of the lights.
That is all there is to it. When not in bloom the beauty of the leaves is sufficient
compensation for the long wait. Color from the inflorescence may last as long
as three months.

The following listings, by genus only, suggest the immense variety in this
family.

Aechmea

This genus includes the famous *Aechmea fasciata,* a plant which looks as if it were sculptured in silver. It is upright and possesses a deep vase from which rises a club-shaped inflorescence studded with pink bracts and blue flowers. The show lasts for months.

A. chantini. The foliage is handsomely banded in white and gray-green. The flowers are red and yellow and the bracts red or pink. Small and larger clones and cultivars of this species are available.

A. fulgens, var. *discolor.* Red bracts and blue flowers followed by long-lasting red berries. *Fulgens* will do well in less light than some of the others.

A. lueddemanniana. An easy plant whose leaves are reddish beneath and the inflorescence black speckled with white. White berries follow the pink flowers.

A. mertensii. Spiny leaves and orange bracts. The white berries turn blue.

A. racinae (Christmas Jewels). Orange inflorescence with yellow and black flowers.

A. recurvata. The flowers are in the vase itself. But the leaves turn red near the cup. Sturdy and pretty, small plant.

There are numerous cultivars of *Aechmea fasciata.* An old hybrid, *A.* x 'Foster's Favorite' has wine-red leaves and blue flowers and berries. There are several forms.

Ananas

The pineapple plant is *Ananas comosus.* There are several cultivar house-plants with variegated leaves that look like small Century Plants. The flowers are purple but the plant is raised for the miniature pineapples which are almost as ornamental as a flower and fun for the hobbyist. Not edible, however. There is also a dwarf species *A. ananassoides nanus* which fits better under the lights.

If you want to try it you may cut off the leafy top of your pineapple fruit, let it develop a callus for several days and then plant it shallowly in sandy soil. Roots will appear in a few weeks. It is not a particularly attractive plant but, as a by-product, costs nothing.

Billbergia

B. nutans is one of the easiest and most popular plants in the family. It requires very little light compared to the others and is a frequent bloomer with pendent, quite prominent yellow flowers with rose bracts. Hence its nickname, Queen's Tears.

The *B. saundersii* species and hybrids have variegated leaves and pendent red and blue flowers.

Cryptanthus

The Zebra Plants or Earth Stars are not for blooming but are compact and have beautiful horizontal stripes in silver and claret, green and tan, etc. Mist often but do not water more than once a week.

Guzmania

These are spreading plants with handsome foliage and club- or spike-shaped inflorescences. *G. lingulata* and *musaica* are fine species.

Neoregelia

The flowers bloom in the cup but the spreading leaves turn violent shades of red near the bases at flowering time. *N. carolinae* has many variations and *N. marmorata* has unusual speckled foliage.

Tillandsia

This is the largest genus in the family and includes *T. usneoides,* Spanish Moss and *T. recurvata,* the Moss Ball, both of which grow profusely in our southern states.

Many of the *Tillandsias* are best raised on slabs of tree fern and these are difficult to maintain unless you are prepared to mist very frequently. They have inflorescences which are lengthy and have narrow tube flowers in blue.

T. lindenii is popular for its blue flowers against pink bracts and its lasting qualities. There are numerous forms.

T. ionantha is typical of some small species which have powdery gray-green dryish foliage which turns flame color at blooming time.

Vriesia

This includes the famous *V. splendens,* Flaming Sword, whose long brilliant red or orange inflorescence lasts for months. There are many variations with handsomely variegated leaves. The new shoot rises from the center. It is a surprisingly easy plant to grow under lights.

Vriesia carinata, a medium-size plant, throws up a brilliant red and yellow feather which lasts for a long time.

V. heliconoides is a small fleshy Bromeliad with light green leaves which puts forth a small edition of *Heliconia* in brilliant red and yellow. This is the showiest of the smaller species and not at all difficult to raise.

CACTI AND SUCCULENTS

Although a few succulents have been listed among our best light gardening plants, it will be some time before the amateur has gained sufficient experience with the vast number of these plants to be able to grow them successfully and, above all, bloom them. By and large the succulents (except the Aizoaceae) are easier than the cacti because they are largely plants belonging to families which have only gradually adapted themselves to desert conditions. Even the cacti have a primitive ancestor still with us which is leafy, the Pereskia. However the cacti and the Aizoaceae (Living Stones, etc., from South Africa), are rather set in their ways and do not take to artificial light very kindly.

In spite of all problems, growers have had more success lately with some of the less difficult cacti—the Rebutias for instance. And we now can make some reasonably reliable recommendations.

General Culture

Soil. Cactus Mix is quite adequate for growing both cacti and succulents. All we have to watch is the pH content. Many cacti require rather limey soil and we should provide it by adding to the mix a quantity of small lime chips to bring them to a nearly neutral 7pH as tested with a litmus paper strip. The mix is porous and has a mechanical consistency which is quite as suitable as desert soil and far easier to handle in the house.

Temperature. Cacti and succulents, more adaptable than orchids, can stand a lot of heat but are accustomed to a sharp drop in temperature at night. The obesity of many cacti serves the purpose not only of water storage but the retention of the day's warmth after nightfall. This produces the dew, or condensation moisture, which coats the surface of the plant and provides it with its chief source of moisture most of the year. A drop in temperature in the house will not normally produce the same amount of dew-moisture as in nature. Therefore we must water the plants more or mist them. I believe that misting regularly during winter, when they require little water, is an effective way of keeping them healthy without a sharp drop in temperature.

Light. Your lamps must be arranged to give the plants the maximum amount of light and the tubes should be as close as possible without burning them. Not being a cactus specialist I do not know the light cycle of each of the genera. But it is well known that many cacti require short days to bring them into bloom. During the fall and winter, when water is withheld, we can keep them on an 8- or 10-hour light day. In the spring, when we increase watering slightly, the day length can be increased to 18 hours, and once the plants have bloomed we can go to a 24-hour day during the growth and watering period.

By these means I think you will avoid etiolation (weak and lengthy growths) which are the bane of cactus growers. You will also have a good chance of blooming your plants.

Water. Anybody who grows cactus and succulents must study the water needs of these plants, as any excess will rot them. Usually watering is gradually started in the spring, increases at bloom time and during the period of growth in summer, and tapers off to near dryness during the fall and winter months. That is when the misting, mentioned above, comes in handy.

Family Cactaceae

The best results so far with cacti under lights have been with certain of the South American species. However, the light gardener would be wise to follow the cultural instructions in one of the many excellent books listing numerous species. Those which are described as requiring some shade in nature, and there are quite a few, will usually do best. It is pointless simply to choose plants by appearance for growing under lights. Cactus nurseries have catalogs and you can order the most suitable species.

Smaller varieties of Echinocereus, Mamillaria, Lobivia, Rebutia, and Notocactus can be recommended. Schlumbergeras and related plants, the Christmas and Easter cacti, are more tolerant of watering but require their dry period and short day in the fall. Rhispsalis, grown more for its odd hanging growth and white or reddish berries, requires moist, humid conditions.

Propagation. The seeds of different species vary greatly in the germination period. In some the wait may extend to months. Simply sow on top of Cactus Mix, water the pot from the bottom until it is thoroughly soaked, cover with a sheet of glass or plastic, and place close under the lights where the seed will be kept warm. A temperature of 80 degrees is about right. .

When the seedlings appear the covering can be removed but the soil must be kept moist at all times. When large enough to handle, they can be pricked out and potted up individually. The young plants will thrive with moisture until a definite leaf or ball is formed, whereupon the cycle of moisture and dryness must begin.

In regard to vegetative propagation I recommend that you consult a book on cactus culture where the various methods are thoroughly discussed. Plants which grow with leaves or segments, like most succulents, can be cut at a joint and laid on moist Cactus Mix—not buried. In due time roots will form.

Family Asclepiadaceae

Culture is the same as for Stapelia. *Ceropegia woodii* has been described elsewhere. The other Ceropegias are less satisfactory and some are very large vines. Caralluma offers us some interesting small shrubs with clusters of mall flowers. Duvalia and Huernia have larger flowers on small plants and may bloom several times a year under lights. Stapelia (p. 219), *Ceropegia woodii* (p. 206).

Family Crassulaceae

The Jade Plant, *Crassula arborescens,* does better in the window and is rather too large for the lights. Most Crassulas are strictly foliage plants. The best for flowering are *C. schmidtii* and *C. cooperi*. They bloom in midsummer without difficulty. Other small leaved varieties grow well but rarely bloom for us.

The Kalanchoes are easy but rather weedy. *K. blossfeldiana* and variations are the fleshy leaved plants one sees in florist shops at Christmas time, covered with red tube flowers. They should be given the same fall short day and rest as the Christmas Cactus. *K. tubiflora* is a most attractive small vine with pink bells.

Aeoniums, Sempervivums, and Sedums do well under the lights if kept sufficiently dry and close to the tubes. They rarely bloom for us.

Family Liliaceae

Agaves and Aloes grow into specimen plants under lights but I have not seen them blooming there. The Haworthias, on the other hand, are quite easy, and will bloom in summer. Water should be withheld in winter.

Family Aizoaceae

Some of these plants need a minimum of water—even less than the cacti. Treat them much the same. Their flowering season is spring and summer. Through much of the year misting is more effective and safer than watering.

GERANIUMS (PELARGONIUMS)

Because of their need for strong sunlight garden Geraniums have not been good indoor plants. A new strain, the "Carefree" Geraniums will bloom under lights and if started from seed in summer or early fall will do so in late winter. But they are still too big and tall, and even though the first truss of flowers may bloom when the plant is only 10 inches high, subsequent growth is rapid and the plant soon becomes outsize.

Except for the challenge there is no reason to depend on this type of Geranium at all since the miniatures and dwarfs have many advantages from the cultural standpoint and are esthetically more satisfactory indoors.

From the point of view of the light gardener these little plants are very close to being miracles. They remain consistently small, bloom easily from November or December until the following August or September, will repeat at least two years in a row, and come in a range of forms and colors which is wholly enchanting. Those who detest the odor of Geranium leaves might consider that it does not travel far and that it is quite unnecessary to smell them every time one looks at them. Even if this fails they are worth the sacrifice.

Miniature and dwarf Geraniums require only a 3-inch pot, for their principal growth is only 3 to 6 inches high. Use sandy soil mix with added lime. A little bone meal is also a good slow-acting fertilizer to include at the start. Place them within 3 or 4 inches of the lights near the center of the tubes. Water daily but be sure that they drain. Fertilize with a balanced chemical solution or an organic. Low humidity does not bother them but they prefer a temperature in the 65 to 75 degree range.

The moment they fail to produce flowers, reduce the watering and allow the pot to dry out well between waterings. Do not fertilize. Trim the plant back to a neat shape and let it rest until ready to bloom again.

At any time cuttings can be made from the tips of branches and set in moist sand or vermiculite in good warmth and light. They grow roots quickly.

Theoretically the miniatures do not grow more than 3 inches high, the dwarfs 6 inches. In practice they may become a bit taller and rather bushier than you might expect. Because the stems are thick and tend to curve into interesting shapes it is easy to train these plants somewhat like Bonsai, setting them in decorative small pots and dishes and pruning them asymmetrically.

Considering that the blooms are always the same—five petals or doubled, the amount of variation in form is astonishing. There are neat singles in white, orange, salmon, pink and red, red with a white eye and so forth—each slightly differently shaped and with a personality of its own. The doubles are more formless but showy.

The cultivars are too numerous to list here and you are referred therefore to the catalogs of specialists. However, worthy of special mention, though not necessarily the best for you, are:

The singles— 'Dopey,' 'Perky,' 'Pixie,' 'Red Comet,' 'Salmon Comet,' 'Sneezy,' 'Snow White,' 'Tiny Tim Pink,' 'Tiny Tim Red.' Variegated Kleiner Liebling does not bloom so well but the handsome green and white zoned leaves and the habit suit it to Bonsai treatment.

The doubles—'Arcturus,' 'Black Dwarf,' 'Jupiter,' 'Merope,' 'Mischief,' 'Mr. Everaarts,' 'Rosy Dawn,' 'Saturn,' 'Twinkle.'

There are numerous others.

GESNERIADS

The African Violet (*Saintpaulia*) was largely responsible for the quick popularity of indoor light gardening. The plant was found to be perfectly adaptable. Another member of the same family, the *Gesneriaceae*, the Florist Gloxinia (*Sinningia speciosa*), from the other side of the world and a much larger plant, also behaved well under the lights. A few other Gesneriads were known and were put to the test with some success. And soon there was a treasure hunt afoot wherever members of this family could be found to see if still others would be satisfactory bloomers with artificial lighting.

In the last ten years numerous new species have been introduced to cultivation among which many have been rejected but a few have been outstanding. Almost all seemed to possess one characteristic—a tolerance of relatively low light intensities. The rejects were principally outsize, small flowered, or somewhat too delicate for the average grower. The better ones have been bred and hybridized to the point where there is a considerable repertoire of workable species and cultivars. At the present time it is the most interesting and satis-factory family for the light hobbyist.

Numerous Gesneriad species grow from Central America to Brazil, in the southern areas of Africa, and from Indonesia to Burma. These are the warm growing plants. In addition, there are species living in temperate or alpine conditions which require a cooler environment than the home grower can provide.

Of course it has not been just the adaptability of the Gesneriads which has made them such favorites. As new introductions arrived we became aware that in this family there was a unique combination of beautiful foliage and flower and that the proportions of many of the plants were just right for their confined positions under the lights.

Types of Gesneriads

The reason why Gesneriads are capable of blooming under fluorescents may be traced to their normal habitat. Whether epiphytic, plants of the forest floor, inhabitants of cave mouths or clefts in the hills, all of them spend much of their time in shade. In this respect they are similar to many orchid species. With few exceptions they like a rich organic soil and considerable moisture for part of the year. In other words, wherever this plant family has chosen to grow and develop it is to be found in conditions which have certain basic similarities. And this accounts for the fact that we can raise so many different kinds, derived from regions geographically far apart and in some respects quite contrasting, in the same light garden and with only slight changes in cultural treatment.

Gesneriads are categorized by the nature of their roots of which there are three kinds—fibrous, tuberous, or possessing scaly rhizomes.

Fibrous Rooted Gesneriads

Since this group possesses roots which are like most nontuberous annuals and perennials the designation is only a means of differentiating them from the other two classifications. *Saintpaulia* and *Streptocarpus* from Africa, *Aeschy-nanthus* and *Chirita* from the Far East, and *Columnea* and *Episcia* from the Americas are all fibrous rooted.

Tuberous Rooted Gesneriads

Rechsteineria and *Sinningia* are in this group. All the tuberous species become dormant if water is withheld from them and sometimes will insist upon doing so whatever the devices we may use to prevent it. This means storage of the tubers, which is a disadvantage. In recent hybrids an attempt is being made to eliminate this feature.

Scaly Rhizomed Gesneriads

This unusual rhizome has somewhat the structure of a pinecone. That is to say that the scaly bulblets are attached to the section of root in an arrangement similar to the scales of a cone. However, they are only slightly graduated in size at the ends, so that the shape of the rhizome with its tightly packed scales is either tubular or somewhat thicker at one end than the other. According to genus, species, and size of plant they may range from a ½ inch to 3 inches in size and are usually produced very freely. *Achimenes* and *Kohleria* have the odd habit of producing a reduced version of the rhizome at the tip of branches toward the end of the season, especially if the plant has not been able to flower.

Each scale will develop into a plant if broken off and planted separately. More vigorous and rapid growth is achieved by using the whole rhizome or a large section of one.

Most of these plants become dormant, and when the top growth has died down the earth is knocked out of the pot and the rhizomes are separated from the rest of the roots. This should be done carefully as they are very brittle. Snip them off cleanly with a scissors rather than try to break them.

They should not be allowed to dry out completely in storage. Keep in a plastic bag with a little slightly moist sphagnum or vermiculite. After several months they will sprout at one end, not from individual bulblets, and can then be potted up just below the surface of the soil. Allowance in the size of the pot must be made for the development of a considerable root system—and a new crop of rhizomes.

Achimenes. Central and South America

For variety of color there is nothing to compare with Achimenes in the whole range of plants presently available for indoor growing. In constant cultivation and hybridization since the middle of the nineteenth century, an enormous number of variations has been produced. Colors are actually available in yellow, red, and blue and a spectrum of shades between. Furthermore, the tints are clear and brilliant.

The leaves are an inch or two in size and saw-toothed, mostly somewhat hairy and in *A. ehrenburgii* almost as silvery as *R. leucotricha*. They are borne opposite each other on the stems which have a hanging habit but are not as long as in *Columnea*. The flowers, which range from quite small to 1½ inches across the front are long-tubed, flaring into five lobes with the three lower ones jutting forward—a very graceful form.

Theoretically the culture is simple enough. The small inch-long rhizomes are planted horizontally an inch below the surface in lightly compacted African Violet Mix as soon as they start to sprout. Three will do for a 6-inch pot for the growth of root is considerable. This usually happens in April or early May and the flowers should appear right through the summer until September or even October. Bloom usually starts when the growth is still quite small.

All that is necessary is to keep them constantly moist, which means literally so, for a single day of dryness may send them back into dormancy. Also it is wise to keep adding eggshell or limestone in small amounts for this is a lime loving plant and will resent the gradual acidifying of the peat. Avoid manures but feed with balanced chemical nutrients in the growing stage and high phosphorus when ready to bloom.

In the fall the leaves start to dry and become unsightly. Sometimes additional rhizomes will grow at the tips of the late branches. In any case, when you finally decant the plant you will, whether you have bloomed it or not, find an ample crop of rhizomes for the following year. These can be stored in a plastic bag until they are ready again.

I have spent a little time on Achimenes because it is such a marvelous plant but I must warn all and sundry that success in the greenhouse is much more common than under lights. In fact, light growers have experienced great difficulty. In the city I suspect the cause is aerial pollution, to which these plants seem to be especially sensitive. Another reason may be a deficiency of light since Achimenes require as much or more than most of the other Gesneriads. Finally, it is just possible that our long day-length under lights is not quite right for them.

Another disadvantage is their summer blooming. Indoor gardeners naturally prefer plants that flower between fall and late spring. Some experiments have indicated that if the blooming period is cut short in early summer and the plants allowed to go dormant they will start to sprout again in the middle of winter. Sooner or later we will tame this beautiful plant and in the meanwhile a few chosen ones have done well with it under lights.

Since the larger plants are best suited to basket culture, a list of the compact ones, as suggested by Paul Arnold, may be of help. These are 'Ambroise Verschaffelt,' white with purple veining; *A. andrieuxi*, a dwarf with violet and white flowers; 'Atropurpurea,' reddish purple;' 'Camillo Brozzoni,' small purple flowers; *A. cettoana*, bluish; 'Charm,' pink flowers; 'François Cardinaux,' lavender and white; and 'Violacea Semi-Plena,' with purple blooms. For two other colors and not excessively large, *A. flava* with yellow flowers, and *A. heterophylla* with orange ones, should be mentioned.

Aeschynanthus. 'Lipstick Plant.' Southeast Asia and the Himalayas

In the last twenty years, as each beautiful Gesneriad was introduced to greenhouse and windowsill growers, it has been greeted with enthusiasm and exaggerated praise. The Lipstick Plants are so gorgeous in bloom that everyone fell in love with them. But though sunlight growers have had good success with them, indoor light gardeners have had few successes. They are spring and summer bloomers which require plenty of light and humidity and are very sensitive to aerial pollution. It is to be hoped that hybrids will be developed which will adapt better to the lights. Meanwhile they make fine foliage plants and, if bloom is rare, it is worth waiting for.

The growth and even the flower is similar to some Columneas. The leaves are thick and oval, opposite on long trailing stems. Flowering with most species and cultivars is clustered at the tip of the stem, which is one reason for not cutting the plant back during its best growing and budding season. The flowers are long-tubed and the shorter lobes are like those of *Columnea* but more rounded. Colors range from orange to deep red. *A. parvifolius* is the most beautiful of a group which have very long deep purple, nearly black, calyces from which the red corollas burst out in startling contrast. *A.* 'Black Pagoda' has interesting variegated foliage. *A. micrantha* is a smaller plant with inch-long deep red tubes borne all along the stem. Some of the plants have been so hybridized and are so variable that even the nurserymen have trouble telling them apart.

Also like *Columnea, Aeschynanthus* is an epiphytic plant and likes to grow in a basket. Lacking that it should be potted up in an azalea pot with Tropical Plant Mix, watered regularly, and fertilized with balanced nutrient. The plant also thrives in coarse sphagnum moss. It should have a position quite close to the center of the lights and within 4 inches of the tubes. Those who have been successful with Aeschynanthus report blooms as often as three times a year. But keep the humidity at 50 percent or better and the temperature 60 degrees or higher.

To propagate simply take cuttings of the young stems, strip the lower leaves, dust with hormone powder, and plant in moist vermiculite. Rooting is rapid.

Chirita. India and China

Of this large genus only a few are in active cultivation, among them the remarkable *Chirita sinensis*. The 6-inch leaves, which are oblanceolate, narrowing gradually into the petiole, are bright green, heavily veined in brilliant silver, and hairy. The thickness of texture gives a leathery effect. The leaves grow in a rosette and peduncles rise from the axils bearing whitish bell-shaped flowers with a three-lobed lip. A form, undifferentiated by name in the trade, has plain green leaves of the same texture. In fact, cuttings may come up either way and nobody seems to know what causes the difference.

This is not an easy plant to maintain or flower and not too many people have been successful with it. The leaves often acquire brown dried areas. The plant must be handled with care for the petioles are very brittle. Yet it is such a beauty and its habit is so very good for light growing that it is worth the attempt.

It seems to do all right in Tropical Plant Mix with an extra dose of lime. An azalea pot seems best considering the form of the plant which is very flat but spreading. Water from the top when the surface of the soil dries out and maintain high humidity. It likes misting with clear water. Temperatures from 55 to 80 degrees are the apparent optimum range. Do *not* fertilize except possibly once every two months with a balanced nutrient containing trace elements. Fertilizer seems to be one of the causes of the browning off of the leaves. I have found it to flourish without any nutrient.

In repotting be careful not to cover the fibrous crown between leaf and root else crown rot can develop.

To propagate, take a leaf and cut the midvein in several places and dust the underside with hormone powder. Lay it on moist vermiculite in a propagation box. Within a short time young plants will develop through the slits.

It is something of a triumph to grow a perfect plant of Chirita even if no bloom ensues. The effect of symmetrical foliage with handsome coloring and texture is sufficient reward. Such a plant, because it is healthy, will probably bloom.

Very different plants are *C. lavandulacea* and its small relative *C. micromusa*. The former is a good open light garden plant and the latter is a terrarium gem. Flowering is in stages up a straight stem. At each joint there grow two opposite pale green oval leaves and from the same place rise whorls of violet-blue and bright yellow flowers respectively. This type of straight line growth obviously has its limits and the plant does not ordinarily sprout again from the base. After flowering it simply dies off. However, it sets seed copiously without your aid, and these are not at all difficult to grow in a warm indoor garden. Six to 8 inches under lights is ample illumination, and season makes no apparent difference. Both plants prefer Sandy Soil Mix with lime. Both are easy to grow and attractive.

Chrysothemis pulchella. Tropical America

Of the two types of *Chrysothemis* in cultivation, one, *C. friedrichsthaliana*, has flowers with a greenish calyx, while *C. pulchella* has an orange calyx. The flowers of both species are yellow with fine red stripes. The difference in the calyx is important because it is persistent for a long time and that is why I consider *C. pulchella* the more attractive plant. In other respects they are very similar. An easy grower with small flowers developing in considerable numbers in the axils, these long lasting calyces are a distinct advantage.

It is a straight-stemmed fleshy plant with 4-inch bright green opposite leaves. As it grows fast it must be trimmed constantly and then will bush out a bit. Culture is very simple. Tropical Plant Mix, a balanced fertilizer, and warmth are the chief requirements. It will bloom as much as eight inches under the lights and should be kept constantly moist. Although tuberous rooted, the best way of propagating is by stem cuttings from top growth. With more testing this may yet prove a Miracle Plant.

Codonanthe crassifolia and macradenia. West Indies and South America

These very similar plants have fleshy green leaves on trailing stems and white flowers—1½-inch tubes with small lobes. The flowers last only a few days but they are produced continuously, and since it is an easy plant to grow it should be more common in our indoor gardens.

A stem cutting of *Codonanthe* will bloom when it is only a few inches long. It can be trimmed and then will produce more stems and bush out a bit. It seems happy in African Violet or Tropical Plant Mix with plenty of watering and humidity. About eight inches from the tubes suits it. Mist regularly.

White is not such a common color in house plants as one might expect, so this Gesneriad is well worth growing.

Columnea. 'Goldfish Plant.' *Central America*

The marvelous flowers of the *Columnea* are a sufficient recommendation for every light gardener to attempt to grow them. Most of them are not easy under lights and are doubly difficult in the city. But once you have mastered them—learned how to treat them in your particular environment—they will be a continuous source of pleasure.

The flowers have a long expanding tube with four lobes. The upper one is long and broad, extending like a hood. The two side ones are like fins, and a lower one is turned directly downward. When the blooms are borne in a more or less upright position they do have a resemblance to a gold or flying fish. They range in size from 1 to 3 inches and display a blaze of deep reds and yellows. When well grown they will flower all along the stems, creating a display which is nearly unique in houseplants. In addition they are among the most long lasting of flowers, often hanging on for weeks. The fruit is also ornamental—a large white button.

Opposite oval pointed leaves are borne on thin or quite thick long branches. The former will trail more than the latter, but essentially it is a trailing plant. This is a distinct disadvantage for the light gardener. Much as he may regret those wonderful 6-foot hanging baskets which are seen at our better house plant nurseries, he knows that an upright or bushy growth is far more adaptable to his conditions. Until recently this was an insuperable problem but hybridizers are gradually introducing plants better suited to our needs. It should be noted that many hybrids listed as everblooming are anything but that under indoor conditions. But the ones we list can be depended upon. In due time there will be more.

The first *Columnea* to give hope of both shrubby growth and everblooming was *C.* 'V. Covert' which has inch-long pink flowers. Not a very showy plant, it is dependable and very pretty when well covered with bloom.

At present the best cultivar for the beginner is *C.* 'Chanticleer.' It is thick stemmed, hairy, and bushy. It is everblooming. The flowers are orange, of medium size, not brilliant.

Smaller leaved and more trailing but with larger, very handsome flowers, orange, beautifully patterned with yellow is *C.* 'Early Bird.' Also everblooming, it is somewhat more difficult than *C.* 'Chanticleer.' *C.* 'Mary Ann' with smaller reddish flowers is also a good one.

Columnea erythrophaea—a Late Addition

This *Columnea,* which has recently joined my collection, is performing so well that I am virtually certain that it is a Miracle Plant. The stems are thick, the leaves dark green and shiny. Flowers are produced in great numbers on quite stocky stems, and buds appear constantly. The blooms are easily 3 inches long and of a burnt orange color, on pedicels 1½ inches long and with a calyx which is ruffled and spread. Altogether, a spectacular plant—much more so than 'Chanticleer.' It appears to be more tolerant of watering than most Columneas.

These are the only ones we can recommend at the present time. There are numerous cultivars and species in the catalogs and you may try them all. If you follow the watering instructions carefully you may be successful with them.

Being epiphytic, Columneas require very light soil and perfect drainage. Tropical Plant Mix loosely packed into the pot is best. As it is a spreader in respect to roots, an azalea pot is better than a deep one. Keep about five inches from the lights—a little nearer if the plant is trailing. Fertilize sparingly with balanced nutrient. Temperatures should be from 65 degrees on up.

The chief problem is watering. Getting the exactly correct balance is very important because if you over-water or under-water the result will be the same—blasted buds. The principle is that Columneas should not be watered until the soil is dry and then only enough to moisten. Observe this rule and you will have flowers.

One way of assuring results is frequent misting. This will take the place of some watering and relieve your anxiety that it is getting too little moisture. The higher the humidity the better.

Note that the buds will hang on for a long time and then, if conditions are right, develop with astonishing speed. Within 48 hours the bud will have grown its full length and opened.

If a plant stubbornly refuses to produce buds at all, stop watering for a few weeks and only mist. Some of the species which are seasonal in spring require a dry period of a month in midwinter. Some of these will put forth even a 4-inch flower which is a reward for a shorter season.

Cuttings, the lower part stripped of their leaves, will root quickly in moist vermiculite. After potting up with sufficient root, the dry regimen should be instituted. The stems will grow much better if little water is provided. Budded cuttings may even bloom. They do in greenhouses. Don't forget to mist.

Diastema. Central and South America

The Diastemas are all small plants with tube flowers flared into five lobes, whitish and more or less spotted with lavender. They have scaly rhizomes and like the others of this group have a dormant period but of relatively short duration. They are particularly suited to terrarium treatment grown in African Violet Mix in with *Gesnerias,* the miniature *Sinningias,* and others.

Light requirements are low. Like the other plants, they prefer warm temperatures and will suffer if the temperature drops below 60.

Diastema quinquevulnerum may, with flowers, grow 5 or 6 inches tall. *D. vexans* is about half as big. The rhizomes propagate freely. In the terrarium the rhizomes can be left undisturbed during the dormant period as long as the soil is not soaked.

Drymonia stenophylla. Tropical America

This *Drymonia* can become a rather large shrub and is included here because it blooms very easily and makes a good foliage plant. It has thick stems and leathery leaves with long petioles. The yellowish white tube flowers grow in the axils of the leaves all year round under lights. Drymonia requires very little light; it will even bloom in a north window. It needs little attention. Tropical Plant Mix, regular watering, and fertilizing will produce a handsome plant. Sections of stem can be propagated easily. Because it grows fast it should be replaced in the home every year.

Episcia. Tropical America

On pages 143–144, among the Miracle Plants, I discuss *E.* 'Moss Agate' and *E.* 'Cygnet,' the most floriferous of the genus, and their culture.

The market has been flooded with hybrids, some having been produced naturally in Central American gardens. Dealers' catalogs contain the names of many attractive species and cultivars. The following are especially worth noting.

E. 'Cleopatra' and *E.* 'Pink Brocade' are very similar plants. The coloring, different from all other Episcias, is white, surrounded by green with a pink border. The leaves are large and this combination is one of the showiest among foliage plants. The plants will bloom in a terrarium. Both are very partial to high humidity and good light. A well-grown plant is magnificent even without the attractive blooms. *E.* 'Cleopatra' has red flowers and *E.* 'Pink Brocade,' orange-red with yellow in the throat. Both are fairly small.

E. 'Cameo' is a recent introduction with shiny leaves combining brown with a rich red. Not easy to bloom under lights.

E. 'Columbia Orange' has small, velvety, bright green leaves and orange flowers. Blooms easily but suckers tremendously.

E. 'Silver Sheen' is like an outsize *E.* '*Acajou*' with very silvery leaves.

Earlier I mentioned *E. dianthiflora*, one of the white flowered parents of *E.* 'Cygnet.' It is a prettier plant than the latter, with small foliage and delightful fringed flowers. You can grow and bloom it with warmth and plenty of humidity.

E. lilacina has blue flowers. I have never seen it in bloom under lights, and though I have tried growing it, it has never done well for me. The flowers are the largest among the Episcias.

E. reptans and hybrids such as 'Shimmer' have a remarkably heavy pile on the leaves which are dark with brilliantly contrasting midveins.

A new plant is *E.* 'Star of Bethlehem' which introduces a two-colored flower, white and bright pink. Very pretty and not difficult to grow but not an easy bloomer.

Gesneria. West Indies

Beside *G. cuneifolia,* one of our miracle plants, the genus Gesneria offers two other gems. One is *G. pedicellaris* which also grows in a rosette but whose leaves are heavily crinkled. Unlike *G. cuneifolia,* it does better outside a terrarium but also requires constant watering. Eight to 10 inches below the lights it will produce its beautiful tube flowers, about an inch long, somewhat pouched toward the base and deep blood red. It will flower at any season of the year. Mist regularly.

G. citrina is a tiny shrub which throws up threadlike pedicels with pendent tubes of purest rich yellow. Very floriferous, it *does* like a terrarium's high humidity. Ten inches from the tubes is sufficient. A perfect charm plant, but very slow growing. A new hybrid, as yet unnamed, has *G. Cuneifolia* leaves and yellow flowers.

There are other Gesnerias, all smallish and either of the rosette or shrubby form. All are worth a try.

Gloxinia perennis. Tropical America

Of the true genus Gloxinia only one, *Gloxinia perennis,* is much cultivated. It is fleshy and large leaved and unless trimmed will get a bit big for the garden. The bluish flowers are rather large campanulate (bell-shaped). Culture is similar to *Chrysothemis.* A nice change from the normal two forms of Gesneriads, tube and flared tube. A short day plant.

xGloxinera. Hybrids of Rechsteineria and Sinningia

There have been a tremendous number of these hybrids mostly crossed by amateurs. Some very beautiful plants were produced with handsome leaves and flowers somewhat larger and more heavily textured than 'Dollbaby,' the *Sinningia* hybrid. I had some which were unnamed and which bloomed beautifully and I would have been happy if they had continued to do so. Unfortunately they soon went dormant and then refused to come out of it. I understand that some amateurs have tubers of these plants which have performed satisfactorily, and a selection is beginning to come on the market. Eventually, I suppose, selection will bring satisfactory results and then light gardeners will have a whole gamut of splendid medium-size plants in a new range of colors. Watch for them in the nursery catalogs. Very early on, Mrs. Frances Batcheller, a leading hybridizer, developed two plants, xGloxinera 'Ramadeva' and 'Krishna.'

These are not easy to bloom but very lovely and 'Ramadeva' has been crossed with 'Dollbaby' to produce 'Cupid's Doll,' an easier grower. 'Ramadeva' was also crossed with 'Cupid's Doll' to produce xGloxinera 'Pink Flare' which is exactly like a rosy-colored 'Dollbaby' and performs as well.

Dr. Clayberg's 'Pink Petite' has proved reliable, as are 'Little Imp' and 'Pink Imp'—crosses with R. leucotricha.

Some of the faulty xGloxineras were much more handsome than these plants and we hope that they will establish themselves gradually.

Culture is the same as for Sinningias.

Hypocyrta. Gesneriaceae. 'Candy Corn.' Central and South America

Hypocyrta wettsteinii is a little shrub with very dark green shiny leaves against which the tomato-red flowers with yellow tips show up beautifully. Like so many Gesneriad flowers these are essentially tubular except that halfway along there is a deep pouch followed by an abrupt narrowing. They are produced in the axils over a long period and, with ideal care, they may be considered very nearly everblooming.

Treatment is the same as for Columneas—African Violet Mix, very light watering, temperatures in the 60s or higher, humidity of 50 percent or better, and fertilization with a balanced nutrient.

H. radicans has longer stems, larger leaves and flowers—the latter up to an inch. H. nummularia's flowers are small, and the tip of the tube, which is so shortened that the opening lies on top of the pouch, is ringed with purple. It is a more difficult plant with a tendency to go dormant and swell at the axils. Very little water should be given during this period, and patience is required until it decides to start growing again. Do not fertilize during the dormancy.

H. perianthomega is a more robust plant, growing 2 feet high and spreading. The pouches are yellow striped with purple which sounds more glamorous than it is. Nevertheless the plant has an odd and pleasing appearance.

Cuttings of the rather woody stems root with ease. In regard to light they are all rather temperamental, and you will have to experiment with different positions until you find the right one.

The new Saylor hybrids, 'Tropicana,' 'Rio,' and 'Black Magic,' are shrubby in growth and more compact than the trailing species. They have aroused hopes that we are on the threshold of a breakthrough on Hypocyrtas and the development of many beautiful variations of these pouch flowers. The three hybrids are sturdy and easy, the flowers large and pretty. They are easy to propagate from cuttings. They have bloomed for me but I am not yet sure how regularly they will perform. Growers should certainly try them.

Koellikeria erinoides. Central and South America

This is a small and unspectacular plant with considerable charm which is a good subject for the terrarium. The hairy thick stem bears whorls of soft green leaves spotted with silver. The flowers are borne in a raceme and are quite small, a dark pink upper lip and a spreading white bottom one which is fringed. It is scaly rhizomatous and will go dormant like *Achimenes* but has no particular season under lights. The treatment is similar to *Achimenes*.

Not too many growers have been successful with this plant but I have found it quite easy if the following method is pursued. The reason why it is happy in a terrarium is not only because of the humidity but the very light, unpacked, relatively lean soil with low moisture content. When it starts to grow in this medium it will bloom a foot from the lights and make a brave show. After flowering the rosettes produce nothing but rhizomes in the tips. Meanwhile, if the plant is happy, its underground rhizomes have spread and these will now put up growth and bloom. While this is going on, lift the old stems out along with their rhizomes and propagate in equally light Tropical Plant Mix with very little watering, in the pot. In the terrarium the new plant, in turn, will bloom and deteriorate and move back in the contrary direction. If the plant was originally in a pot in the terrarium, let it roam over the soil surface. It is not weedy and is easily removed.

Dormant rhizomes can be laid just under the surface of a bed of moist vermiculite and will sprout in due time. A well-grown plant is a true gem.

Kohleria. Central and South America

This wonderful genus has soft hairy leaves, often with a reddish glow, and large flared tube flowers with uniquely beautiful reticulation of the veining on the lobes. *Kohleria eriantha* presents a spire of brilliant burnt orange flowers but is rather too tall for the light garden, as are *K. bogotensis* and *K.* 'Long-wood,' both with red flowers. I have caused them to bloom by placing them between a light unit and a windowsill so that they had the benefit of both sources of illumination. But for our special purposes the species listed below are better.

Plant enthusiasts, like fishermen, are prone to exaggerate their success. Kohlerias, we often read, are easy to grow and bloom. The first is true but, at least under lights, the second is a dubious statement. I have found them capricious, developing nothing one year but promising foliage, and the next year bursting into flower as expected. Some are reputed to be long day plants. Yet *eriantha* has been described as requiring a short day. The matter is not settled as yet. I have bloomed them with long days yet suspect that, for best results, there may be a short day phase which is important for triggering bloom.

Another peculiarity is that, though possessing rhizomes, these are not produced freely and I have had large plants which showed little sign of them. Occasionally, as with *Achimenes*, the rhizomes appear in the axils of the leaves and can be treated the same as if they had developed in the soil.

A third anomaly is that the plant rarely goes completely dormant and will continue to show green at all times, though watering must be reduced during the resting period in late fall and winter.

Kohlerias should be planted in African Violet Soil in tallish or broad azalea pots so that they can either spread or droop. When they flop over the edge of a pot the stems soon reverse themselves and reach for the light, which is a saving grace.

Grow them fast by giving ample moisture and plenty of organic feeding. This will strengthen the stems and bring flowers to bloom more quickly. At any time cuttings can be made of the growing tips. Planted directly into mix and kept well watered they will root quickly and may even flower from a stem in bud. For the same reason repotting at six-month intervals is advisable. This is a voracious plant which soon exhausts its soil and must be kept on the move at all times in spring and summer.

K. amabilis. Hairy green leaves spotted with brown. Handsome pink flowers dotted with maroon. Long blooming summer plant small enough for a large terrarium.

K. lindeniana. Erect growth; leaves olive veined with silver. White flowers with a violet throat. Fragrant (exceptional in this family).

K. 'Rongo.' This Batcheller hybrid produces startlingly veined maroon flowers. Grows erect but can be pinched back. I have found it to be the most reliable and long lasting bloomer. Dr. Clayberg's new hybrid, 'Connecticut Belle,' bids fair to be the most compact and floriferous of the lot.

A number of low growing hybrids worth trying are on the market. If only we could induce this fine genus to bloom regularly in winter.

Nautilocalyx. South America

Three of the species are grown mostly for foliage. The leaves of *N. bullatus* are dark green, of *N. forgetti,* green with red veins, and *N. lynchi* red. They are all of simplest culture, growing like weeds in Tropical Plant Mix. Watch out to keep constantly moist and not to expose them to very high temperatures.

N. villosus, as its Latin name implies, is hairy all over. The leaves have a tendency to curl, and the plant looks untidy after it has bloomed. However, it blooms freely with white tube flowers with a touch of blue. As long as it is kept very wet it will thrive under the lights.

Phinaea multiflora. Tropical America

This tiny plant is best suited to terrarium culture and should be treated like the Gesnerias. It has fuzzy leaves which form a 2-inch-high mound from which the pedicels of the flowers stand up absolutely straight. On top of each pedicel appears a little white cup of a flower. Blooming periods are irregular but I have found that sometimes they will keep going for months. Then they die down and the rhizomes must be stored until they show signs of life.

However, there is another way of keeping replacements coming along. Like some of the Gesnerias, *Phinaea* self-pollinates and forms large capsules which must be removed to keep the plant neat. These are full of seed, can be dried, the seed planted, and a new series of plants started. Thus, when a mature plant goes dormant you will have successors ready to take its place. If the pods are left on it will self-sow but stop blooming.

Rechsteineria. Central and South America

The *Rechsteinerias* enjoyed a vogue for a while which waned when the light gardening repertory was increased by a number of fine plants which did not go into a long dormancy. However, both the species most in cultivation are very handsome plants and should be in every light garden.

R. cardinalis. The 2-inch-long tube flowers are deep red. A flowering stem will bloom for months, gradually elongating and trailing, unless supported, until it becomes unsightly or the tuber goes dormant. Sometimes, if the stem is removed close to the bulb, a new shoot will appear and produce another round of flowering. Stem cuttings root easily.

R. leucotricha. Queen of the Abyss. I rate this as among the most beautiful of light garden plants, yet there are few who will agree with me. The complaint is that the flowers are small and inconspicuous. To me they are exquisite and the color combination with the leaves is pure rococo.

When the tuber sprouts, usually in early spring, the stem rises up vertically, covered thickly with silvery fur. When it is a few inches high, it puts out two leaves which are like silvery furry ears and, immediately, a cluster of buds develops. These elongate until they are 1½ inches long and are powdery pink. Then the flowers continue to enlarge. If other stems start up while the first is blooming, cut off the latter and the process will be repeated. Later on the leaves will grow 4 to 5 inches long and occasionally there is additional bloom. Eventually the plant will go dormant. Stems with leaves propagate easily.

Culture is almost exactly like Gloxinia. When the leaves look tired, watering should be reduced until the tuber is completely dormant. Then it can stored in the pot or in a plastic bag until it sprouts again.

During growth in African Violet Mix, moisture should be constant and the plants should be fertilized with a balanced nutrient. As the plants grow older, watering must be somewhat reduced in order not to rot the tuber.

As with Gloxinia the tubers can become large and woody requiring the starting of new plants. *R. leucotricha*, in particular, can develop enormous tubers. I have had one as big as a turnip, and these do last somewhat better than *R. cardinalis.* Light requirement is about five inches under the lights. They like good humidity and fine misting. Waterdrops will discolor the leaves of *R. cardinalis* but not *R. leucotricha*, which seems to enjoy a regular spraying.

Other handsome Rechsteinerias to try, if you have the room (for they are pretty big) are *R. cooperi, macrorhiza, verticillata, cyclophylla,* and *lineata.*

Seemannia latifolia and sylvatica. South America

This is a good plant for a medium-size terrarium for it is essentially a creeper raising its stems with whorls of grayish green leaves only a short distance above the ground. The flowers are borne on wiry angled pedicels and are short, fat, and tubular with a smaller opening. The description is hardly inviting but the actual flower glows with an appealing reddish-orange color and the habit is graceful.

These are scaly rhizomatous plants which go into a semi-dormancy but need not be lifted as long as the soil is just moist. These rhizomes are like thin little worms and very delicate. They are essentially summer flowerers and will signal their determination to rest by a gradual dying out of the leaves from the base upward. Overwatering in this period can be fatal. If raised outside a terrarium, a humidity of 65 percent is called for and temperatures above 65 degrees. Very popular during the year of their introduction to light gardeners in this country, they have proved a little difficult, principally because the attentuated rhizomes make the following of dormancy rather tricky for the beginner to handle. Light requirements are for a position about six inches from the tubes.

Sinningia speciosa (Gloxinia). Brazil

For a long time the magnificent Gloxinia (a genus name improperly applied to *this* genus) was the most popular of Gesneriads. It was the result of either a hybridization or a mutation of slipper Gloxinias which appeared in Europe in the nineteenth century. The slipper became a rotate flower with six to eight lobes. Through further hybridization the flowers have been greatly increased in size and are now available in a bewildering range of colors and zonings which have made quite passé those old favorites the Emperor and Empress strains which are still the most commonly seen in florist shops.

Recently, except as gift plants, they have lost favor with many house-plant amateurs because of their excessive size, the length and brittleness of their leaves, and their habit of dormancy. However, they are beginning to make a comeback as nurserymen hybridize them toward smallness rather than bigness, and increase the duration of growth and flowering. Fischer Greenhouses and Lyndon Lyon have been leaders in this field.

Gloxinia tubers are generally bought in a dormant state and need no attention until a sprout appears. Then plant in an azalea pot about three times as broad as the tuber, in African Violet Mix, moderately well packed. The top of the tuber should be just on a level with the soil. Water well the first time and then keep just moist until the leaves are well developed.

When growth accelerates, feed regularly with a balanced nutrient. Keep the leaves close to the lights. Should the illumination be insufficient the leaves will reach upward. It is just right when they lie flat. As the buds develop, keep them within about 4 inches of the lights. Switch to a high phosphate/potash fertilizer. Never allow the plant to dry out during its growth and blooming period.

Gloxinia growers generally allow their plants to die down gradually after flowering. Since a single plant occupies so much space and will go dormant soon, I hasten the process by simply removing the green growth and setting the pot aside.

It is a quite mistaken theory that Gloxinias, and similar tuberous plants, need dormancy in order to gain strength. This is so far from being the case that it can be said that they are inactive during this period and probably lose rather than gain. The dormancy is just a habit derived from constant exposure of the genus to periods of drought. Little or nothing is gained by allowing the plant to take its own time drying out. Watering must stop immediately after the stem is cut.

The pot can now be set aside until, after a month or more, it starts to sprout again. During each growth period the tuber grows bigger until it becomes woody and less productive, whereupon it is wise to start new plants with seed or leaf cuttings. Cross-pollination is easy and seed plentiful.

Grow Gloxinias in high humidity and at warm temperatures—lowest 65 degrees. The chief cause of rot in Gloxinia tubers is caused by water settling in the top of the tuber, hence the custom of keeping it at soil level. During summer periods of high humidity and temperature do not allow any standing water in the saucer. The soil should be just moist, otherwise wilt may ensue.

Because they are relatively large plants, two other Sinningias should be mentioned in this section while the smaller species will be treated in the following one.

Sinningia regina has large, 6-inch, dark green leaves with white veins. The large dark purple flowers nod and the lower lobes project. Many hybrids have been made with the Florist Gloxinia, producing white, pink, and red slippers.

Sinningia eumorpha, a somewhat smaller plant, is white flowered. The Pink Eumorpha is a hybrid. Here, again, new hybrids with other species are turning up constantly in the trade.

The culture of these plants is like that of the Florist Gloxinia.

Sinningias Miniature

The best of the miniature Sinningias and the hybrids, such as 'Dollbaby' and 'Cindy,' are described among the Miracle Plants. In size all these range from a little over an inch in height to at most 5 inches. S. *pusilla* and *concinna* are the smallest, S. 'Freckles' and 'Bright Eyes' reach 2 to 3 inches, and 'Dollbaby' and 'Cindy' may reach 5 inches. The flowers of the larger plants are much larger in volume and more flared so that they are quite showy when several are blooming at one time. S. *hirsuta* has the greatest spread of any of these plants but the flowers are short stemmed.

Sinningia concinna is a little bigger than S. *pusilla,* more purple, and with distinct dots in the throat. Culture is like that for S. *pusilla* except that it is an altogether more sensitive plant: everything that will set S. *pusilla* back is likely to kill S. *concinna* altogether. Temperatures must be warm and even, the soil very light and just moist. It will not tolerate too much fertilizer.

The humidity must be high. But if conditions are watched closely it is a continuous bloomer and very beautiful.

Sinningia hirsuta is a hairy-leaved plant with numerous pale bluish flowers. It is a slow grower to maturity. The culture is the same as for Gloxinia. Well grown, it is very handsome—much like a species African Violet.

A large number of hybrids are crosses between the above two plants and S. *pusilla* and S. *eumorpha*. They have resulted in the following fine cultivars which just fail to make the Miracle Plant list.

Sinningia 'Bright Eyes' and 'Freckles,' both creations of Dr. Clayberg, are similar. Both are about halfway in size between S. *pusilla* and S. 'Dollbaby.' 'Bright Eyes' is whiter, less purple than 'Freckles' and the latter has purple dots in the throat. I consider 'Freckles' the easier plant and have bloomed it months on end in terrarium conditions. Of the intermediate size plants it is the best and would have merited Miracle Plant rating if it were not for the softness of the leaves, their sensitivity to mold, and the difficulty in propagating. Sometimes 'Freckles' will produce offsets from its tuber and these can be potted up separately. Culture is the same as S. *pusilla*.

S. *pumila* is a hybrid developed by Dr. Clayberg. There is a diploid and a tetraploid form.

S. 'Wood Nymph' (Lyon).

There are others and I have not had experience with all of them. The majority will be superseded by improved strains. Watch for and try new hybrids of this type. They are very promising.

Smithiantha (Naegelia). Mexico

Smithianthas bloom easily for me, starting about November and lasting for two months. Then their fat rhizomes go dormant until June whereupon they spend the rest of the time growing. That is the difficulty, although there is some compensation in the handsome heart-shaped leaves, exquisitely scalloped, velvety, and toned in shades of red bordered by greens. There is also the problem of size for they tend to grow easily to 18 inches. Again, if you have the room, the spire of more than inch-long fat bells in purest yellow, in rich reds and mixtures, is a most spectacular sight.

Culture is quite simple. A single rhizome will serve a 6-inch pot with African Violet Mix. If the growing plant is kept very close to the lights it will sometimes stay fairly compact and bloom early but it will tolerate rather low illumination until the flowering stems develop fully. After blooming, the leaves die down and the rhizomes are removed. They are best stored in a plastic bag with a little moisture and should be replanted, horizontally, when they sprout again. If you have the patience to wait for it, this is a splendid genus.

There are some dwarf strains on the market now with which some amateurs have had success. I have found them less easy to bloom than the normal big ones but, undoubtedly, better clones will be found and propagated. If Smithiantha can be made a little longer blooming and a bit more foolproof at the same time that it is dwarfed, it will make a very fine plant indeed.

Streptocarpus. Africa and Asia

The genus has approximately 150 species, the most interesting of which, for our purposes, are African. Among the ones we cannot grow in light gardens at present are those which have a single enormous leaf, sometimes a yard long, and which produce a cluster of flowers from the base. Those that we can grow are more civilized, and though not easy plants, they are handsome and merit every effort to grow them.

Streptocarpus will do well in our Tropical Plant Mix with a liberal addition of lime. I had been growing *Streptocarpus* successfully for quite some time before I discovered that experts considered them to be hostile to peat moss. I have continued to do so with no worse results. Why they have trouble and not I is still a mystery. My method is to use Tropical Plant Mix a little short on peat and with the addition of considerable amounts of eggshell—about two teaspoons to a 3-inch-diameter pot. I keep the soil quite moist for 'Constant Nymph' and rather dry for other hybrids. Growth is rapid and flower production just fine.

S. rexi hybrids. These are the majority of the hybrids now in cultivation, including 'Constant Nymph' (Mrs. Batcheller's) and its variations. All these plants are fibrous rooted and their long narrow crumpled leaves grow directly out of the soil. This habit makes them particularly subject to crown rot due to overwatering, watering the interstices between the leaves, or wet soil in the same places. They are shade loving plants which grow at some altitude in the mountains of South Africa and prefer temperatures in the 60 to 70 degree range, above which they may cause trouble, though not necessarily.

Grow them 6 inches below the lights in a position where they receive particularly good air circulation. Water well during active growth but the moment this stops allow the pot to nearly dry out each time before the next treatment. The best fertilizer is an organic solution. I have found that a considerable amount of eggshell added to the soil is beneficial.

A healthy hybrid spreads rather rapidly in the pot and soon becomes a tangle of leaves and a blaze of continual flowering. Although this *Streptocarpus* group likes potbinding, there are limits, and the usual thing is to remove the plant and cut it into longitudinal sections which are planted separately after a good dusting with a fungicide. This appears to disturb the parent excessively and I have experienced considerable loss in this way. Hence I use another method which can be recommended not only for *Streptocarpus* but for any plant which is similarly constructed.

Division should be made *only* at a time when the parent is in active growth, evidenced by a number of young light green leaves. Study the plant well and pick out an area on the periphery which contains young leaves and some semblance of constituting a unity. With a long, thin, very sharp knife cut a semicircle through the crown of the plant (a thin fibrous layer separating leaves from roots), driving the knife deep. Then, working from the outside, with a spoon or a miniature trowel, lift the root and leaves out in one piece with as much soil as possible.

The hole which remains behind should be left open and the soil along the edges pressed back so that it remains that way. The visible areas of sliced crown in the hole should be heavily dusted with Fermate or another fungicide. The hole should be left undisturbed for some three weeks, during which time watering should be done from below the pot, and the leaves actively misted. Then the hole can be filled with moist soil. A minimum of damage will be done to the parent by this method.

The cutting should be similarly dusted and planted in just slightly moist soil. Extreme care should be shown to have the level of the soil exactly even with the fibrous crown. Keep moderately warm—70 degrees, water sparingly from the bottom, and mist as often as possible. If any leaf starts to rot at the base of the new plant, remove it cleanly, clear the soil away from the area, dust with fungicide, and cut down the watering still more. The opening must be left undisturbed for a few days.

These instructions are valuable because *Streptocarpus* of this type are worth the trouble as they will bloom continuously most of the year and the flowers are unique.

The flowers in this group are long trumpets, borne one or more to the stem, with wide spreading lobes, 'the upper two being somewhat reflexed. The Wiesmoor hybrids come in pinks, blues, and white with distinct designs in the throat, rather like inverted fleur de lys. 'Constant Nymph,' the Miracle Plant, is of this type. *S. rexi* is smaller than the hybrids, the flowers large and lavender in color.

Streptocarpus for the terrarium are *S. cynandrus*, blue flower; *S. kirki*, purple flower; and *S. rimicola*, white flower.

S. holsti has purple watery stems and jade green leaves an inch long. *S. saxorum* has fuzzy gray leaves, also small and turned down in such a way that they look thick. The first has little brilliant blue flowers in panicles. The second has single lavender trumpets on threadlike pedicels. Both plants are difficult to impossible for blooming under lights. It is probably a matter of day length. They do beautifully in greenhouses or on the windowsill. Both are spring bloomers.

I have found that *Streptocarpus* goes through a difficult period from July to September and that there are days when there is danger that the whole plant will go limp and possibly rot. Possibly this is due to excessive heat and, if this is the case, air-conditioned rooms will prevent it. It is advisable to cut down watering to a minimum the moment any sign of flaccidity in the leaves appears.

All the *Streptocarpus* propagate easily from stem or leaf cuttings. Those with long leaves are a bonanza for the propagator. Each leaf may be cut into wedges with sections of midvein and planted in damp vermiculite.

The following three *Streptocarpus* are suitable for terrarium culture.

S. cynandrus. Blue flower.

S. kirki. Purple flower.

S. rimicola. Tiny, with white flowers.

Seed culture. The method is the same as for other Gesneriads. However it presents the problem of seeds which are extremely small. They should be dusted over sphagnum-vermiculite mix and kept both moist and warm during germination. Seeds planted in midwinter will usually bloom the following fall.

ORCHIDS

There is no family of plants, in my opinion, which has a brighter future under lights than the Orchid. It is an enormous family, with a minimum of 20,000 species to which have been added innumerable cultivars, totaling a far greater number of choices than any other family in cultivation. Of these we already know many which have been grown successfully in light gardens and yet constitute only an infinitesimal part of the whole.

The flowers are unique in form and infinitely varied. A remarkable number are richly perfumed. Among those available are some which are among the longest lasting blooms in our whole repertoire.

The number of light gardeners who have had experience with the Orchids is still relatively small. This is partly due to the conservatism of the orchid societies and the tradition of greenhouse culture. Furthermore, there is the matter of cost. Being slow growing plants, an average species Orchid may be priced at five to ten dollars and a fine hybrid very much higher.

Yet there are numerous plants which can be bought for two to five dollars and there are the usual exchanges among hobbyists which cost nothing. The long-lasting qualities of orchid plants justifies paying somewhat more and, as the reproduction of Orchids by the new method of meristem culture (producing a new plant from the growing tip) becomes more widespread, even the finest clones will soon sell for far less than at present. Then the great merit of orchids as light gardening plants will come into fuller recognition and the spread of their culture indoors will be very rapid.

Orchids also have their drawbacks. Most of them have a dormant period. And they are, except for a few genera, singularly lacking in charm of foliage. This last trait is one we will have to live with and which is somewhat compensated for by compactness. But dormancy can probably be overcome eventually by breeding. There is every likelihood, in the long run, that strains will be developed which will produce pseudobulbs throughout the year and be more or less continuously in bud or flower. Two groups of Orchids will remain for a long time inaccessible to the home grower—the cool growing epiphytes and terrestrials. But this still leaves such a large field to be explored that the variety offered by other families appears minuscule by comparison.

Orchids are different in so many respects from other flowering plants that I am strongly tempted to indulge in a description of their unique features. But this is not the place for such diversions and the reader should consult the many books on this subject. Nevertheless, the discussion will be rather lengthy because of the special methods of culture. The following are some general remarks applying to all Orchids likely to be grown under lights. And these are followed by specific listings and cultural recommendations. Every indoor gardener should be experimenting with these wonderful plants which *do* bloom under lights.

Choosing the Right Orchids

More discouragement is caused the would-be grower of Orchids under lights by poor initial purchases than anything else. To choose a plant on no other basis than its beauty is to invite disaster, as those which grow well in the light garden must meet certain specifications at present. The lists at the end of this section should be helpful.

The cultural recommendations, which are in a number of respects very different from greenhouse treatment, will give some clues to other species and cultivars which may be tried with some prospect of success. The experienced grower can, of course, accomplish very difficult feats with his Orchids but it is certainly wise for the beginner to raise the most adaptable types before branching out into the unknown.

Temperature Requirements

Contrary to common opinion, Orchids are often very cool growing plants. In fact, there are terrestrial species living close to the Arctic Circle and both terrestrials and epiphytes at high altitudes on mountains. Even in the tropics some of the finest species grow at altitudes of 5000 feet or higher. Thus the majority prefer temperature levels which average below those which are suitable for Gesneriads and many other tropicals.

Ideal temperatures for the cool Orchids are claimed to be between 45 and 60 degrees Fahrenheit, of intermediates between 50 and 65, and warm growers between 60 and 75. Indoor light growers have found no way as yet of growing the cool Orchids. The intermediates are possible and the warm ones, as long as their light requirements are not too high, are the best.

These designations (cool, intermediate, and warm) are commonly used in orchid catalogs in listing species but they are neither rigid designations nor necessarily reliable. Considering home conditions, including cellars, the indoor light grower may be able to provide an intermediate range of 60 to 75 degrees, the low in winter and the high in summer. The warm range would then be 70 to 85. For living rooms the latter is the more attainable. Within the full temperature range we must find plants which are sufficiently adaptable and, if possible, will allow us some leeway at the upper limits.

Tolerance of higher or lower temperatures depends in part on the condition of the medium we use, the humidity of the air, and our watering techniques. Rather more is known about the needs of the more popular botanical Orchids than the cultivars but the latter are, on the whole, more adaptable.

Orchids prefer a 10-degree drop in temperature at night. This is fairly normal in northern climates and presents no special problem. The chief difficulty is with high summer day temperatures. Cooling through good ventilation, plenty of ambient evaporation, and the use of air conditioning equipment will help.

Cold Shock

Some intermediate Orchids will not set buds unless they are subjected to a period of abnormally cool temperatures. Dendrobiums are notorious in this respect. These plants can be kept outdoors until the temperature drops to 45 degrees. The indoor grower may try storing the plants in the refrigerator for two or three weeks in midwinter. Be sure, however, that the temperature does not go below 40 degrees. I have tried this a few times with success. The plants should not be watered at all during this time. The pseudobulbs will shrivel somewhat but, when warmed and watered, very little buds will appear within a few weeks.

Light Day

An Orchid that blooms in wintertime must be suspected of belonging to the long night category, but in most instances, we have as yet no means of knowing whether this is the case. In the greenhouse the seasons change the same as they do in nature, and when an Orchid flowers in winter the grower has usually concerned himself not at all with the question whether this is due to time of year or to natural day length. It will be some time before we know the truth.

In the tropics the short day length is usually seasonal in a different sense than in the higher latitudes. The difference between summer and winter sunny hours is relatively small. More drastic changes are created by topography. Certain plants will grow only on one side of a hill where the length of day suits them at some time of the year which may be either summer or winter. It is, therefore, often ignorance of day length requirements which creates difficulties for greenhouse growers, and the success in certain locations in the growing area may be related to the amount of shade at certain seasons. Thus this important matter is essential knowledge for all growers, and further study of the problem would be most valuable.

A good day length for long day Orchids is 16 hours. But where there is any uncertainty on this point it is wise to maintain 15 or 16 hours in summer and taper off to 10 or 11 hours in winter. In any case, when Orchids have sheathed but fail to fill out, it is wise to put them on a short day regimen for a month or two.

Light Intensity

In nature Orchids run the full gamut of light intensity from the brightest sun to the deepest gloom in which any plant can bloom. Under lights the maximum intensity we can provide with standard fixtures is about 1500 footcandles or equivalent. This means a bank of at least six 48-inch tubes 2 inches apart with maximum reflection. This will be sufficient for growing many of the *Cattleyas* and small vandaceous Orchids. Those which need less light present no problem.

However, we should consider that such a concentration of tubes with ballasts is rather too warm. So, if the ballasts can be set at a distance, there will be considerable gain in effectiveness. Proper amounts of air movement are also important in cooling the area. Of course, we continue to have difficulties with tall Orchids as with other plants whose lower parts are rather distant from the lights. High Output and Very High Output tubes in sufficient number are overcoming this problem gradually but we still need experience. In the next few years growers will find ways of blooming even the tallest and most light demanding Orchids, such as the *Vandas*.

Soil for Epiphytic Orchids

I have tried all the media recommended for Orchid culture and find that they have one overwhelming disadvantage for a grower who raises a number of plant families in the same garden, giving them a regular watering. This is that they retain too much moisture which rots the roots and produces black rot in leaves and leads (new growths). For some time I have been using pebbles with fair success, usually granitic or feldspathic. Potting is no problem with them, and the plant can be removed for inspection of the roots without damage. But, more important, I do not have to keep as close track of my waterings. Knowing that the medium dries out rapidly, I can water every day except during dormancy. Even a heavy spray of the pebbles in the morning will take care of the plant's needs. The Fennell Orchid Company sells a porous slag which is also excellent. Similar material occurs as road ballast, and I have collected very good porous stone of this type. A final advantage—this medium costs you nothing. The other media described below are those normally used by Orchid growers.

Osmunda. The fibrous roots of a number of terrestrial ferns, it comes in dried pieces which can be cut and packed into the pots after thorough soaking. The advantage of osmunda is that for a period of a year it will supply sufficient nutriment for an Orchid plant. After that, because it tends to break down, repotting is necessary. It is very moisture retentive, especially when packed hard as recommended by all the old-time orchidists. When it is dry on top it may be a soggy mess near the bottom of the pot.

I have found that it proves satisfactory in the house when packed rather loosely and when there is plenty of broken crock below.

Fir Bark and Redwood Fiber. Fir bark, which can be bought in various sizes made from Douglas Fir, is an excellent medium for Orchids. A low pH is compatible. As it contains very little nourishment, regular fertilizing is necessary. It permits good air circulation in the pot so that there is less danger of stifling and clogging.

Redwood Fiber, often sold as Palco Wool, is a soft material which is useful for small plants and as a means of denser packing. But I find that this is a definite disadvantage in practice.

Tree Fern and Fiber. Except when chunked, I have found this absolute poison for Orchids in the house. Shredded, it packs solid and is very moisture retentive. No fertilizer is needed for a year with this material.

Mixes. Most large Orchid nurseries sell mixes which consist of bark, fiber, vermiculite or perlite, and charcoal.

pH. Orchids usually prefer a pH of 5.0 to 5.5. The organic materials listed meet this specification.

Pots

For terrestrials under lights, clay pots are best and, as Orchid roots like to spread, the short, wide Azalea type is best.

The main consideration in respect to epiphytes is to secure sufficient aeration for the subsoil roots. Knowing how the roots are growing is of utmost value for judging other aspects of culture. Thus a clear plastic pot has great advantages. Not only can we see what is going on but it is possible to open up the sides, by means of a heated metal instrument, with holes and slashes. The benefit to the plant is immediate and noticeable. Orchids like to grow in and out of the medium, and soil roots easily change into aerial roots as they emerge. Thus a healthy Orchid will send out its roots right through holes.

There is another advantage to plastic. Orchid roots attach themselves to a porous surface such as a clay pot. This interferes with the easy removal of the plant for repotting and for the closer examination of root. Pulling a plant out of a plastic pot is easy and can be done often without injury to the roots, the ones which have spread through the holes being carefully eased out with the rest.

If clay pots are used, the bottoms should be knocked out and the hole stuffed with a crushed piece of light chicken wire. Some orchid supply houses carry special pots which are slashed along the sides. They are very superior to those which are not.

Whatever the means, make sure that your pots are very airy. This is the best guarantee of healthy growth. The matter cannot be stressed too often.

The size of pot varies according to the habit of the plant but you can pot small and gain space. On the other hand I do not believe that a larger pot per se is damaging to the plant. What has probably caused this impression is the tendency of the larger amount of compost to retain moisture too long. But the small potting is certainly safer as long as aerial roots receive regular misting, preferably with a weak dilution of an organic or high nitrate fertilizer.

Basket containers are difficult to handle indoors. They drip, they dry out excessively fast and then must be drenched thoroughly. Besides, they do not fit easily under lights except in a cellar where they can be hung below ceiling fixtures.

Potting and Repotting

Orchids should usually be repotted each year. Some growers pick the moment when new leads have just started. Others prefer to do their whole collection in the spring. If no great damage is done to the roots, almost any time before maturity of the pseudobulb is probably safe.

Remove all the old medium from the roots and snip off any dead ones. You will recognize these by the collapse of the root covering. You may find that you have very little root left after trimming and that the plant will need extra support. This is particularly true if you are potting loosely as I recommend. In this event, take a length of stiff wire and make a coil at the end which will fit into the bottom of the pot. The straight extension, when set into the pot, and the coil covered with medium will act as an excellent stake to hold the plant in place.

Orchid roots are brittle and few in number. It is important that the medium fill the space between them. With pebbles this is no problem but with the other media it is advisable to use a potting stick. This is a stake with a blunt point. A hammer handle trimmed down to a partial point is a good large one. Dowels of different sizes can serve for smaller pots.

The medium is first loosely set around the roots and then the stick is used to work the material inward from the sides of the pot. The point is inserted close to the wall and then levered inward against the medium. This forces it toward the center without damaging the roots. Additional medium is poured along the edge of the pot and worked toward the center until you are satisfied that the packing is sufficiently solid.

The level of the soil should come just to the top of the roots and should not bury the connections between the pseudobulbs or the aerial roots. This rule can be relaxed when there are a number of back bulbs whose leads are angled. But the newer growth must always ride high.

Fertilizer

Orchid growers recommend a 30-10-10 chemical fertilizer dissolved to one-fourth the strength suggested on the label. It can be applied with each watering. However I find that this concentration easily burns roots and aerial roots in the house. One-twelfth the label dilution is safer, or fertilize only every fourth watering.

As bud sheaths form, a higher phosphate/potash formula can be used.

Humidity

A relative humidity of 60 to 75 percent will make a great difference for the better in your Orchids. Fifty percent is about the minimum for good culture.

Fine misting is very beneficial. Try to do it twice a day.

Watering

Orchids collapse from excess watering more often than from any other cause. A common experience for the beginner is to find his Orchid ailing and to decant it from its pot only to discover that all the roots are dead. What this should teach him is that the effects of overwatering are cumulative. At first the plant can absorb part of the moisture, but as the roots deteriorate, the ability to absorb declines and the excess increases. A frequent symptom of rootlessness is shriveling of the pseudobulbs. The neophyte is inclined to interpret this as due to a shortage of water. Actually it is the result of the process we have described. The pseudobulbs die of thirst because they no longer have the means to drink.

In discussing soils and pots I make abundantly clear the importance of good aeration and quick drying out. Better a plant lacking enough than one having too much moisture. Do not hesitate to remove a plant from its pot to check up on moisture conditions when in doubt. The sign of proper watering is healthy growing roots, the aerial roots white and fleshy, the tips shiny and green, the subsoil ones fat and juicy.

If your plant has lost all or most of its roots and the pseudobulbs are still healthy, you may yet save it. Dust the rooting areas with hormone powder and tie the whole plant into a clear plastic bag. Hang it where it gets some light. Roots often develop with this treatment.

It is impossible to specify how often or at what intervals watering is needed. This will depend on the species, the size of the pot, and the soil consistency. But even for those plants which are considered moisture loving during the growing period (except the terrestrials) the compost should be allowed to dry out thoroughly between waterings. The only difference between the dry and the wet Orchids is that the period of dryness for the former is longer. If humidity is sufficient you run little risk of harming the plants by favoring the dry side.

Those Orchids which require a dry rest period, Dendrobiums for instance, should be kept bone dry except for a daily misting, until they show by new growth that dormancy is over.

Misting

I have already referred to the benefit of regular misting. Orchids cannot have too much of it as long as no moisture remains on their leaves when darkness comes. Only one warning—I am speaking of mist, not spray. There is no surer way of producing rot than allowing water to collect in the axils of the leaves. This warning also applies to regular watering. Why this should not be injurious in nature I do not know. Rain is not choosy where it hits a plant. But it is certain that in the house it can be deadly.

Terrestrial Orchids

Terrestrial Orchids grow in rich organic soil and have roots similar to other plants. Most of our northern Orchids are terrestrials and a great number also grow in the tropics. Of those in cultivation, the principal tropical genera are the Paphiopedilums, or Lady Slipper Orchids, and the Cymbidiums. Almost all the Cymbidiums require too cool an environment for indoor growing. That leaves the others pretty much in command of the field.

Of the Paphiopedilums the easiest are those which are warm growing. Mr. Fred Bender of New Rochelle, N.Y., has been outstandingly successful in raising both warm and cool types in his cellar light garden. The warm growers are mostly species but the cool ones have been bred and hybridized to such an extent that an immense number of cultivars exist. The flowers are of enormous size and very long lasting. They are winter bloomers—from November to April.

Terrestrial Culture

Either brown osmunda or fir bark with chopped oak leaves is often used. Under lights it is probably wiser to purchase a terrestrial mix from an orchid nursery. Our Tropical Plant Mix is also a satisfactory compost.

Light requirements are relatively low. You can grow these plants under two 48-inch tubes about six inches away.

Water right through the pot. The soil should be moist but not wet. As nutrient, a balanced formula once or twice a month is adequate. Paphiopedilums like misting and plenty of air movement. Warm growing plants require 60 to 65 degrees at night and not more than 80 degrees during the day. Occasional higher temperatures are tolerated. At night the temperature for the cool growers should go down to 50 to 55 but during the day they can endure the same warmth as the others.

Warm Growing Paphiopedilums

The most popular Paph is *P. 'Maudiae,'* the graceful green and white striped Lady Slipper. The others are mostly species, though breeding has led to superior strains. Alphabetically listed some of them are *P. barbatum, bellatulum, callosum, charlesworthii, concolor, delenatii, godefroyae, niveum, tonsum,* and *venustum.* Nurserymen who raise and breed Paphiopedilums as a specialty can advise you of a number of other warm species, and the most warm growing of the famous hybrids.

Cool Growing Paphiopedilums

There are beautiful species in this range but they are far outnumbered by the hybrids. These are legion, and in a short discussion it would be vain to try to list them. Visit a nursery and consult catalogs. Best of all, join the local Orchid society and get information directly from amateur and professional growers. Superior Paphs are expensive and it is pointless to be hasty in choosing plants.

The Sympodial Epiphytic Orchids

Cattleyas, Miltonias, Oncidiums, and Odontoglossums are among the numerous Orchid genera which put forth an aerial bulb, called a pseudobulb, to which the leaves are attached and from which the flowering peduncle grows. Each pseudobulb flowers only once in most species. It then puts forth a rhizome which eventually terminates in another pseudobulb, and so on, forming chains. The back bulbs, as they are called, act as water and food reservoirs for the new pseudobulbs. Removing them weakens the new growth and reduces its chance of flowering.

However, when the chain is long enough—four or more—it is usually harmless to cut halfway through the rhizome connecting the older group with the four front pseudobulbs. These back bulbs will usually put out a new growth, whereupon the cut can be completed and the group potted up making a separate plant. In many species and cultivars, when they are well grown, pseudobulbs will develop from two or more units of the chain. Sections of back bulbs can also be immediately removed and hung in an airtight plastic bag with good expectation of root development and new growth. Though not as satisfactory as the other method, it will serve when a plant has outgrown its pot and reduction in size becomes imperative.

Cattleya

The sympodial plants include, in the Cattleyas, the most popular Orchids for cutting and for corsages. Here, too, there is the greatest diversity among the cultivars. Cattleya has been crossed with Laelia, which much resembles it, and these two, either together or singly, hybridized with *Sophronitis* (SLc.), *Brassavola* (Blc.) and *Epidendrum* (Epic.) to mention a few of the many genera, to produce an enormous range of plants.

Some assert that the Cattleya group is the easiest to grow under lights but consistent results, I believe, are much better with Phalaenopsis and Paphiopedilum. Many of them require quite cool conditions and considerably more light than we can supply them. If the nurserymen would do some work testing the light reaction of their plants, we would certainly be able to develop a repertory of bloomers in this huge group. Too many people buy Cattleyas in bud, bloom them under the lights, and then claim virtues which they do not possess. Repeated bloom is the only proof useful to the light gardener.

Most of the corsage type Cattleyas are much too tall for fluorescent light growing. They are very big plants and the flower stalks grow still higher. Of more interest to light growers are those crosses which result in shorter pseudo-bulbs and sprays of flowers which, though not as large as the corsage type, offer much more variety of form and substance. Recent Laeliocattelya introductions, called Cocktail Cattleyas, are proving more adaptable to light growing than older hybrids.

The Cattleyas, and their relatives, can be grown in any of the principal epiphytic media, the peculiarities of culture being that potting be moderately tight but that there be ample aeration and a complete drying out between waterings. I have warned against tight potting under lights and this still holds, but because of the rather loose root structure of these plants and their height, they must have a reasonably firm anchor. Pebbles will hold them in place and a wire support, as suggested, will help.

Most of the Cattleyas and their hybrids require the best light you can give, about 1000 footcandles, humidity between 60 and 80 percent, and temperatures in the 60- to 80-degree range with a 10-degree drop at night. Misting is very beneficial.

The bud of these plants is enclosed in a sheath which splits when the former has developed sufficiently. Because of low humidity in the house and lack of air movement these sheaths often harden under lights and the bud has no means of escaping. Also it may turn brown or even start to rot. In any of these situations the bud may be saved by carefully splitting the sheath at the top and stripping it down. If this is done gently the bud will be unscathed and none the worse for being exposed. This suggestion is applicable also to plants which do not have such a large sheath as the cattleya, Miltonias, for instance. With these smaller, tighter sheaths, the operation is quite delicate and greatest care must be taken not to injure the bud with the sharp instrument used to split the sheath.

Monopodial Epiphytic Orchids

Phalaenopsis and Vanda are two leading genera among many which have a monopodial growth. The development is something like that of a vine, a sort of fleshy stem with alternate long-lasting leaves. The flowering peduncles rise from the axils of the leaves. Aerial roots, which are attached to a tree support in nature, appear at different levels. Vanda requires much more light than we can supply. However, there are a number of vandaceous plants and vanda crosses which are quite small and which give promise of being better performers. Check this with your orchid nursery.

Phalaenopsis

Phalaenopsis, the Moth Orchid, is the easiest of these monopodials to grow under lights. It has the advantage of being a warm grower, of being quite short, of needing relatively little light, and of having very long lasting bloom. Hybridizing has resulted in plants with a big spread and huge flowers. Recently, however, there has been a trend toward compactness and more interesting colors, and there are numbers of species which are almost miniatures.

From the axils of the leaves rise long arching peduncles which bear toward the end a succession of five to twenty flowers, each one 2 to 5½ inches across, depending on the cultivar. The five tepals form a mothlike shape usually broader than long, and in the center there is a jutting lip, smaller than the tepals, in a like or contrasting color. The range of tone is from white to bright pink, some yellows and purples, candy stripes, specklings, and some exquisite contrasts of red lip on white flower, pink on yellow, red on pink, etc. The texture of the flowers is heavy and rich.

Some plants will put forth flowering stalks two or more times a year. After first bloom a stalk may send out one or more side branches in succession. For this reason the stalk is never cut until it dies down naturally. The individual flowers may last up to three weeks, a single spray for two months and, with branching, the stalk may last much longer. Whereas other large Orchid plants are difficult to fit under the lights, the long sprays of Phalaenopsis can be managed with ease.

Choose an Azalea type pot as the rooting is not very deep. However, they spread rapidly and you must allow extra room. The leaves of mature plants range from a few inches to a foot in length. For the little ones you must judge pot size by eye. Mature plants of large size require a 6- to 8-inch pot, and ultimately you may need a 10- or 12-incher.

Use ¼-inch fir bark for small plants and ½-inch for the large ones, packing it carefully with a potting stick around and between the roots without damaging them. Many growers repot their young plants every six months and the mature ones annually in the spring. This frequent potting is necessary because of the tendency of the bark to clog with time and hold more moisture than is desirable. The medium must allow air circulation at all times. Standing moisture will cause rot.

A temperature of 65 degrees or higher is preferred and a relative humidity of 70 percent or better. Good air circulation must be maintained. As to light, most will grow well a foot from the lights at the center of the tubes.

The whole matter of moisture is ticklish with Phalaenopsis as with most orchids. Use a wand and flush the pot. Never allow water to rest on the leaves or in the axils for they are particularly subject to botrytis rot. If you do get water there, take a paper towel or tissue and soak it up. Even when you mist, which benefits them greatly, be careful to allow no accumulation of large drops.

When you buy a plant, check the root system immediately. There should be very little shriveled material. The live roots should be white and fresh looking, indicating rapid growth. If you are at the nursery, let the plant be decanted right there. If the roots are in poor condition, you need not accept it, and if they are vigorous, no harm will be done.

The problem of root growth being so important, even though you may do some damage, you would be wise to examine their condition a few times in the early stages of ownership. Healthy aerial roots are no indication of the state of the lower growth. The examination should take place when the compost is dry. If you look at the roots you will learn more quickly just how much you should water. It is surprising to decant a seemingly dry compost and find that the lower part of the pot is soaking wet. Just as with Gesneriads, the plant enjoys moisture but abhors soggy conditions.

Feed with high nitrogen soluble fertilizer diluted to one-twelfth the recommended strength every two weeks. Use an organic fertilizer every two months.

As the budding stalk grows longer the pot can be moved outside the light garden with the stalk pointing toward the lights, the tip 6 to 10 inches away. This will lengthen the spray and place buds and bloom in the best position. As the stalk lengthens the pot can be moved farther away.

In your choice of a hybrid you should be guided by the grower or by a successful experienced orchid amateur, for only they can tell you, among the welter of new crosses and old, which will best meet your needs. If possible, buy mature plants in bloom to start with. It is most unfortunate that orchid catalogs specify the size of flower and sometimes their number on a spray, but do not include such useful information as size of the mature leaf or whether the blooms are long lasting or relatively continuous.

Of the top size plants in whites and pinks some of the best sires have been 'Grace Palm,' 'Gladys Read,' 'Cast Iron Monarch,' and 'Doris.' But these are being rapidly superseded by new parents more remarkable for form and color than for size. Rather more manageable and decidedly more interesting plants have resulted from matings of these and other giants with species. Some smaller plants are recent crosses between species.

The species are usually less reliable bloomers than the cultivars but include a number of smaller plants. Variation in color, form, and size among them is very great as with most Orchid species. They are worth mentioning here because when they occur as one parent of a cross, the progeny are usually of manageable size.

P. cornu-cervi. Flowers 2¼ inches. Yellow blotched with brown.

P. equestris. 1½ inches. White flushed with rose.

P. fuscata. 2 inches. Yellow barred with brown.

P. intermedia. 2 inches. Pink.

P. lueddemanniana. 3 inches. White to yellow, sometimes barred. This plant has many forms and is often used in hybridizing.

P. mannii. Unusually shaped golden yellow flowers.

P. mariae. 1½ inches. Tepals whitish, lip purple.

P. sumatrana. 2 inches. Creamy white with zebra stripings in reddish brown.

P. violacea. 2 inches. White to greenish. Purple lip.

A List of Orchids to Grow Under Lights

Although hundreds of different species and cultivars have been raised under lights, the chief cultivators up to now have been Orchid hobbyists, while the average light gardener has shied away from them. In the firm belief that this family offers more variety than any other, I am listing below some of those which have succeeded and are worth trying. In having done so I will be accused of all sorts of omissions, perhaps of very obvious choices. But everyone should realize that the choice is so vast that errors of this sort are unavoidable. The fact that a plant has been grown and bloomed under lights does not necessarily make it an ideal recommendation.

Each of these species and any number of hybrids deserve individual attention like that which we have given the Gesneriads. But we still know too little about our subject. The experimentation has been diffuse and the results not sufficiently definitive except in a few instances. On the whole I have chosen warm growing plants of moderate size, but the reader must realize that there is no end to the number of possibilities and that new cultivars are constantly appearing. It will take a few more years before we begin to mine the treasure from this lode.

Most of these plants will tolerate the conditions under which we grow Gesneriads.

Acampe dentata, pachyglossa, and *papilossa.* Warm growing miniatures.
Aerangis biloba, citrata fastuosa, friesorum, kirkii.
Aerides affine, lawrenciae, odoratum, quinquevulnerum.
Angraecum compactum, eicherlianum, falcatum, phillippinense, veitchii.
Anoectochilus hispida, regalis, sikkimensis. Foliage and flower for the terrarium.
Ansellia africana. A more modest size *Ansellia.*
Ascocentrum hendersonianum and *miniatures.*
Aspasia epidendroides, lunata, principissa. Very fragrant.
Bifrenaria. Seek out the smaller species which are also fragrant.
Bletia patula and *purpurea.* Terrestrials.
Brassavola caudata, cuculata, glauca, and *nodosa.* The last is famous for its perfume and ease of culture.
Brasso-cattleyas and *Brasso-laelio-cattleyas* (Bc. and Blc. for short). The smaller pseudobulbed hybrids can be grown.
Broughtonia sanguinea. A lovely reddish orchid.
Catasetums. These fabulous orchids, which cast their pollinia if properly triggered, are warm growing and easy. Choose the smaller plants for the light garden.
Cattleya hybrids. The following is a mixed bag of medium size or easy plants. Many of them are very fragrant. Large hothouse or commercial types are not recommended.
   C. aurantiaca hybrids, *wolteriana, fascelis, fulvescens, guatamalensis, luteola, nobilior, citrina.* Named clones 'Helen Garcia,' 'Enid Alba,' 'George Baldwin.'
Chondorhyncha discolor.

Chysis species.

Comparetia falcata and *macroplectrum.*

Cryptochilus sanguinea.

Cycnoches chlorochilon, loddigesii, ventricosum. Rather too large for light gardens.

Dendrobium. Warm growing and short caned species, especially D. compactum and Phalaenopsis.

Diacrium bicornutum.

Doritis hybrids. Similar to Phalaenopsis.

Epidendrum cochleatum, the Clamshell Orchid. Other Epidendrums, *allemanii, bractescens, fragrans, gracilis, ionophlebium, microbulbon, paleaceum, porpax, pseudepidendrum, radiatum,* and *tampense.* There are many others.

Erycina diaphana.

Gomesa recurva.

Hexisea bidentata. Bright orange red flowers. Easy with high humidity.

Kingiella decumbens and hybrids with Phalaenopsis.

Laelia acuminata rosea, anceps, autumnalis, crispa, gouldeana, cinnabarina, jongheana, and *milleri.*

Laeliocattleya (Lc. for short). In many colors and forms. Not excessively large in many instances. Look for the "cocktail orchid" listings derivative from plants like Lc. 'Psyche.' New hybrids are appearing all the time. They are very floriferous, often blooming from a continuous production of pseudobulbs.

Lockhartia oerstedtii. One of the easiest. Numerous little yellow flowers in the axils of bracts. A long bloomer. Other Lockhartias are worth trying.

Ludisia discolor var. Dawsoniana. Most beautiful of all orchid foliage. Ideal for the terrarium.

Miltonia. The Pansy Orchid. The huge true Pansy hybrids are difficult under lights. Easy and floriferous are *M. clowesii, regnellii, roezlii, vexillaria,* and *spectabilis.* Hybrids between these species are vigorous and among the best plants for the beginner. They bloom twice a year for me.

Notylia. Almost all species grow easily with relatively little light. Fragrant.

Oncidium. The majority of the Oncidiums are spray orchids with yellow or brown flowers. *O. ampliatum* grows easily under lights but the spray may be 3 feet long and as it develops the pot must be moved out from under the lights with the flowering stalk exposed to as much light as possible. Other tall growers, such as *O. sphacelatum,* must be treated in the same way.

O. kramerianum (and *papilio*) has exquisite blossoms formed like a complex brooch. *O. ornithorhynchium* is a small plant with pink flowered sprays. The tiny *O. pusillum* and *O. pumilum* bear large yellow flowers. These can be kept warm and moist in chopped osmunda and tree fern. There are hordes of exquisite small plants which vary greatly in their temperature requirements. The warm growing ones are best for the lights.

Ornithocephalus bicornis and *fuscus.*

Paphiopedilum. The Lady Slipper Orchids. Terrestrials. The intermediate growers are green leaved, the warm ones mottled. The latter are generally easier for the indoor grower and require a limey mix. Among the excellent species are *callosum, insigne, lawrenceanum,* 'Maudiae' (green and white stripes), *spicerianum, sukhakuli, venustum.* The cooler, green-leaved varieties are innumerable. Very robust, many of them will grow well under lights if the temperature does not climb over 85 degrees. Magnificent size and long lasting bloom characterize these plants.

Pescatorea cerina, odorata, wendlandii.

Phaius grandifolius. Nun's Orchid. Tall but easy. A terrestrial.

Phalaenopsis. The Moth Orchid. Many species and innumerable hybrids are available with new ones appearing constantly. You can find them in all sizes and a bewildering range of forms and colors. They bloom for a long time.

Rodriguezia secunda. Also intergeneric hybrids.

Saccolabium acutifolium, calceolare, dasypogon, giganteum.

Stenoglottis. A charming terrestrial and easy.

Trichocentrum species.

Trichocidium albo-coccineum.

Trichopilia suavis, tortilis, and others.

In addition to the above there are many new intergeneric hybrids which, when a cool and warm grower are mated, result in plants which are much easier for the indoor light gardener to grow than either of the parents. Especially notable are the new vandaceous (plants growing like Vanda on a single stem) hybrids, some of which are quite small and bear nodding masses of numerous flowers in brilliant colors.

Although the large families have already contributed so much, we have by no means exhausted their potential. Indoor light gardening is a young art and it requires years of horticultural experience to evaluate the reactions of different species and cultivars. Furthermore, any such revolutionary change as that from outdoor and greenhouse gardening to light gardening results in many surprises. Plants act very differently and in ways which are unexpected. We often overlook a plant because we think that its natural environment is much too different from our artificial one. But then, one day, curiosity causes us to experiment with it. Lo, and behold, it turns out to be a winner for reasons we cannot explain.

The plants which follow in the next section are selected from a number of families. And it is here that much of the future promise of an increased repertory for indoor light growers lies. The field is so wide and the number of possibilities is so great that no one knows where to begin. The ones we list have been with us for some time and proved their worth.

Chapter 16

MISCELLANEOUS PLANTS

It is fortunate that light gardening is not entirely dependent for bloom on the few families just described. Because each of them has been of sufficient importance to horticulturists to be studied and grown by organized societies, other families which may in the end offer a great deal to light gardening have been neglected. Because there are so many other possibilities, selection of material with a reasonable chance of growing and blooming under lights has been difficult. Those which have already proved successful are lumped together here.

Many old favorites are not included. Let us take *Aphelandra squarrosa,* the Zebra Plant, as an example. It is widely sold in florists' shops as a gift plant where its green shiny leaves with bright white stripes and its spire of yellow flowers attract the customer. It serves its purpose and will bloom for a period. But if we put it under lights we will find it rather tall for the method. It will finish flowering, drop its lower leaves, and become a scrawny plant indeed. It may flower again but from an arrangement of stem and leaf which has become unattractive. If you start a juvenile plant it is not impossible to grow it to maturity but usually it will not flower.

Two groups are also listed here, the Annuals and the Carnivorous Plants. A few of the first are included among the Miracle Plants. We do not have much experience with annuals and there is plenty of room for experiment. The better ones will bloom for a longer time under lights than out of doors. Carnivorous plants are curiosities in which any plant grower is interested.

GARDEN PLANTS FOR THE HOUSE

Garden plants have the attraction of the familiar and, in the bargain, are often more brightly colorful than our tropical bloomers. Light gardeners would like to grow them but are daunted by a lack of information. Their culture under lights is still in the experimental stage and it will be some time before we will be able to give instructions which are specific and reliable.

An obvious disadvantage of the garden plants is that they are definitely seasonal—at least in the garden. Once the annuals and perennials have bloomed themselves out they are finished and this usually takes only a few months. On the other hand, there is nothing to prevent the light gardener planting them in midsummer and enjoying them all winter long and that is as satisfactory as many of our favorite tropicals.

Another problem, though, is light requirement. Except for a few, they are sun lovers and, though we may succeed in blooming them, they reach for our tubes and then fall over on weak stems. Also they have a very rapid root development which has a tendency to be rather shallow so that, unless we are willing to allow considerable pot space, they become dangerously pot-bound. You will start a Zinnia and it will, in due time, bloom very nicely. But it doesn't fill out well and become bushy as it should.

To a remarkable degree light duration can compensate for a lack of intensity. At our usual longest day length of 16 hours we can bloom the garden with the disadvantages I have noted. It has also been found that they can be exposed to a 24-hour day, in other words, continuous light. They grow more rapidly from seed, bloom, and remain more compact under these conditions. Enough experience has been collected on this subject to contradict the former scientific gospel that a night rest is essential to plants.

That is all very well, but the plants to which a full growing cycle of 24-hour light has been applied is not, to my knowledge, very large. It may be the universal solution but I am unwilling to give the impression that we know this to be the case now. In any event, most light gardeners are averse to keeping the lights going around the clock not only for economic reasons but because it is difficult in most situations to segregate the continuous light garden from any other one on a shorter day. Until the tubes are more efficient, culture must be considered from a 16-hour viewpoint.

I feel safer using garden loam, sterilized, with a proportion of one-fifth perlite added. Many annuals do best in rather poor soil and will grow much too fast and far in a rich one.

Sow directly into this soil, place the propagating box close to the lights, and prick out, when the seedlings appear aboveground, into more spacious quarters. Finally, pot them up in the same mixture when they have grown a couple of inches. At all times keep the plants very close to the tubes—not more than 3 inches away, and well watered.

When choosing from the seed catalogs always opt for the smallest plants.

More and more miniatures are being hybridized because average gardens are less extensive than formerly, and this coincides very neatly with the needs of the light gardener.

The following is a partial list of garden plants which have been successfully grown under lights.

Agathea coelestis	*Hypoestes sanguinolenta*
Alyssum	*Impatiens*
Aquilegia	*Lantana*
Aster, dwarf (cool)	*Linaria*
Balsam 'Tom Thumb'	*Lobelia*, dwarf
Brachycome (Swan River Daisy)	Marigold, dwarf French
Browallia 'Sapphire'	*Microsperma*
Calandrinia speciosa	*Mimulus*
Calceolaria, dwarf (cool)	*Nemophila*
Calendula, dwarf	*Pentas*
Candytuft	*Petunia*
Clerodendron fallax	*Portulaca* (it does amazingly well)
Coleus	*San Vitalia*
Exacum	*Thymophylla* (Dahlborg Daisy)
Felicia	*Torenia*
Gazania, dwarf	*Zinnia*, mini

I have grown all of these and, as long as they are kept close to the lights, almost touching, they do as well as out of doors. Many other annual and perennial plants can be started in this way and planted in the garden later but are too tall growing for a light garden.

There is some evidence that certain of the perennials which go into dormancy in the garden remain active under lights just as some of the tropical plants. In any case the season of planting matters not at all under lights. You can seed in midsummer for winter bloom.

Mr. Leonard Miller of New York has been engaged in the seemingly quixotic effort of growing all kinds of wild flowers, annual and perennial garden plants. The reason for some of his successes as well as his failures is that he grows in a cool cellar. It is hard to believe that on a 16-hour light day *Aquilegia canadensis,* the wild Columbine, not only grows and blooms profusely but sheds seed from which new plants come into bloom in constant succession. He has also had the patience and skill to grow Florist Cinerarias and Primroses.

Everything therefore is possible. Light gardeners have naturally concentrated on the tropical blooming plants but with the result that much of the other horticultural material has never been given a real try. If you like and want to grow annuals and perennials, go right ahead. You may be able to add another useful plant to the light gardener's list.

Allophyton mexicanum. Scrophulariaceae (Mexican Foxglove).
Mexico and Guatemala

As to foliage this wonderful little plant looks very much like *Gesneria cuneifolia* when young. The rosettes consist of rather narrow long obovate leaves which are shiny and serrate. As the plant develops the lower leaves drop off and the rosette climbs, rising on top of a rather thick woody stem until, after growing itself out because of size or exhaustion, we replace it from an ample stock of seeds.

The flowers are typical of the family and similar to many of the five-lobed Gesneriads. About ⅜ inch long they are purplish fading to a pinkish white. From the whorls of leaves thin stiff peduncles rise a few inches and at the tip appears a cluster of buds which open one by one. Usually there are several peduncles in bloom at one time. The flower sets seed without any visible outside agency and, if left to mature, a thin-shelled oval pod is formed which turns brown. They can be stored and used as needed.

Allophyton prefers a soil consisting of 3 parts sand and 2 parts humus, well packed. Place it 5 inches from the lights in a 3-inch pot and keep constantly moist. Humidity, as for all our tropicals, should be over 50 percent for best results but *Allophyton* will tolerate dry air and still bloom. Feed sparingly.

The flowering of a healthy plant is almost continuous.

Anthurium scherzerianum. Araceae. Tropical America

In spite of being a huge and widespread family, the *Araceae* supply very few flowering plants for the indoor gardener. But among these are two of the best, and one could be tempted to choose *Spathiphyllum*, because of its hardiness, over *this* wonderful *Anthurium*. The former is only disqualified from being classified a Miracle Plant by its size—a little large to be considered ideal. The latter is certainly the showier plant and the flowers are extraordinarily long lasting.

The flowers of the arums are tiny and cover the spadix (the Jack-in-the-Pulpit) while the spathe, a shaped or colored modified leaf, is the showy part. *Anthurium scherzerianum* is a near relative of those enormous, seemingly lacquered, flowers seen in florist shops in brilliant oranges and reds. Ideally the leaves of *A. scherzerianum* should be no more than 6 inches long, a lengthened heart shape, and quite leathery. They rise either from the compost or, as they grow older, from a thick slow growing trunk. The pedicels of the "flowers" are 5 inches long, reddish in color, and the flowers, which are heart-shaped, the spadix pendent from the top, are 2 to 3 inches across.

The type has been much bred and crossed so that there are various shades of blood red, scarlet, rose, and red with white spotting. And although there are designated variations, they are rarely labeled as such at the nursery. Thus the particular clone one acquires has much to do with success, some being more vigorous and floriferous than others. Do not give up with this plant. If one fails to be satisfactory try another from a different nursery. Once you have a good one it will be one of your permanent favorites.

Besides its large size and brilliant coloring, the flower has the distinction of being among the longest lasting. A 2-month time span is quite normal. There is no profusion of them for they appear one, or at the most two at a time (except in large plants) but they are quite showy enough as individuals. A good plant will always be provided with a bloom or bud under lights.

A. scherzerianum should be potted in osmunda. For some this may represent a mental block for only Orchids usually require this material. You can buy it from most Orchid nurseries. But it will usually survive in coarse sphagnum or an African Violet Mix with the addition of an extra part of peat.

The osmunda, which comes in chunks (it is the root of various ferns) should be soaked overnight and very tightly packed around the roots of the *Anthurium*. Fertilizing is not necessary with this medium but organic solutions will encourage superior growth and flowering. Buy a young small plant in flower and use a maximum 3-inch clay pot. The medium should be kept moist at all times but the pot should not stand in water.

Keep the leaves within 5 inches of the lights away from the center of the tubes. Low temperatures are to be avoided and 65 to 80 degrees is ideal. It is not sensitive to high temperatures. Maintain 60 percent humidity or better and mist once or twice a day if possible.

In due time the plant will put forth suckers which can be cut off and potted separately. Root cuttings set in peat and vermiculite may sprout if kept in the 80-degree range. But the suckers are your best bet. A slow growing plant, it should last in your small pot for at least five years and produce enough material for propagation.

Biophytum sensitivum. Oxalidaceae

This little plant looks like a miniature Cycad or is mistaken for some sort of Acacia because of its whorl of apparent fronds with many leaflets. It is just 3 inches high many months after germination and I do not know as yet how high it can grow. Out of the center of the whorl grow stiff stems bearing little puffs of pink which pass in a day and are replaced very shortly by a starlike open capsule full of seeds. Collect these and start new plants. It is a most interesting subject for terrarium planting and a charmer when set in a Japanese pot.

It seems to be satisfied with any mix and to like moderate moisture. It is only a bit particular about light. If grown close to the tubes the leaves turn reddish and the plant stops growing. It is happiest when about fifteen inches away. At night some of the fronds fold upward and some downward so that it is a bit scraggly. But in the morning it reassumes its perfect symmetry. A charming plant you should not miss.

Bouvardia. Rubiaceae. Central America and Mexico

Bouvardias have a long history of popularity as cut flowers and especially for wedding bouquets. They are medium-size shrubs with tube flowers in clusters, each flower four-lobed and deliciously fragrant. Very few hobbyists have tried them under lights but they deserve to be used more widely as they are winter bloomers and among the few fragrant ones..

Buy juvenile plants and keep underpotted to prevent excessive growth. Use Sandy Soil Mix with dry manure or a good organic fertilizer added. Keep them moist and give them low house temperatures. They like it in the 60s and, though they will tolerate the 80s, are not very happy about it. In September give them shade or a short day of 9 hours to induce bud formation.

When flowering is finished allow a rest by reducing water and ceasing to fertilize. Also trim at this time. As soon as growth starts again water and fertilize. Young jointed cuttings root easily in peat and sand or vermiculite mixtures.

Bouvardia longiflora 'Humboldtii' is the standard white. The flowers are very long and especially fragrant.

B. ternifolia, which is smaller, is also easier and has the advantage of coming in a number of colors. Cultivars are 'Christmas Red,' 'Fire Chief,' 'Giant Pink,' and 'Joy,' which is white.

Browallia. Solanaceae. Annual. Tropical America

Browallias are handsome constant bloomers in the light garden and can be kept going for many months, then replaced with new seedlings to fill out the year.

B. speciosa major (Columbia) grows easily from seed, and when started in August will bloom all winter. The leaves are shiny and pointed, the flowers tubed and widely flared, the color violet blue. They can be planted in Sandy Soil Mix and will grow easily under the lights.

B. americana has smaller flowers in blue or white. *B. americana nana* is a dwarf cultivar.

B. viscosa 'Sapphire' is a dwarf with bright blue flowers very freely produced. This is the variety most often seen in light gardens.

Like most annuals these should be grown near the lights and allowed to dry somewhat between waterings. Vermiculite and perlite can be used instead of the sand.

Campanula isophylla. Campanulaceae

The *Campanulas* are little trailing plants (at least those which are raised as houseplants) which mostly bloom from spring to fall. During the growing and blooming period they are quite easy, only requiring regular watering. But when fall comes they must be kept quite dry and in rather a cool place or they will rot out. To provide for the future, cuttings can be started which will behave contraseasonally and guarantee a new crop.

The potting mix should contain some ground limestone or chips and about equal quantities of humus and sand. Fertilize with very mild balanced nutrients.

C. *isophylla* is bluish; C. *isophylla alba* is a fine white form; C. *fragilis*, which is blue, is also worth trying.

Carissa. Apocynaceae (Natal Plum). South Africa

Carissa grandiflora is a common cultivated shrub in Florida where it is used as a hedge on account of its dense greenery and long sharp thorns. Treated as a specimen it will grow into a very big shrub. It has white pinwheel flowers 2 inches across followed by a red fruit from which the locals make a jelly. Variety *nana compacta* is a smaller plant though it can still attain 3 or 4 feet if permitted to do so. Recently the University of Miami achieved a further diminution with a cultivar called 'Petit-Point,' only 6 inches high and a good candidate for bonsai treatment.

The dwarfs and juveniles of the original plant make excellent light garden plants which are capable of flowering and fruiting throughout the year.

Give them Sandy Soil Mix with a large dose of shell or eggshell. Use organic fertilizers and water well when in active growth. Give maximum light. The plant should be trained horizontally so that the leaves receive as much light as possible—which is also a good way to grow them for ornament. Cuttings of young growth will root in damp sand or sphagnum-vermiculite mix. For blooming the temperatures should not go below 50 degrees.

Carnivorous Plants

Those interesting oddities of the plant world, the carnivorous plants, are quite easy to grow under lights. All of them require the same cultural conditions.

They must be segregated in a terrarium of their own in which the medium is fresh sphagnum moss. The temperature must be at least 65 degrees within the container and the humidity must be maintained at a high level. The sphagnum should be always moist, and the water used should be distilled or allowed to stand for a few days to rid itself of chlorine completely. Do not fertilize. Keep the terrarium covered most of the time and the plants within a foot of the lights.

A plant which is now available everywhere that plants are sold is Venus's Flytrap, *Dionaea muscipula,* the one with leaves which close over insect victims. The flowers are white, somewhat like those of Oxalis, on long rather thick pedicels. You can feed it minute insects or bits of raw meat but are advised not to. It can lead to rotting if your judgment of the size of a meal does not agree with Dionaea's. The plant spreads and can be divided.

Darlingtonia, the Cobra or California Pitcher Plant, the most spectacular of our native carnivores, can be acquired from nurseries on the West Coast. Of the other Pitcher Plants, *Sarracenia purpurea* and *rubra* are the only ones small enough for a terrarium.

Then there are the Sundews, the various *Drosera* species with charming pink or white flowers. These perch on top of the sphagnum spreading their innumerable viscid hairs, each tipped with a bead of syrup.

Pinguiculas, the Butterworts, grow on the soil with a rosette of leaves which are covered with a thick jellylike substance. The flowers, erect on thin pedicels, are yellow or blue and cornucopia-shaped.

These plants plus some sphagnum tolerant ferns are quite sufficient for a conversation piece terrarium.

Ceropegia woodii. Asclepiadaceae (Rosary Vine). South Africa

This is such a well-known little vine that its inclusion in a list of Miracle Plants, as if it were some sort of paragon, may appear to be carrying things too far. But we do not usually think of it as a flowering plant at all and raise it mostly for its pretty heart-shaped leaves, rather thick, like little cushions, and veined all over with silver. In a greenhouse or on a big porch it looks really insignificant but when it is set in proportions more appropriate to its own, namely our light garden, it assumes a certain importance and one begins to notice the odd little flowers. Furthermore it is only under lights that it is likely to bloom almost continuously.

The flowers, ¾-inch long at best, are pale lavender and shaped like a round bulb and straight nozzle. From the tip of the open tube four feathery wires seem to form a little cage.

The plant grows from a little corm which increases in size with time. Everything about it is calculated to withstand drought, the leaves thick as lozenges and the bulblets which develop in the joints between the paired leaves. A 3-inch pot is ample. Sandy Soil Mix or even Cactus Mix will suit it. Drainage must be very good.

Although *Ceropegia* reacts to moisture like *Euphorbia bojeri,* it must never stand in water. The liquid must drain through and be allowed to dry a little between applications. But certainly a necessity for maintaining bloom is that it should never dry out completely, a touchy matter but usually workable if the pot is watered lightly once a day in summer and every two days in winter. It likes a misting. Set it 6 to 8 inches from the lights. Warm temperatures assist continuation of bloom. Use only organic fertilizer.

As soon as you acquire the plant, buy at a variety or nursery supply store a small fan trellis, one that is 8 inches wide at the top and about a foot high, with two points which set firmly into the soil of the pot. Then start training your plant, tying on the lengths of vine as they grow and arranging them as symmetrically as possible. Keep the pot facing the fluorescent tubes —the best place is in the outer rank—so that the leaves will all face forward.

With careful training, weaving in and out of the wires and around the points, the whole surface of the trellis will be covered. By this time flowering should be well on its way, appearing in the axils of the leaves and, if the plant is happy, constantly repeating in the same place. There may be as many as thirty, even forty, blooms at a time and the whole piece will then be as handsome a decoration as you could wish.

I have mentioned that *Ceropegia* blooms best in warm temperatures. This means 65 degrees or better. It will withstand much lower temperatures without suffering. But since we are interested in flowering, the level which concerns us is that at which this activity will cease. When a plant such as *Ceropegia* continues to flower for a very long time we should not expect it to resume quickly once it stops. Then we must give it a rest. Everything depends on keeping the dynamic growth of the plant at a high pitch. This means not only flowering but the constant increase in the length of the vine. The moment this ceases we must not try to force any longer. Rest becomes a necessity, and spontaneous new growth is our signal for the start of a new cycle.

Eventually bulb and vine will become too big for the pot, although this should be well beyond the usual pot binding. You can then transplant it to a larger container. But this is rather pointless as the sizes of leaf and flower are unsuitable for any larger trellis. However, it *is* possible, provided that you have calculated proportions carefully so that it will continue to present a decent appearance.

Most people would prefer to start a new plant, which is exceptionally easy in this case. Before the old vine has reached its limits in the pot remove lengths of stem each with a bulblet attached and plant directly in a new growth pot. Set the bulb in a slight depression in the soil so that its top is above the surface and pin it down with a hairpin (a most useful indoor gardening tool) or a piece of bent wire. Deep planting is likely to rot the bulb. Water sparingly. Initial growth will be slow but before long another handsome trellis picture is on its way.

Clerodendron thomsoniae. Verbenaceae. West Africa

This magnificent vine is a great favorite in botanical gardens and greenhouses where it can run rampant and is loaded all spring and summer with masses of blood red corollas protruding from brilliant white inflated calyces. Hardly a candidate, you would think, for the light garden. Fortunately it tolerates trimming to such an extent that it can be kept to a modest size like a small shrub.

Success with this plant depends on two factors. One is its requirement of a thorough rest for a few months in midwinter. From November through February it must be dried out completely. The leaves all fall off, of course, but the stems stay green. In mid-February start watering, and after leaves come, fertilizing with a balanced formula. Flowering peduncles develop almost immediately and are followed by months of bloom.

Even when I knew this trick, trials with a number of plants from different nurseries failed to bloom. Finally I found one which performed and whose progeny have proved equally reliable. This clone was characterized by somewhat heavier, more quilted leaves than the others. As the other clones which failed were all capable of blooming in a greenhouse environment there is no means of advising you how to pick out a plant which will bloom. Mine was bought from Logee's Greenhouses.

Plant in Tropical Plant Mix and maintain the top of the leaves within 5 inches of the tubes. Between the end of dormancy and the end of its blooming period *Clerodendron* will almost double in height in the process of putting forth the flowering peduncles. At the end of the season cut the plant back to 8 or 9 inches, preserving if possible a number of branches. Then it will have room to grow. The root system is very large so a 6-inch pot is a minimum for a good blooming plant.

Cuttings of young growth root very easily in moist vermiculite and even in water.

Crassula schmidtii. Crassulaceae. South Africa

This is a charming small plant which consists of a tuft of narrow, fleshy, long pointed leaves from which there arise scapes bearing many small bright rose and white striped flowers. During a blooming period the scapes may succeed each other, and if the dead flowers are not trimmed off they will retain their color for a long time after drying. Bloom is usually sometime during the summer, contrary to many South African succulents. There seem to be no day length problems under lights.

A 3-inch pot is quite sufficient. Propagation is by separation of the rosettes or laying a leaf on moist vermiculite. Pot in Sandy Soil Mix. In winter water only once every two weeks but as the days lengthen this can be increased to once a week. Give a balanced nutrient once a month starting in the spring but eliminate entirely from November onward.

The only problem I have had with *C. schmidtii* is due to its being a succulent (literally) host for mealybugs which are peculiarly persistent on this plant. Remove them with cotton and rubbing alcohol being careful to work into the axils of the leaves. Repeated treatments will rid you of the pests. Malathion or oily solutions will kill the plant in short order. But VC-13 can be used in the soil.

Crassula rupestris and *C. cooperi* will also perform occasionally under lights.

Crossandra undulaefolia. Acanthaceae. India

Crossandra's trusses of brilliant salmon orange flowers, the three lobes spreading widely from the narrow tube, contrast beautifully with the dark shiny green foliage. It is really a small shrub and quite sturdy, yet the culture is much the same as the Gesneriads and it is a year round bloomer.

Seeds, started in vermiculite and milled sphagnum, take as much as thirty days to germinate. During that time they should be kept in bright light and the seed bed enclosed so that humidity remains high. The seeds are large enough to plant one or two to a small pot. When growth starts, the pots should be kept within an inch or two of the tubes, the leaves misted regularly and an organic or balanced chemical fertilizer fed to them. Legginess can be prevented by early pruning.

Thereafter the plants will carry on in African Violet Mix. They like medium temperatures in the 60 to 80 degree range and a 65 to 70 percent relative humidity.

Crossandra can grow to be quite a large shrub if permitted. Therefore prune it as flat as possible and keep it rather pot-bound. Flowers setting seed will discourage further blooming.

New plants can be started readily from cuttings of new growth. Enclose the pot so that there is high humidity for a period. Do not forget to treat the bottom tip of the cutting with a growth stimulant and be sure that at least one joint is buried in the medium. Keep well watered at all times until roots are formed.

Cymbalaria muralis. Scrophulariaceae (Kenilworth Ivy). Europe

Your nurseryman should really toss this one in free as it is a nuisance in the greenhouse—a little vine, hardly big enough to trellis, which will wander around your garden and freely produce its purplish little spurred flowers with a yellow throat. It will grow in any sandy mix and likes rather bright light. A number of other similar Cymbalarias are native to Italy, and sometimes turn up in cultivation. Worth having for the light garden.

Fuchsias

Normally Fuchsias, plants which grow and bloom in summer, must be carried over the winter in a semidormant state or restarted with cuttings either in the fall or the spring. They are such magnificent blooming plants that every one of the hundreds of cultivars is desirable. It is regrettable that some are unsuitable for the light garden because of the hanging habit and others because they just do not perform well under fluorescents. But the light garden has one advantage the windowsill never possessed—it has no seasons, and if a Fuchsia will perform for us at all we can depend on good winter as well as summer flowering. When indoor light gardening becomes sufficiently popular there will certainly be a movement to develop hybrids which will adapt to the new conditions and enlarge our repertoire.

Fuchsias in the light garden can be potted in African Violet Mix, kept constantly watered and misted as often as possible. Humidity should be 60 percent or better and the air constantly in movement. Temperatures not higher than 75 degrees are preferred. Although considered rather undemanding about light, they will need plenty of it in your light garden. Fertilize with organic solutions.

When received from a nursery the plant should be trimmed and all flowers and buds removed and, indeed, until growth is actively resumed, nip off the new buds—for a Fuchsia will try to bloom even when there is very little or no leaf or stem growth. Watch for white flies and mites, especially the former. Vapona strips will eliminate the first and Kelthane dipping the second.

Cuttings can be rooted in perlite or vermiculite spring or fall. It is wise to replace the plants yearly.

Provided culture is right the following Fuchsias have no seasons under lights and are constantly in bloom but, for this very reason, they require constant attention. This is an instance where the type which will do well under lights is definable. It must be, for the present at least, a plant which has single blooms, is on the small side, and usually has reddish foliage.

Fuchsia magellanica and its forms can grow into a shrub of great size but the juveniles are easily trimmed.

F. triphylla 'Gartenmeister Bohnstedt,' the Honeysuckle Fuchsia, has deep orange blooms without the petticoat, and foliage which is green to maroon with red veins. This is the easiest of the lot and will bloom constantly summer and winter. I do not list it as a miracle plant only because it is rather sensitive and will open its flowers if it is happy and, at the slightest sulk, keep dropping them. By adjusting its position under the lights, watering properly—in short keeping a close watch on its moods—it is possible to tame it to perfect behavior, whereupon it becomes a most ornamental and dependable plant.

F. 'Mme Dacheau,' 'Mrs. Marshall,' 'Little Beauty' (Black Prince), and 'Buttons and Bows' either remain small or bloom when very young. *F.* 'Bluette,' a single with rose sepals and blue corolla, has proved a good performer under lights.

Although I do not know anyone who has had experience with them under lights I suggest that *F. parviflora, rosea* and *thymifolia* may be found satisfactory as they are all rather small, less ingrown plants than the big hybrids.

Gardenia jasminoides. Rubiaceae. Cape Jasmine. China

Gardenia plants appear in variety stores as well as nurseries in the middle of April. They are usually in bud and the temptation is great to try these shiny leaved plants with the fragrant white blossoms. The disappointment is in proportion if the buds brown and drop off or the plant brings into the house a fine crop of white flies.

Both of these problems are now easily avoidable. For the light garden a small plant is best. Bring it home, wash it off well with borax soap in lukewarm water, and set the pot in a deep saucer or bowl so that it has constant wet feet. It will do well several inches from the lights toward the ends. Fertilize occasionally with high nitrogen formula and once a year treat with a small amount of Sequestrene for iron. Normal light garden temperatures, high humidity, and plenty of misting will suit it. The mistake in the past has been to treat this plant to a drying out between waterings.

If carried around the year in the house, flowering may well start by late November. The old rule about pinching back early buds is hardly necessary under lights, and left alone the plant will give you a longer season of bloom. Cuttings root easily in Sandy Soil Mix under the lights.

Gardenia radicans is a miniature plant with smaller blossoms which are as fragrant as the big ones.

Gynura aurantiaca. Compositae (Velvet Plant). Java

Gynura has been a popular houseplant for a long time because of its shapely leaves which are velvety and rosy purple. Under lights it will produce its tufted burnt orange flowers.

Very easy to grow, Gynura's tendency is to grow fast and trail. Under lights it can be controlled by drastic pruning and pot-binding. Then it becomes a flat bushy plant and its foliage stays solidly compact.

Keep it moist, not wet, within a foot of the lights in Tropical Plant Mix. Give it a balanced fertilizer. Cuttings root with ease in moist vermiculite.

Trimming such a plant amounts to cutting off branches which become longer than you desire. This will encourage new growth from the roots and side growth. Pot binding keeps the plant from growing fast.

Hoya. Asclepiadaceae (Wax Plant). East Asia

Hoyas are popular in greenhouses because they ramble about with little or no attention and seasonally produce handsome clusters of waxy fragrant flowers. As houseplants they are more often grown only for their thick waxy leaves which, in some kinds, are variegated. In country houses, where they can be hung in baskets allowing their long stems to hang down, some varieties will bloom occasionally but in the city until recently flowering was quite impossible.

Light gardeners have discovered the virtues of *Hoya bella* which is quite different in appearance from the others and which will bloom dependably indoors. Bella has small dark green leaves less thick than the others and has a branching habit. The flower clusters are large, consisting of white stars with pink centers. Careful culture will bring them into bloom throughout the year.

Unless it is very large it should be confined in a pot no larger than 3 inches in diameter for it likes pot binding. Pack the roots in tight with Tropical Plant Mix and water regularly. Because of its way of branching it should be hung from the fluorescent fixture itself or from the reflector so that the branches extend under the lights although it will often bloom at the tips of the branches some 12 inches away from the tubes. Because the branches elongate excessively and get in the way of other plants, trim it back early in its growth in order to achieve multiple branching of shorter lengths. Fertilize regularly along with your other plants.

The flower cluster appears at the end of a short peduncle growing from a leaf axil. Never remove this peduncle because it is the source of repeated flowerings. The problem with this Hoya, then, is to achieve a balance between the need to maintain compactness and the desire to preserve as many blooming peduncles as possible. Since the flowers are most attractive it is worth the trouble. The important thing is not to fuss over the culture of this plant but treat it like any other, forgetting if possible that it is a succulent. Under the lights it responds to this treatment by blooming more often.

Impatiens. Balsaminaceae. Sultana. Zanzibar

Due to the development of a dwarf hybrid strain which is particularly shade tolerant, Impatiens now grows well under lights and is in continuous bloom. It is called the Imp Series and comes in a full range of the standard colors. In fact these are less watery-hued than most.

Start the plants from seed in July for winter bloom in Sandy Soil Mix. Keep them close to the lights to maintain the dwarf growth. As they grow you will find that, like other garden plants, they need plenty of space for roots. A 4-inch pot, at least, is required but the blooming mileage is worth the space. Don't give them much nutrient for if they starve a bit they will remain more compact.

Impatiens balsamina, Garden Balsam, is also available from seed in a dwarfed strain. It requires the same culture as Impatiens.

Both these plants can be propagated from stem cuttings with leaves in moist vermiculite.

Jacobinia carnea. Acanthaceae. Brazil

Jacobinia carnea is a favorite of botanical gardens where it grows in the tropical house to a height of 4 feet or more and bears big spikes of pink flowers very similar at first sight to those of Monarda or Bee Balm.

The behavior of this plant under lights is astonishing for it will bloom when only 3 inches high, putting forth an inflorescence which would look exaggeratedly large if it were not for the 3- to 5-inch-long leaves that frame it.

Cut off the dying flower mass and the stem will immediately sprout four to six flowering stalks. Remove all but two and plant each one in Tropical Plant Mix, keep moist and within 6 inches of the lights, and before you know it you will have new flowers from every one.

This manner of handling the plant is necessary because if left undisturbed it will simply grow too large for the light garden. Therefore we cannot speak of it as an ever-blooming plant under lights. But it has many of the virtues of our Miracle Plants and, if the procedure is followed religiously, you can have *Jacobinia carnea* blooming in one pot or another throughout the year and occupying very little space considering its brilliance of color and size of flower.

The only caution about this plant is in regard to watering. If excessively watered the lower leaves will turn yellow. It likes to be moist but not wet. Allow the surface to dry out between waterings. Fertilize heavily.

A yellow species, *Jacobinia umbrosa,* is available from nurseries and should be equally attractive and easy.

Jasminum sambac. Oleaceae. Arabian Jasmine. India

Arabian Jasmine has that very desirable quality of being fragrant. 'Maid of Orleans' is the cultivar most commonly grown. It is a vine capable of growing to 5 feet or more and it would be of little interest to us were it not for the fact that it can be very much trimmed and then becomes like a little shrub, somewhat branched and rather woody. The dark green, shiny leaves, pointed at either end, are relatively sparse. Flowers appear close to the stem, singly or in little clusters. They are narrow white tubes with petals reflexed to the horizontal and spreading up to an inch across. The angling is very much like a pinwheel. The odor is rich and spicy.

It requires Sandy Soil Mix, occasional fertilizing with a mild balanced formula, sparse but continuous moisture. Eight to 10 inches from the lights suffices. But the humidity must be as high as possible. If this is not available you will have to mist it regularly. Bloom takes place at all times of the year and there is no dormancy. Growth is slow and flowers are produced with very little top activity.

From the start, train this Jasmine very much like a Bonsai by shaping it through pruning. Don't let it get out of hand or it will soon become unsightly. Kept small and retarded it will become quite woody and the stems will assume interesting shapes.

Other Jasmines are *J. gracile* with larger flowers but more difficult to train and bloom, *J. mesnyi,* which is bright yellow but only blooms in the spring and *J. officinale,* the Poet's Jasmine, which has finely cut leaves and rather weak growth.

Other Jasmines

The English-speaking world calls almost any fragrant tube flowered vine a Jasmine. For this reason I include here some quite unrelated species, all of which are, indeed, fragrant and worth trying in the house. Culture is much the same as for the true Jasmines.

Cestrum diurnum and *C. nocturnum* are members of the family *Solanaceae* and natives of the West Indies. They are shrubby with white fragrant flowers.

Gelsemium sempervirens of the *Loganiaceae* is the Carolina Jessamine, a widespread native plant in our South. It has sparse, rather dull leaves but 1-inch bright yellow trumpet flowers. It will bloom off and on but requires the maximum in fluorescent lighting.

Trachelospermum jasminoides, Apocynaceae, Confederate Jasmine, is a Chinese import with small starlike flowers, the petals somewhat twisted. Not easy under lights.

Kalanchoe. Crassulaceae. Madagascar

As houseplants most of the Kalanchoes are grown for their foliage. The exceptions are *K. blossfeldiana* which is a popular Christmas bloomer, and *K. uniflora,* Coral Bells, which appears to bloom best in spring. Both are short day plants and require that the light hours be cut to 10 for a few weeks in the fall. Most people know the firecracker flowers of *blossfeldiana,* but *uniflora* is rarer. The latter is, on the whole, a more reliable plant. It is a trailer which grows easily and can be trellised like a little vine. Its pink bells are produced in great profusion and the period lasts a long time.

The culture of Kalanchoes, other than the short day period, is of the simplest. Give them Sandy Soil Mix, manure water during the growing period, and long days under the center of the lights. After blooming they should rest for a couple of months and watering can be cut to once every two weeks, or the minimum which will keep the leaves from shriveling up.

K. flammea is similar to *blossfeldiana* but larger and *K. manginii* has little red bells and somewhat resembles *uniflora.* Both are also worth trying.

Linaria. Scrophulariaceae. (Annual). Toadflax. Worldwide.

Dwarf varieties of this charming Snapdragonlike flower are offered by seedsmen. Usually they come in mixed colors. Choose the strain by size—not over 10 inches. The colors are very many, the flower being provided with a long spur and the yellow mound on the lip being a bright yellow. Culture is simple and bloom rather long lasting. They can be reseeded for year-round color.

Plant the seed in sandy mix and place directly under the lights. Germination is within 8 to 10 days. Keep moist, and when ready transplant to a 3-inch pot of the same mix. After blooming, Linarias will often drop seed in the pot and start a new growth on their own.

By the way, many of the Linarias are perennial but, so far, we have not had any experience with them. They are likely to be rather big plants.

Lobelia erinus. Lobeliaceae. South Africa

There are many cultivars of this dwarf trailer with deep blue flowers borne profusely throughout a long season. You can buy clumps for a few cents in spring when they are offered by nurserymen as edging plants. Plant them in Sandy Soil Mix with lime added and give plenty of room for root growth. Maintain moisture and treat them occasionally with manure water. Keep them rather to the side of the lights within 6 inches of the tubes. Being rather trailing plants they are best planted with some support under the pot or in a stemmed vessel.

Seed is easy to propagate and can be started at any time of the year. If planted in August you can have midwinter bloom. In addition to blue varieties there are those in pure white, and a red with a white eye.

Lopezia coccinea. Onagraceae. Mexico

This is a small, delicate shrub with minuscule leaves and two winged rose flowers which are quite insignificant. But there is a glow to the latter and when this plant is in bloom it makes a rather good show. Given careful treatment it can grow up to 2 feet in the house but it is advisable to keep it pruned not only for convenience but because the flowers will appear in better proportion.

Sandy Soil Mix is called for and a drying out between waterings. Put it in your brightest spot in the light garden and mist occasionally. It requires very little misting and dislikes lime. The flowering is principally in winter but I have had it bloom from fall to spring.

Malpighia coccigera. Malpighiaceae. Barbados Cherry. West Indies

Do not be upset if your little plant of *Malpighia* does not display the holly leaves which are half its beauty, for these only appear when it has grown beyond the juvenile stage. This lovely mimic is something of a split personality. The flowers, which are different from any other shrub you can think of, actually have a curious resemblance to the small *Oncidium* Orchids. They are pink, very complex, very airy, and lie among the emerald leaves like jewels.

It grows in Sandy Soil Mix, prefers to be at least 5 inches from the lights, should be kept moist but not wet and fertilized with a balanced formula. On the whole I prefer to pot this plant in sand mixed with leaf mold or humus. It is not quite partial to the peat. Although I have raised and bloomed *Malpighia* and will always try again, I have not yet found a sound explanation for its occasional sudden dropping of leaves and quick death. But I suspect that it likes rather cool roots which must never dry out completely and is very unhappy if it does not receive just the right amount of light, which usually means not too much. I also think that good air movement is important. Cuttings root rather easily.

Oxalis. Oxalidaceae. Sorrel. Worldwide

Most Oxalis have cloverlike leaves in threes, each segment of which is heart-shaped. *O. regnelli,* which I list under the Miracle Plants, bears the segments in triangles. Not all of them are as easy as *regnelli,* and some, being tuberous, go dormant in the fall, requiring storage until they sprout again in the spring. Those which are stemless usually have long weak peduncles and petioles which flop over after a while. Also, since the flowers are of short duration and are produced in great quantities, the plants are generally loaded with those which have finished their work. Plucking and trimming, therefore, is a constant chore if one wishes to keep the plants in decent shape.

Culture is of the simplest. Sandy Soil Mix and plenty of watering with a balanced fertilizer are all they need. But they must be kept fairly close to the lights to maintain upright growth and bloom. Tubers multiply rapidly which obliges one to repot, sometimes every six months. Temperature makes little difference but good humidity is beneficial. Keep wet at all times.

Of the other Oxalis the following three are the most useful to light gardeners.

Oxalis hedysaroides rubra, Firefern, is a lovely little fibrous rooted shrub with deep red leaves divided into stemmed segments. The segments do not fold down the middle at night as do most of the Oxalis. Instead they have up and down movement and it may happen at any time of day. So one of the fascinations of this plant is to watch its leaves moving individually at every change of light or air. They are also sensitive to touch and will drop if fingered or sprayed.

The flowers are sulfur yellow and small. The stems propagate easily in moist vermiculite.

Oxalis martiana aureo-reticulata. The gold-veined Oxalis is one of the most beautiful of small foliage plants. It is equally good on the shelf or in a terrarium. The flowers are deep pink and are produced in fair quantity. Keep very moist and the chances are that it will not go dormant. Propagates pips.

Oxalis ortgiesii has thick succulent stems bearing handsome quilted leaves, notched at the tips and red below. The flowers are yellow. Give this one less water than *regnellii* and keep it a foot from the lights. Bloom is constant. As it is fibrous rooted it does not go dormant. But it can become rather tall and spready with time. Cuttings root well.

O. peduncularis has tiny succulent foliage and orange flowers. It is a prostrate grower. Otherwise treat like *ortgiesii.*

In the nursery lists you will find a number of other Oxalis. All are easy to grow and good bloomers but the tuberous ones go into dormancy. *Oxalis gigantea* is fibrous rooted, a single bare stem which sprouts large yellow flowers and tiny green leaves. It *does* go to sleep at odd moments but is a curious plant and takes up little space.

Pentas lanceolata. Rubiaceae. Egyptian Star Cluster. Tropical Africa

A pretty, rather coarse herb, *Pentas* has straight tallish stems bearing pink, red, or white umbels of small flowers. It has been much recommended of late but grows too tall for most light gardens. Because of the long stems it must usually be staked and it does not take too kindly to pruning. Still it blooms easily in Sandy Soil Mix with light watering and kept rather close to the lights. It does best if the temperature is cool, at least at night.

Being something like an annual in habit it also needs very little nutrient. Young cuttings root easily.

Peristrophe angustifolia, Var. aureo-variegata. Acanthaceae. Java

This is a charming little shrub with 2-inch leaves brightly variegated in green and yellow. It has the tendency to grow out rather flat after having lifted itself up about six inches. The flowers are two-lipped, silken, and a light purple.

Planted in African Violet Mix, set toward the end of the lights, and kept well watered, it will grow and bloom for a long time. If any plain green leaves appear remove the stem up to that point to encourage continued variegation. Cuttings root easily. The spread is about fifteen inches for a well-grown plant. It is rather subject to white flies, but a blast with a household bomb will finish them off and does not seem to affect the leaves.

Portulaca grandiflora. Portulacaceae (Annual). Brazil

It is only after repeated experiments that I have dared recommend Portulaca for the light garden. This popular outdoor annual is a creeper with large silky flowers in the brightest of tints in the range from yellow to red. It thrives on poor soil, withstands drought, and prefers a position in full sunlight. The success I have had with this plant offers additional proof that one should never take anything for granted when it comes to light gardening. I have often been fooled by tropical plants which flowered easily the first time but proved on repeated attempts to be very difficult and temperamental subjects.

Seedsmen now provide dwarf varieties of Portulaca which are more upright in growth than the usual garden cultivars. The seed germinates very easily but has a tendency, even when close to the lights, to elongate, branch, and fall over. So culture requires a second stage. Take 2-inch cuttings from the sturdiest plants, remove a few lower leaves, dust with hormone, and set them in moist vermiculite. Roots develop usually in less than two weeks and two or three can be put in a 2-inch pot.

Using Tropical Plant Mix with some eggshell, and compacting it around the roots, they will grow straight and bloom beautifully about four inches under lights. Water only when the soil is dry and give them fertilizer only once every two weeks. When they have bloomed from the tip, which is usually when they are 3 to 4 inches high, cut them back so that they will branch. They will now have thick enough stems to support the new growth. Take stem cuttings whenever you need new plants.

In the garden Portulacas have had one disadvantage. If you were a nine-to-five worker you would never see them in bloom since they open around ten and close at five. Under lights, *mirabile dictu*, they don't go to bed till around 9:00 P.M.

Roses, Miniature

Miniature Roses are so popular that we must mention them if only to warn you about them. In the first place, most of these plants have tiny flowers on what are quite capable of growing into large plants. Second, they require quite cool conditions and great care in watering when they stop blooming. Third, they attract various forms of mites and spiders. Finally, they need all the light you can give them and more. Because of their special needs it is very advisable to read the literature on the subject and seek the aid of those who have been especially successful in raising them. I know few who have been successful in growing them under lights and a host who have tried over and over again, attracted by their charm, and are still as far from solving their problems as at the beginning.

Ruellia. Acanthaceae. North and South America

Ruellias when quite small bear large tube flowers which flare into five lobes. The colors are blue, purple, and red. *R. makoyana* and *R. amoena*, the most commonly cultivated, are red. The leaves, green with white veins and red reverses, are opposite on the stem, which branches on older plants, and the flowers grow in whorls in the axils. Both North and South American plants will bloom in winter. The former are occasionally available from greenhouses or southern seedsmen.

Plant in Sandy Soil Mix and keep well watered, fertilizing with organic solutions. A position 4 inches below the lights is sufficient. They can be trimmed nicely. Keep them warm and humid. Cuttings will root easily.

Ruellias attract spider mites but do not suffer from Kelthane dips or sprays.

Scilla violacea. Liliaceae. South Africa

The flowers of this *Scilla* appear with regularity in the spring and, though rather insignificant and greenish purple in color, give me the justification for including them among the blooming plants. It is such a satisfactory one that it would be a shame to leave it out.

The chief beauty is in the leaves which are narrow, 6 inches long, beautifully mottled with dark green over light silvery green, and deep red beneath. The bulbs are small and propagate rapidly so that in a couple of years you can have a handsome potful.

They are very easy to grow in Sandy Soil Mix at the ends of the lights and can be allowed to dry out partially between waterings. Manure or other organic water supplied monthly is sufficient. The plant does not like very hot summer days and prefers cool, though not cold, temperatures.

Spathiphyllum. Araceae. Tropical America

This is one of the easiest of all plants to grow and flower. It will take more abuse than almost any other plant, suffering watering and dryness with equal stoicism. Accustomed to shade, like many of the other aroids, a position near the light garden is sufficient and this is probably the only plant in our repertoire which will bloom under office ceiling lights.

The flower is closely related in color and form to our wild Callas—that is, a white spathe with a yellow spadix. The bloom is principally in winter but may turn up at any time during the year. They need very little fertilizer. Soil can be any packaged houseplant mix or African Violet Mix. They will grow in sphagnum or osmunda as well.

S. *clevelandii*, a doubtful botanical name, is the one used in florist shops for one of the most satisfactory species. The leaves are a foot long and rather narrow.

S. *floribundum* has round shiny leaves and somewhat broader spadices. From 6 to 8 inches high, it is just right for the light garden but requires more humidity and warmth.

S. *candidum* is a similar, smaller plant.

The *spathiphyllums* are particularly useful in floor gardens, providing interesting tropical foliage and bright white flowers with very little light. They are propagated by cutting of the offsets, which are freely produced, at root level.

Stapelia. Asclepiadaceae. Carrion Flower. South Africa

The Stapelias are a large genus of South African plants which resemble columnar spineless cacti and bear flowers that are large in relation to the size and height of the stems. In the greenhouse or out-of-doors in the South they bloom in the fall but under lights they can be induced to generate buds throughout the year. In most species the flowers last a couple of days at most. Nevertheless, they can be recommended because the form and coloration is unique in the plant world.

The most popular of the Stapelias is S. *nobilis* which has four-angled leafless stems up to 6 inches long. The flower is 11 inches across, star-shaped, buff with burgundy stripes. Naturally, the bud is huge and looks like a turnip-shaped balloon. The corolla springs open petal by petal in a matter of half an hour and lasts two or three days. It has an unpleasant odor close up and attracts flies, but at a distance of a few feet the smell is unnoticeable.

Planted in a small pot, say 3 inches, Stapelia will trail its stems along the shelf. The flower will lie half on its surface as it does in nature.

Although S. *nobilis* is the most spectacular of the genus, other members are better light garden plants and quite showy enough. S. *hirsuta* produces a 4-inch burgundy-colored star covered with inch-long hairs. S. *variegata* has crisp yellow stars dotted with red and an inner superimposed structure called an annular ring which looks something like a Life Saver. Both these plants have 5- to 7-inch stems and will bloom intermittently throughout the year. There are many other interesting species which should be tried.

Stapelias should be planted in Sandy Soil Mix in a 3- or 4-inch pot. Even when big they require very little room for their roots. Water at least once a week and keep the plants within 4 inches of the tubes. Fertilize every three months with 20-20-20 solution. If the plants are underwatered the stems will retain their green color but shrivel. Watering will plump them out immediately. If they are overwatered the stems will become pulpy and turn yellow. Cut off any rotten stem and just don't water for a while. On the whole though, Stapelias are quite tolerant of water and will bloom more often if kept moist.

In the tribe of the *Stapeliae* there are many genera which offer plants of almost equal interest to the light gardener. *Duvallia, Huernia, Caralluma, Piaranthus,* and *Hoodia* are just a few of these. Some are quite small plants but all produce unusual-looking flowers of relatively large size. All of these plants grow much more rapidly than the cacti.

To propagate, simply fill a pot with vermiculite and set sections of the stem, the end dusted with hormone powder, into it. Allow the vermiculite to soak up water from the bottom the first time and then water only once every three weeks. Very fine roots and new growth will develop quickly. Then repot in regular Sandy Soil Mix.

Thunbergia alata. Acanthaceae. Black-eyed Susan Vine. Tropical Africa

There are not many vines suitable for growing under lights. Either they must be able to bloom on rather short lengths or permit pruning back to shrubby growth. Black-eyed Susan Vine fulfills the first requirement. Within eight weeks of sowing in a 2½-inch pot it will put forth its showy creamy yellow flowers with the deep purple throats. In doing so it hangs down from the shelf but will have sufficient light to continue. It can be started at any time during the year and kept within reasonable size by pruning from time to time. Although usually a late summer flower, in the greenhouse it will bloom most of the time under lights.

Thunbergia can be planted in ordinary African Violet Mix and must be kept well watered. It will tolerate pot binding to a considerable extent. Humidity of 70 percent or more and warm temperatures of 65 degrees or better encourage flowering. I prefer to use organic fertilizer with this plant.

The color and size of the flowers make this a very desirable addition to the light garden which, relative to the amount of bloom, is not a space monopolizer.

Torenia. Scrophulariaceae. Wishbone Flower. Annual. Eastern Asia

This popular garden and pot plant can be easily grown under lights. Catalogs list them by size and color rather than species. Growing about a foot high they bear rich velvety blue flowers with a white or golden throat, the shape a vertically narrowed funnel which is flared at the opening. The stamens, rising out of the throat, face each other like the two ends of a wishbone. There is also a white form.

Torenias can usually be bought at the nursery in the spring but are also easy to raise from seed like any annual. Give them Sandy Soil Mix (you can also try African Violet Mix) and allow plenty of room for root growth. For winter bloom plant in July, for late spring in January. Give them plenty of water during active growth.

Chapter 17

THE CULINARY HERB GARDEN

The city cook has long suffered from inability to acquire fresh herbs on the market and has been restricted to the use of the dried products. This is not an unmitigated disaster, for certain herbs are better in the sauce dry than fresh —Tarragon, for instance. But there are many uses to which the dried herb cannot be put. Now fluorescent light has solved most, though by no means all, of the problems. We still cannot raise the really tall plants—at least not in the usual modest-sized home light garden. But we can grow most of the kitchen herbs and have them all year round—a distinct improvement over the outdoor garden. In fact, the country gardener who wants fresh herbs in winter must turn to light gardening.

WHERE TO PLACE THE HERB GARDEN

In a house the cellar is always an ideal place for an herb garden. But for convenience, in apartments especially, it belongs in the kitchen. There, it can be set under the kitchen cabinets on a permanent worktable. Placed against the wall it is not in the way and utilizes space which is usually wasted. All the herbal requirements of the household can easily be raised in a space 12 inches by 24 inches. Cooking gases do not seem to affect the plants unfavorably.

EQUIPMENT

All you need is the following:

1. A two-tube, 24-inch fluorescent fixture with reflector. This is standard commercial equipment and can be bought or ordered in any electrical supply store or from Sears.

2. A 24-hour electric timer to turn your lights on and off with an interval of sixteen hours illumination daily.

3. A plastic tray 22 to 24 inches long and at least 12 inches wide.

4. Some means of supporting the pots above the bottom of the tray. This can be pebbles or crushed charcoal. But much better is a sheet of plastic crate about one-half inch thick. This is clean material and light in weight. You can buy it from plastic dealers.

5. A plastic bread box with clear domed cover for propagating.

6. Two-inch square plastic pots for the first transplant and 4-inchers for the permanent potting of the larger plants.

7. You can use garden soil but it should be sterilized before use. Indoor gardeners have not found it as satisfactory as the artificial soils. You are better off with a bag each of sphagnum moss (milled), perlite, and vermiculite. All three can be bought at garden centers and gardeners' supply houses. The perlite and vermiculite are also available in small packages at variety stores. You will also need some lime in the form of crushed eggshells or packaged horticultural lime.

8. A bottle of fish emulsion fertilizer and a can of 20-20-20 chemical fertilizer. Plants in the house need more fertilizer than out-of-doors.

PROPAGATING

Whenever any of the plants listed below can be propagated by cuttings you will have a head start and better results if you buy a plant or two and make cuttings, treating them according to the instructions in our section on propagation.

Plant seeds in a bed of moistened milled sphagnum moss in your plastic bread box. Make little rows across the narrow part, plant, and label the box on the outside with the names of the seeds in each row. A dozen seeds are usually sufficient and more for your needs. Another simple way to begin is to use Jiffy 7s or One-Step Seed Starters (Park Seed Co.). These are compressed fibrous discs which expand when soaked in water. Plant one or two seeds in each just below the surface.

Whichever method you use, place your propagating tray with the cover nearly touching the lights. Keep the top closed if the medium is just moist but open it up for a while if the plastic becomes densely clouded or drops appear, indicating excess moisture. After the seedlings come up leave the top partly open and transplant as soon as there are four real leaves. Later on some of the herbs suffer in transplanting.

MIX FOR THE POTS

For most herbs a mixture of 1 part sphagnum moss, 1 part perlite and 1 part vermiculite is suitable. In a few instances I have given cultural directions (below) which call for a leaner mixture.

LIGHT

Use Cool White commercial tubes or one each Warm White and Daylight.

THE HERBS

The major commercial herb gardens issue catalogs which list the characteristics of the plants, their culinary or medicinal uses, and give some tips on culture. Many plants are included which are much too coarse and big for indoor gardening.

Basil

A must in the culinary herb garden. Fresh, it is fine in salads and especially with tomatoes. Dried, it can be used in most sauces. It is also one of the easiest to grow. The most suitable kind for light gardening is *Ocimum minimum*, the Bush Basil, which is green and small leaved. Seeds germinate and grow easily under lights. When it is 4 inches high start cutting for table use and, as it becomes pot-bound, switch from a 2-inch to a 4-inch pot. There it will last a year, supplying quantities of leaves. If you want it to continue to bush do not allow it to flower.

One plant is really all you need because cuttings root within a week in moist vermiculite and will do almost as well in water. Keep the plant moist at all times.

Chervil, Curly

Chervil is considered by gourmets more delicate than Parsley. Actually the flavor is quite different. Whereas Parsley is slightly bitter and musty, Chervil has a faint taste of licorice. Use as a garnish, and in salads and sauces. It can be dried or frozen.

Seeds germinate easily within a few days. For this plant I prefer a rather richer medium, say one part peat moss, one part perlite, and one part vermiculite. As it is a shade-loving plant it does well under the lights and need not be near the center of the tubes once out of the seedling stage. Do not pot bind, but move to a 4-inch pot as soon as it has developed four or five large leaves. Keep moist. The botanical name is *Anthriscus cerefolium*.

Chives, Onion (Allium schoenoprasum)

Light gardening really does nothing for Chives which, as we know, grow well on a windowsill. Starting from seed is not advisable because a couple of years are required to mature the plants and they require a winter freeze to come back fresh in the spring. You are better off to buy the little clusters of growing bulbs and leaves from your grocer or vegetable man and just keep them growing under the lights. Cutting them regularly, for egg dishes, spreads, mashed potatoes, etc., keeps them sprouting. But once they start to die down there is not much you can do. A couple of months in the refrigerator may rejuvenate them but it is hardly worth the trouble.

Dittany of Crete (Origanum dictamnus)

The leaves have a pleasant minty odor but no special use in the kitchen. Dittany does make a nice bushy little plant and will propagate from cuttings.

Lavender, English (Lavandula officinalis)

This is another plant which has no culinary purpose but you may want to grow it for its fragrant dried leaves which are used to perfume linen. Seedlings have an annoying way of damping off even in sphagnum moss, but if you can get a plant or two going and keep it trimmed it will make a nice shrub and may even produce its fragile bluish flowers. Contrary to many herbs, this one must be kept quite dry. Water lightly only when the soil in the pot is dry all through. Propagation from cuttings is easier than from seed. The Munstead strain is dwarf.

Lettuce

The house is not really the place to grow lettuce of any kind because of its bulk in growth and use. But you may find it fun to try the dwarf Bibb Lettuce which will grow nicely in a 4-inch pot and will provide a succession of leaves if it is trimmed regularly. Grow it from seed and keep it moist.

Marjoram, Sweet (Majorana hortensis)

Although familiar by name to nearly everybody, Marjoram's use in cooking is little known. The flavor is that of a very mild Oregano. Where the latter is overpowering and is most useful in specifically Italian dishes, Marjoram is so delicate that it can be used plentifully with eggs, sauces, in salad dressings, in herb coatings for meats, and in soups.

The seeds sprout within a few days under the lights and we have had no trouble with its reputed tendency to damp off. Transplanting should take place after the first four true leaves are formed. Trimming can start when the plants are about four inches high. Cuttings root easily. The plant stays compact and the little leaves are most attractive.

Mint

There are various kinds of mint offered by the herb farms of which the most familiar are the true peppermint and spearmint. We are generally advised that the only use of these herbs is in candy and juleps. But try them fresh in salads—they're great.

Mints grow by runners that root on the surface. Buy a plant and you can start a mint plantation by pinning down the stems in the soil of nearby pots. Most of them will do quite nicely in quite moderate light but should be kept moist at all times. The tendency is to straggle.

Mentha pulegium, Pennyroyal, is worth knowing for its delightful fresh minty odor and delicate flavor. It is great as a garnish and as a salad green.

Parsley (Petroselinum crispum)

It is surprising how well Parsley does under the lights. It germinates rapidly and should be moved to a 4-inch pot where it will flourish for a season. When it dies down start another round of seed. Keep moist and in bright light.

Rosemary (Rosmarinus officinalis)

This is a perfect pot plant under lights. Grow Rosemary from seed or from cuttings which root within a few days. None of the other herbs lives so long. If you trim with care and art you may, in a year or two, be able to shape it into a perfect little Bonsai tree, with gnarled trunk and needlelike leaves suggesting an ancient fir tree. The very pungent leaves are somewhat piney and wonderful with lamb or fish dishes. Only one cultural direction is necessary. Keep it constantly moist. If the soil dries out the plant will die. It does quite well at the ends of the tubes in rather poor light. The prostrate Rosemary is far less vigorous in the house.

Sage (Salvia officinalis)

Everybody knows that Sage goes with pork. But, in small amounts, it is a tasty herb with veal and chicken, and should be used more often. The plant is a perennial which grows 12 inches tall with furry gray leaves and pretty blue flowers. We have had trouble with seed damping off, but if you plant enough to start with there will always be a few survivors—enough for the house. Keep the plants moist and in the brightest spot under the lights. Trim to make it bush.

Savory, Winter (Satureja montana)

Adding Savory to the water in which you cook dried and lima beans prevents flatulence and adds pungency. Use it also in herb coatings for pork and veal. It always seems to be used in the dried state.

Seeds germinate quickly and well. Once you have a plant, propagation can be by means of cuttings and pinning stems down into the soil of a nearby pot (soil layering). Keep in a very bright position under lights and fairly dry. Unlike Summer Savory, the winter variety will grow into a nice little shrub with time.

Strawberry

We have had success with 'Alexandria,' a Strawberry which produces fruit the first year from seed. Ours started to bloom and set fruit in twelve weeks and the crop was continuous and plentiful. Anybody who doubts that indoor grown fruit is as good in flavor as it is from the garden should try Strawberries. It's a thrill to gather them in midwinter.

The Alexandria is a runnerless plant which looks beautiful in a 4-inch pot with its upstanding leaves. Place it near the center of the lights (although it will do quite well at the ends) for best results, keep well watered, and give it plenty of dried cow manure or fish emulsion as fertilizer. Cool temperatures, below 80 at the most, encourage bloom and fruit.

Tarragon (Artemisia dracunculus)

My favorite herb is also one of the more difficult ones to grow in the house. The wonderfully aromatic sweet leaves are far more fragrant when dried. So you will need a good crop to amount to anything.

Seed propagation does not work so you must buy a plant. Get one in the spring so that you can get it started in full vigor under the lights. If you buy in the fall when the plant has partly died down it will not recover. But when young it will get used to the lights and continue to grow. Start cuttings of replacement plants immediately. Tarragon requires a rather peaty mix of two parts peat, one part perlite, and one part vermiculite. It also requires your brightest light.

Thyme

The many kinds of Thyme, all delicious, have endless uses in the kitchen. The only problem is producing enough of the tiny leaves. Most of them are creepers requiring a gritty soil. To your regular mix add one part lime chips and keep on the dry side in bright light. It is best to buy plants and to take cuttings or soil layer the stems.

Chapter 18

PLANTS FOR CHILDREN

Reared from their tenderest years on a steady diet of television heroes and commercials, inducing a child to take some interest in plants is a project calculated to daunt most parents and teachers. On the other hand, the artificiality of urban living, in which a greater percentage of the population is involved each year, makes the preservation of a link with nature increasingly urgent. The lettuce and radish school of child botany no longer suffices; indeed, it never was very effective. Happily, new techniques of indoor horticulture and the exciting plants which can be grown as never before will make the task easier. Here are some suggestions for dealing with the problem.

To start with, it is not enough to maintain plants in other rooms of the house or apartment—they must be in the child's own room, and the earlier in his life the better. Provide the simplest of fluorescent light stands and a few well chosen plants. Do not crowd them. In so doing half the battle has been won for he will grow up with them and be conscious of them as constituting part of the normal "furniture" of his world. Children treasure the familiar and you will find that the withdrawal of a plant will be really missed.

You may raise the significance of plants a notch above an object—closer to a pet—by speaking of them not as "they" but by their names. Use a shortening of the common or Latin name when it sounds right or is suggestive—Freckleface for the Freckleface Plant or Hypo for *Hypocyrta*. In this way the plant achieves a degree of personality in the child's mind.

Those who detest personalizing plants, as practiced by some *adults*, should recognize that for a *child* this is an essential part of the identification process— not a piece of whimsy. I should also like to remind them that all the cultivars have names which are nothing but the caprice of their originators. 'Freckles,' 'Prince Valiant,' and 'Sneezy' are no better or worse than the nicknames we may suggest, or a child may himself invent and enjoy using. Certainly teaching him to say *Hypocyrta nummularia* at four years of age makes no sense at all, particularly as the average parent cannot either spell or pronounce the name correctly.

When we acquired a large round cactus heavily covered with spines our children immediately named it Willis, after a character in one of Heinlein's outer space stories. The spines turned brilliant red when sprayed with water. When this happened the children said that Willis was blushing and they loved to show off this trick to their friends. Without any special encouragement this identification of a plant with a fictional character laid the groundwork for an enduring affection regarding plants in general.

From about five years a child will readily and cheerfully learn to carry out certain responsibilities in the household. He can be induced very easily to take care of the plants himself. Since children like a sense of possession, keep a little watering can, a small amount of fertilizer, packaged soil, and an extra pot or two in his room. Use only these for taking care of his plants. Start by handing him the watering can so that he can join in. You will find that sheer curiosity and imitation will cause him to take over the other chores with very little effort. Gradually it can become a habit to care for the plants as he does for his animal pet, discovering that the need for food, water, and even trimming, are very similar.

If there is a slackening in care just inquire if the plant is not too dry or whether it has been fed this week. Do not expect his span of interest to be greater in this case than in playing with any one of his toys. Sheer forgetfulness may be all that is involved. Assume the job yourself for a day or two. Do not force and do not chide. Parental solicitude is fine but it should not be manifested by worrying and warning. There would be no better way to make the child lose interest, for he then judges that the matter is not his own but the concern of an adult. If he asks questions, do not shrug them off but find the answers; they are available in books. There is nothing deadlier than the effect of a parent refusing to answer out of ignorance and the unwillingness to do anything about it.

Children love activity and things which are small in keeping with their own dimensions. So children's plants should be little ones in little pots (light garden plants are ideal) and they should *do* things or have some special attraction such as closing their petals at night, rooting by runners along the surface of the soil, or having leaves that shrink from the touch. Naturally they should also be easy to maintain.

These are my criteria for choosing those listed below as among the plants which are suitable.

Dollbaby (flowers, seeds)
Dwarf Pomegranate (for flower and fruit)
Euphorbia bojeri (flowers and spines)
Miniature African Violet (for flowers)
Oxalis (leaf movement)
Queen of the Abyss (texture of leaves)
Rosary Vine (leaves and flowers, vining habit)

Strawberry Geranium, Saxifraga sarmentosa

This easy plant has beautifully veined leaves and runners which grow little plants at the tips. These can be planted in little pots while still attached to the parent so that a single plant may have a ring of offspring.

Kalanchoe beharensis

A plant notable for the thickness of the leaves and a surface texture which is like a tight hard pile. It should be grown in Sandy Soil Mix with maximum light.

Freckleface Plant. Hypoestes sanguinolenta

The leaves are speckled with pink dots. A fast grower. Cuttings root with the greatest ease in African Violet Mix. The flowers are pretty, too.

Any of the Miracle Plants not mentioned here are also excellent for the purpose of interesting children in plants.

These and similar plants can also be raised in the classroom. Attracting the attention and interest of the children will depend on the knowledge and the interest of the teacher. The forms of flowers, methods of cross-pollination, seed formation, and germination *can* be made fascinating to anybody. The only serious stumbling block—and this applies particularly to the American male, even in childhood—is the persistent tradition which relegates an interest in plants other than crops to females. When this prejudice has been removed it is certainly as easy to teach plant lore as, say, mineral or animal lore. Once the barrier is breached there should be no difficulty in securing the participation of students of both sexes in the care of the plants, in the course of which they will see the abstract information they are receiving become reality.

APPENDIXES

Short Glossary of Botanical Terms Used in This Book

Axil—The joint between any parts of the plant above soil level. Where two branches meet. Where the petiole of a leaf meets the stem.

Bract—A modified leaf, often growing just below a flower or even partly enclosing it as in Bromeliads.

Calyx—The outer perianth of the flower. The divisions are called sepals and usually have the same number as the flower has lobes or petals. The calyx persists after the flower drops off.

Clone—See full discussion on pages 134–135. A plant resulting from vegetative propagation.

Corm—A solid bulb.

Corolla—The inner perianth. It consists of the separate or joined petals.

Diploid—An organism which in an embryonic state has a normal double complement of chromosomes.

Epiphyte—A plant that grows on trees, not in the ground.

Habit—The general pattern of growth in a plant—its appearance.

Hybrid—A cross of two species.

Inflorescence—The flowering part of a plant.

Meristem—The ultimate rows of cells in a growing tip; nascent tissue.

Monopodial—Used in describing orchid plants; an orchid with a single stem much like a vine.

Panicle—A loose compound inflorescence, each flower having its own pedicel.

Pedicel—The stalk of a single flower.

Peduncle—A stalk bearing more than one flower.

Perianth—The flower, consisting of the corolla and calyx.

233

Petiole—A leaf stalk.

Raceme—A simple inflorescence of pediceled flowers arranged one on top of the other.

Rhizome—A subterranean or prostrate surface stem which roots at the nodes.

Scape—A naked flowering stem rising from the ground.

Sepal—A division of the calyx.

Spadix—A fleshy flower-bearing spike like the Jack in Jack-in-the-Pulpit.

Spathe—A large bract enclosing the spadix like the pulpit in Jack-in-the-Pulpit.

Stolon—A runner or any basal branch which is inclined to root. A kind of rooting sucker.

Sympodial—Refers to orchids which produce a series of pseudobulbs.

Tepal—The word used for sepals and petals combined when they are not readily differentiated, for instance with Lilies.

Tetraploid—An embryo with double the diploid number of chromosomes. Tetraploids are fertile and often especially vigorous. Hybrids with an unequal number of chromosomes are infertile.

Truss—A terminal cluster of flowers.

Tuberous—Having the appearance of a tuber or growing from a tuber.

Umbel—An inflorescence consisting of a cluster springing from the same level. Usually it is flat topped.

Vandaceous—Like the growth of a Vanda (*Orchidaceae*) or similar to Vanda. Of monopodial growth.

Where to Buy Plants

BROMELIADS

Alberts & Merkel, Inc., Boynton Beach, Florida 33435. Catalog 50¢.

Bennett's Bromeliads & Bonsai, POB 1532, Winter Park, Florida 32789.

Cornellison Bromeliads, 225 San Bernardino, North Fort Myers, Florida 33903.

Fantastic Gardens, 95505 West 67th Avenue, South Miami, Florida 33156.

Holmes Bromeliad Nursery, 19395 S.W. 248 Street, Homestead, Florida 33612.

Hummel's Exotic Gardens, 3926 Park Drive, Carlsbad, California 92008.

Lowe, Paul P., 23045 S.W. 123 Rd., Goulds, Florida 33170. List 10¢.

Marz Bromeliads, 10782 Citrus Avenue, Moorpark, California 93021. List 12¢.

Perner's Bromeliads, 302 East South Cross, San Antonio, Texas 78214.

CACTI AND SUCCULENTS

Abbey Gardens, 18007 Topham Street, Reseda, California 91335. Catalog.

Cactus by Mueller, 10411 Rosedale Hwy., Bakersfield, California.

Cactus Seed Co., POB 162, Toronto 9, Canada. Seed list.

Cactusville, Edinburg, Texas 78539.

Desert Plant Co., Box 780, Marfa, Texas 79843.

Henrietta's Nursery, 1345 North Brawley Avenue, Fresno, California 93705.

Jack's Cactus Gardens, 1707 W. Robindale Street, W. Covina, California 91790.

Johnson Cactus Gardens, Box 458, Paramount, California 90723.

New México Cactus Research, POB 787, Belen, New Mexico 87002.

The Plantsman Greenhouse, 2142 Gerritsen Avenue, Brooklyn, New York 11229.

Wright, C., 11011 Tarawa Drive, Los Alamitos, California 90720. List 25¢.

GERANIUMS (MINIATURE)

Carobil Farm, Church Road, Brunswick, Maine 04011.

Cook's Geranium Nursery, 712 North Grand, Lyons, Kansas 67554.

Edelweiss Gardens, Box 66, Robbinsville, New Jersey.

G. & F. Geraniums, Lac du Bonnet, Manitoba, Canada. Catalog $1.00.

Logee's Greenhouses, Danielson, Connecticut. Catalog 50¢.

Merry Gardens, Camden, Maine 04843. Catalog $1.00.

Norvell Greenhouses, 318 Greenacres Road, Greenacres, Washington 99016. Catalog.

Wilson Bros., Roachdale, Indiana, 46172. Catalog.

GESNERIADS

Antonelli Brothers, 2545 Capitola Road, Santa Cruz, California 95062. Catalog. Principally Gloxinias.

Arndt's Floral Gardens, 20454 N.E. Sandy Blvd., Troutdale, Oregon 97060.

Buell's Greenhouses, Eastford, Connecticut 06242. Catalog $1.00.

Button, Milburn O., POB 232, Crestwood, Kentucky 40014. List 10¢.

Constantinov. Violets By, 3321 21st Street, San Francisco, California 94110. Saintpaulias.

Craven's Greenhouse, 2732 West Tennessee, Denver, Colorado 80219.

Dee's Garden, E-3803 19th Avenue, Spokane, Washington 99203.

Easterbrook, L., Greenhouses, 10 Craig Street, Butler, Ohio 44822.

Engert's Violet House, 7457 Schyler Drive, Omaha, Nebraska 68114.

Evlo African Violets, 3917 Copeland Lane, Fremont, California 94538.

Feece, Susan, Route No. 3, Walkerton, Indiana 46574.

Fischer Greenhouses, Linwood, New Jersey 08221. Catalog.

Frathel's Originations, 252 Clay Avenue, Rochester, New York 14613.

Gesneriad Jungle, 2507 Washington Pike, Knoxville, Tennessee 37917.

Granger Gardens, Route 2, 1060 Wilbur Road, Medina, Ohio 33256.

Harborcrest Nurseries, 1425 Benvenuto Avenue, Victoria, B.C., Canada.

Hobby Nursery, 5230 Franklin Blvd., Sacramento, California 95820.

Houser, Don H., 2507 Washington Pk., Knoxville, Tennessee 37917.

Kartuz Greenhouses, 92 Chestnut Street, Wilmington, Massachusetts 01887. Outstanding list of Gesneriads, Begonias, etc. Catalog 25¢.

Lake's Violets, 4265 N.W. 11 Street, Des Moines, Iowa 50313.

Lauray of Salisbury, Undermountain Road, Salisbury, Connecticut 06068. Fine and varied list of plants.

Lyon, Lyndon, 14 Mutchler Street, Dolgeville, New York 13329. Botanical Gesneriads and Saintpaulias. List.

Madison Gardens, 6355 Nuddke Ridge Road, Madison, Ohio 44057.

Mary's African Violets, 19788 San Juan, Detroit, Michigan 48221.

Norvell Greenhouses, 318 Greenacres Rd., Greenacres, Washington 99016. Catalog.

O.K. Violets, 82220 Secor Road, Lambertville, Michigan.

Park, Geo. W., Seed Co., Greenwood, South Carolina 29647. Catalog.

Payne's Violets and Gesneriads, 6612 Leavenworth Road, Kansas City, Kansas 66104.

Quality Violet House, Route 3, Box 947, Walkerton, Indiana 46574.

Richter's Greenhouses, 9529 Indianapolis Blvd., Highland, Indiana 46322.

Ridge, Harvey J., 1126 Arthur Street, Wausau, Wisconsin 54401. Gesneriads and supplies. List 10¢.

Rose Knoll Gardens, Assumption, Illinois 62510.

Routh, Mrs. Bert, Lewisburg, Missouri 65685.

Schmelling's African Violets, 5133 Peck Hill Road, Jamesville, New York 13078. Also supplies.

Scotsward Violet Farm, 71 Hanover Road, Florham Park, New Jersey 07932. Botanical Saintpaulias.

Spidell's Fine Plants, Junction City, Oregon 97448. Catalog.

The Green House, 9515 Flower Street, Bellflower, California 90706.

Tinari Greenhouses, 2325 Valley Road, Huntingdon Valley, Pennsylvania 19006. Outstanding list.

Tropical Gardens, Rte. 1, Box 143, Greenwood, Indiana 46322.

Tropical Nursery, 10343 No. 99 Highway, Stockton, California 95025.

Tropical Paradise Greenhouse, 8825 West 79th Street, Overland Park, Kansas. Catalog 50¢.

Volkart, Mrs. Leonard, Russelville, Missouri 65074.

Volkmann Bros. Greenhouses, 2714 Minert Street, Dallas, Texas 75219. List.

West Coast Gesneriads, 2179 44th Avenue, San Francisco, California 94116. Fine list.

Whistling Hill, Box 27, Hamburg, New York 14075. Botanical Gesneriads. List.

Wyrtzen Exotic Plants, 165 Bryant Avenue, Floral Park, New York 11001. List.

HERBS

Caprilands Herb Farm, North Coventry, Connecticut.
Greene Herb Gardens, Greene, Rhode Island 02827.
Hemlock Hill Herb Farm, Litchfield, Connecticut 06759.
Merry Gardens, Camden, Maine 04843.

HOUSEPLANTS, MISCELLANEOUS

Armacost & Royston Inc., POB 25576, West Los Angeles, California.
Burgess Seed & Plant Co., 67 East Battle Street, Galesburg, Michigan 49053.
Dee's Garden, 19th Avenue, Spokane, Washington 99203. Listings 10¢ each.
Edelweiss Gardens, Box 66, Robbinsville, New Jersey 08691.
Garden Nook, The, Box 5023, Raleigh, North Carolina 27600.
Greenland Flower Shop, Port Matilda, Pennsylvania 16870. List 25¢.
Lauray of Salisbury, Undermountain Road, Salisbury, Connecticut 06068.
Logee's Greenhouses, Danielson, Connecticut. Catalog 50¢.
Loyce's Flowers, Rt. 2, Granbury, Texas 76048. Stamp for list.
McCombs Greenhouses, 900 N. Hague Avenue, Columbus, Ohio 43204. Catalog 25¢.
Merry Gardens, Camden, Maine 04843. Catalog $1.00.
Norvell Greenhouses, 318 S. Greenacres Road, Greenacres, Washington 99016.
Novel Plants, Bridgeton, Indiana 47836. List 10¢.
Plant Oddities, Box 127G, Basking Ridge, New Jersey 07920.
Roehrs Exotic Nurseries, R.D. 2, Box 144, Farmingdale, New Jersey 07727.
Seaborn Del Dio Nursery, Rte. 3, Box 455, Secondido, California 92025.
Garden Nook, The, Box 5023, Raleigh, North Carolina 27600.
Tropical Gardens, Box 143, Greenwood, Indiana 46142.
Tropical Paradise Greenhouse, 8825 West 79th Street, Overland Park, Kansas 66104.
Williford's Nursery, Rte. 3, Smithfield, North Carolina 27577. Catalog 16¢.

ORCHIDS

Alberts & Merkel, Inc., Boynton Beach, Florida. Catalog 50¢.
Casa Luna Orchids, Star Route 1, Box 219, Beaufort, South Carolina 29902.
Fennell Orchid Company, 26715 S.W. 157 Avenue, Homestead, Florida 33030.
Fort Caroline Orchids, 13142 Fort Caroline Rd., Jacksonville, Florida.
Freed, Arthur, Orchids Inc., 5731 So. Bonsall Drive, Malibu, California 90265. *Phalaenopsis.*

Hager, Herb, Orchids, Box 544, Santa Cruz, California 95060.

Hausermann's Orchids, Inc., Addison Road and North Avenue, Elmhurst, Illinois 60126. Catalog.

Ilgenfritz, Margaret, Orchids, POB 665, Monroe, Michigan 48161.

J&L Orchids, 20 Sherwood Road, Easton, Connecticut.

Jones & Scully, Inc., 2200 N.W. 33rd Avenue, Miami, Florida 33142. Catalog.

Kirch, Wm., Ltd., 2630 Waiomao Road, Honolulu, Hawaii 96876.

Lager & Hurrell, 426 Morris Avenue, Summit, New Jersey 07901. Catalog $2.00.

Lowe, Paul P., 23045 S.W. 123 Road, Goulds, Florida, 33170.

McLellan, Rod, Co., 1450 El Camino Real, South San Francisco, California 94080.

Penn Valley Orchids, 239 Old Guelph Road, Wynnewood, Pennsylvania 19096.

Schaffer's Tropical Gardens, 1220 41st Avenue, Santa Cruz, California 95060. *Paphiopedilums* and *Phalaenopsis*. Catalog.

Thornton's Orchids, 3200 N. Military Trail, West Palm Beach, Florida 33401.

TERRARIUM PLANTS AND SUPPLIES

Many of the best terrarium plants can be purchased from the *Gesneriad* nurseries and from other exotic gardens. Bonsai supplies are often useful. The following short list contains some useful names:

Allgrove, Arthur Eames, North Wilmington, Massachusetts 01887. Catalog 25¢.

Armstrong Associates, Inc., Box 127, Basking Ridge, New Jersey 07920. Carnivorous plants. Catalog 25¢.

Barrington Greenhouses, 860 Clemente Road, Barrington, New Jersey 08007.

Bolduc's Greenhill Nursery, 2131 Vallejo Street, St. Helena, California 94574. Exotic ferns.

Comstock Nurseries, POB 158, Grosse Isle, Michigan 48138. Bonsai. Catalog.

Japan Artisans, 15 West Ferry Street, New Hope, Pennsylvania 18938. Bonsai pots.

Oakhurst Gardens, POB 444, Arcadia, California 91008. Carnivorous plants.

O'Hara, Helen, Glen Head, Long Island, New York 11545. Feather Rock. Miniature plants.

Savage Gardens, POB 163, McMinnville, Tennessee 37110.

SEEDS

The most interesting experiments may be made with annuals and tropical perennials of small size which are not in general cultivation under lights. For catalogs of much greater extent and variety the English seedsmen are incomparable. The horticultural societies of different countries will usually supply the names of seedsmen.

Al & Son Company, POB 2256, Cleveland, Ohio, 44100. Catalog 25¢.

Arndt's Floral Garden, 20454 N.E. Sandy Blvd., Troutdale, Oregon 97060.

Brudy, John, Rare Plant House, POB 84, Cocoa Beach, Florida 32931.

Burpee, W. Atlee,Co., Hunting Park Ave., Philadelphia, Pa. 19132.

German, H. G., 103 Bank Street, Smithport, Pennsylvania.

Herbst Bros., 1000 N. Main Street, Brewster, New York 10509.

Morgan, Shirley, 2042 Encinal Avenue, Alameda, California 94501. List 30¢.

Olds Seed Co., Box 1069, Madison, Wisconsin 53701.

Park, Géo. W., Seed Co., Greenwood, South Carolina 29647. Catalog.

Saier, Henry E., Dimondale, Michigan 48221. Catalog 50¢.

Vaughan's Seed Co., 5300 Katrine, Downer's Grove, Illinois 60515 and Chimney
   Rock Road, Bound Brook, New Jersey 08805.

Many of the plant societies have seed funds. The lists are printed in their
publications.

Fluorescent Lighting Equipment and Gardening Supplies

FLUORESCENT LIGHTING EQUIPMENT

ABC Supply Co., 220 West 83rd Street, New York, New York 10024.

Armstrong Associates, Inc., Box 127 BK, Basking Ridge, New Jersey, 07920.
   Catalog 25¢.

Burgess Seed & Plant Co., 67 E. Battle Street, Galesburg, Michigan 49053.

Craft-House Manufacturing Co., Wilson, New York 10706.

Crea, Frank, 1274 Adee Avenue, Bronx, New York 10469.

Emerson Industries, Inc., 132 Adams Avenue, Hempstead, L.I., New York.

Flora Greenhouses, Box 1191, Burlingame, California 94010.

Floralite Company, 4124 East Oakwood Road, Oak Creek, Wisconsin 53221.

Green House, The, 9515 Flower Street, Bellflower, California 90706.

Greenhouse Specialties Co., 9849 Kimker Lane, St. Louis, Missouri 63127.

Greeson, Bernard D., 3548 North Cramer, Milwaukee, Wisconsin 53221.

Growers Supply Co., Ann Arbor, Michigan 48103.

H. P. Supplies, Box 18101, Cleveland, Ohio 44117.

Hall Industries, Inc., 2323 Commonwealth Ave., N. Chicago, Illinois 60064.

House Plant Corner, The, Oxford, Maryland 21654. Catalog 20¢.

Lifelite Incorporated, 1025 Shary Circle, Concord, California 94520.

Lighting, Inc., POB 2228, Raleigh, North Carolina 27602.

Lord & Burnham, Irvington-on-Hudson, New York 10533.

Neas Growers Supply Co., POB 8773, Greenville, South Carolina 29604.

Park, Geo. W. Seed Co., Inc., Greenwood, South Carolina 29646.

Radar Fluorescent Co., 63 15th Street, Brooklyn, New York.

Rapid Lite, 245 South Broadway, Yonkers, New York 10705.

Robbins Electric, Inc., 77–79 Throckmorton Street, Freehold, New Jersey 07728.

Rosetta Electric Company, 21 West 46th Street, New York, New York 10036, and 73 Murray Street, New York, New York 10013.

Shaffer's Tropical Gardens, 1220 41st Avenue, Santa Cruz, California 95060.

Shoplite Co., 566J Franklin Avenue, Nutley, New Jersey 07110. Catalog 25¢.

Sutton Electric Supply Corp., 221 East 59th Street, New York, New York 10022.

Tube Craft, Inc., 1311 W. 80th Street, Cleveland, Ohio 44102.

Verd-a-Ray Corporation, 615 Front Street, Toledo, Ohio 44102.

INDOOR GARDENING SUPPLIES, MISCELLANEOUS

Many firms scattered throughout the country carry supplies which are needed for indoor gardening. They describe their stock in trade as Greenhouse Supplies, Florist Supplies, and Nursery Supplies. Most of the firms listed under *Where to Buy Plants* and *Fluorescent Lighting Equipment* also carry some gardening supplies.

Ambassador All Glass Aquariums, Inc., 4403 Broadway, Island Park, New York 11558. Fused glass terrariums.

Amchem Products, Inc., Ambler, Pennsylvania 19002. Rootone.

American Plant Food Co., Inc., 5258 River Road, Bethesda, Maryland.

Aquarium Stock Co., Inc., 27 Murray Street, New York, New York 10013. Glass and plastic aquariums. Branches in other cities.

Atlas Fish Emulsion Fertilizer, Menlo Park, California 94025.

Baccto Organic Peat, 1 Decker Square, Suite 325, Bala Cynwyd, Penna. 19004.

Burpee, W. Atlee, Co., Hunting Park Ave., Philadelphia, Penna. 19132.

Chapin Watermatics, Inc., 368 N. Colorado Avenue, Watertown, New York 13601.

Chester, J. C., Mfg. Co., 59 Branch Street, St. Louis, Missouri 63147. Plastic terrariums.

Friendly Gardeners, Inc., Box 1, Lake Oswego, Oregon 97034. Organic fertilizer.

Geiger, E. C., Box 2852, Harleyville, Pennsylvania 19438. Automatic misters.

Greeson, Bernard J., 3548 N. Cramer Street, Milwaukee, Wisconsin 53211. Large list of supplies.

Hoffman, A. H. Inc., Landisville, Pennsylvania 17538. Fertilizers.

House Plant Corner, The, Box 165S., Oxford, Maryland 21654. Catalog 20¢.

Hydroponic Chemical Co., Copley, Ohio 44321. Hyponex fertilizers.

Industrial Plastic Supply Co., 324 Canal Street, New York, New York 10013. Plastic boxes, domes, etc.

Koffard, Reed S. Co., POB 453 R., Van Nuys, California 91408. Misters.

Mosser Lee Company, Millston, Wisconsin 54643. Sphagnum moss.

Natural Development Co., The, Box 215, Bainbridge, Pennsylvania 17502. Organic fertilizers.

Paragon Time Control, Three Rivers, Wisconsin. Automatic timers.

Para-Wedge Louver Corporation, 549 Hempstead Turnpike, West Hempstead, L.I., New York 11552. Para-wedge louver manufacturers.

Park, Geo. W., Seed Co., Inc., Greenwood, South Carolina 29646.

Peters, Robert B., Co., Inc., 2833 Pennsylvania Street, Allentown, Pennsylvania. Chemical fertilizers.

Rivermont Orchids, POB 67, Signal Mountain, Tennessee 37377. Orchid supplies.

Saffer, Al, & Co., Inc., 130 West 28th Street, New York 10001. Greenhouse supplies. Large catalog.

South Shore Floral Co., Quentin Place, Woodmere, New York. Miscellaneous gardening supplies.

Sponge-Rok Sales Co., 7112 Hubbard Avenue, Middleton, Wisconsin 53562. Perlite.

Sudbury Laboratories, Inc., Box 1075, Sudbury, Massachusetts 01776. Soil testing equipment.

Tropical Plant Products Inc., Box 7754, 1715 Silver Star Road, Orlando, Florida 32804. Orchid supplies.

Veith, Fred A., 3505 Mozart Avenue, Cincinnati, Ohio 45211. General supplies.

Wick Pots, Inc., 7602 30th St. West, Tacoma, Washington 98466.

Plant Societies and Their Publications

African Violet Society of America
Box 1326 FG
Knoxville, Tennessee 39901
$6.00 annual dues brings five issues of *The African Violet Magazine.*

The American Begonia Society, Inc.
10331 South Colima Road
Whittier, California 90604
Membership and subscription to *The Begonian,* a monthly publication, is $4.00 a year.

American Gesneria Society
Worldway Postal Center
Box 91192, Los Angeles, California 90009
Dues $4.00 (Joint $4.50) per year.
GSN (*Gesneriad Saintpaulia News*)—a splendid publication with much information and many advertisements of equipment and plants.

The American Gloxinia and Gesneriad Society, Inc.
Mrs. Charlotte Rowe, Membership Secretary,
Box 174, New Milford, Connecticut 06776
Annual membership $5.00
The Gloxinian is published bimonthly.

American Orchid Society, Inc.
Botanical Museum of Harvard University
Cambridge, Massachusetts 02138
Annual dues $12.50
American Orchid Society Bulletin is published monthly. An outstanding publication in every respect.

The Bromeliad Society, Inc.
Box 3279
Santa Monica, California 90403
Annual dues $7.50
Journal of the Bromeliad Society is published six times a year.

Indoor Light Gardening Society of America, Inc.
Mrs. James Martin, Membership Secretary
1316 Warren Road
Lakewood, Ohio 44107
Annual dues $5.00.
Light Garden is published six times a year—a must for the light gardener.

Saintpaulia International
Mary Hofer, Membership Chairman
19788 San Juan
Detroit, Michigan 48221
Annual dues $4.00 includes *GSN* (see under American Gesneria Society).

House Plants—A Recommended Reading List

Ballard, Ernesta D., *Garden in Your House*. New York: Harper & Row, $6.95.
Baur, Robert C., *Gardens in Glass Containers*. New York: Hearthside Press, $6.95.
Brandon, Dorothy, and Schneider, Alfred, *Max Schling Book of Indoor Gardening*. New York: Astor-Honor, $6.50.
Brooklyn Botanic Garden, *Gardening in Containers*. New York: Brooklyn Botanic Garden, $1.00.
————, *House Plants*. New York: Brooklyn Botanic Garden, $1.00.
Budlong, Ware, *Indoor Gardens*. New York: Hawthorne Books, $6.95.
Cherry, Elaine C., *Fluorescent Light Gardening*. New York: Van Nostrand–Reinhold, $6.95.
Cruso, Thalassa, *Making Things Grow: A Practical Guide for the Indoor Gardener*. New York: Knopf, $5.95.
Elbert, George, and Hyams, Edward, *House Plants*. New York: Funk & Wagnalls, $7.95.
Fenten, D. X., *Plants for Pots: Projects for Indoor Gardeners* (juvenile). Philadelphia: Lippincott, $4.95.
Field, Xenia, *Growing Bulbs in the House*. New York: St. Martin's Press, $3.95.
Free, Montague, *All About House Plants*. New York: Doubleday, $5.95.

Graf, Alfred B., *Exotica #3: Pictorial Cyclopedia of Exotic Plants—Guide to Care of Plants Indoors.* Rutherford, N.J.: Roehrs, $54.00.

Johnston, Vernon, and Carriere, W., *Easy Guide to Artificial Light Gardening for Pleasure and Profit.* New York: Hearthside Press, $4.50.

Kramer, Jack, *Flowering House Plants Month-by-Month.* New York: Van Nostrand-Reinhold, $5.95.

———, *Gardens Under Glass. The Miniature Greenhouse in Bottle, Bowl or Dish.* New York: Simon & Schuster, $4.95.

———, *1000 Beautiful House Plants and How to Grow Them.* New York: Morrow, $12.95.

Kranz, Frederick and Jacqueline, *Gardening Indoors Under Lights.* New York: Viking Press, $5.95.

Langer, Richard, *The After-Dinner Gardening Book.* New York: Macmillan, $4.95.

Lee, Elsie, *At Home with Plants.* New York: Macmillan, $5.95.

McDonald, Elvin, *The World Book of House Plants.* Cleveland: World Publishing Co., $8.95.

Nehrling, Arno and Irene, *An Easy Guide to House Plants.* New York: Hearthside Press, $2.95.

———, *Propagating House Plants: For Amateur and Commercial Use.* New York: Hearthside Press, $4.95.

Schuler, Stanley, *1001 House Plant Questions Answered.* New York: Van Nostrand-Reinhold, $6.95.

Selsam, Millicent E., *How to Grow House Plants* (juvenile). New York: Morrow, $3.30.

Sullivan, George, *Plants to Grow Indoors* (juvenile). New York: Follett, $1.00.

Sutcliffe, Alys, *House Plants for City Dwellers.* New York: Dutton, $4.50.

Whitehead, Stanley B., *Book of House Plants.* New York: Warne, $7.95.

Sample Catalog Listings of Fluorescent Lamps

The following list serves the purpose of familiarizing the reader with the designations used in the catalogs of lamp manufacturers, the relative prices, and lumen output. I have used 48-inch lamps throughout except for the 96-inch Super High Output tubes. Prices are approximate list per single tube in 1972. Lumens are "approximate initial."

GENERAL ELECTRIC

Medium Bipin — 40-watt
Starter Required — 48-inch

F40 CW	Cool White Mainlighter	Lumens	3150	Price	$1.20
F40 CW/S	Cool White Staybright	"	3250	"	1.40
F40 CWX	Deluxe Cool White Mainlighter	"	2200	"	1.55
F40 WW	Warm White Mainlighter	"	3200	"	1.55
F40 WWX	Deluxe Warm White Mainlighter	"	2150	"	1.55

F40 SW/N	Soft White, Natural	"	2100	"	1.75
F40 D/S	Daylight Staybright	"	2650	"	1.60
F40 CW	Cool White reflector,				
	135-degree, window	"	2600	"	3.45

G.E. SLIMLINE

Single Pin
No Starter Required

F48 T12 CW	Cool White	Lumens	3000	Price	$1.90
F48 T12 WW	Warm White	"	3000	"	2.05
F48 T12 WWX	Deluxe Warm White	"	1970	"	2.15
F48 T12 SW/N	Soft White, Natural	"	1890	"	2.25
F48 T12 D	Daylight	"	2500	"	2.05

G.E. POWER GROOVE

110 Watt   48 inches.
Recessed Double Contact   Requires special electrical
No starter required   equipment.

F48 PG 17/CW	Cool White	Lumens	7000	Price	$5.45
F48 PG 17/CWX	Deluxe Cool White	"	4800	"	6.05
F48 PG 17 D	Daylight	"	5600	"	6.05
F48 PG 17 WW	Warm White	"	6400	"	6.05

The Westinghouse line is less extensive but very similar in specifications and prices. The following are two Super High Output catalog listings. Recessed Double Contact. Special Equipment required.

F96 T12/CWX/SHO	215 Watt, 96",				
	Deluxe Cool White	Lumens	11,000	Price	$6.10
F96 T12/CW/SHO	219 Watt, 96", Cool White	"	15,500	"	5.45

There are also Warm White, White, and Daylight SHO lamps.

SYLVANIA

40 watt   48-inch
Medium Bipin   No starter required

| F40 GRO | Gro-Lux | | | Price | $4.30 |
| F40/GRO/WS | Gro-Lux Wide Spectrum | | | " | 1.60 |

DURO-TEST
Naturescent

| 40-watt 48-inch, Med. Bipin Code 4820 | | | | Price | $3.49 |
| 60-watt 48-inch, Rec. Dble. Contact High Output | | | | " | 8.21 |

Vita-Lite

40-watt 48-inch, Med. Bipin Code 4821   Price $4.79

Plant Lite Bulb

75-watt R-30 Med. socket   Price $4.99
150-watt R-40 Med. socket   "   4.99

GENERAL ELECTRIC COOL BEAM FLOOD

 75 watt 75PAR38/2FL   Price $5.95
150 watt 150PAR38/2FL   "   6.00
300 watt 300PAR56/2MFL   "   11.75

G.E. MULTI-VAPOR METAL HALIDE LAMPS

Special fixtures necessary as well as wiring.
 400 watts   Mean lumens 23,700   Price $26.80
1000 watts   "   "   71,000   "   59.50
1500 watts   "   "   123,000   "   65.00

G.E. LUCALOX LAMPS

250 watts   Mean lumens 23,200   Price $53.00
400 watts   "   "   42,300   "   55.00

INDEX

(Pages in italics refer to charts and illustrations)

Orchids (*cont.*)
culture, 185–91
dormancy, 184
epiphytic, 187, 192, 193
fertilizer, 189
light intensity for, 186
list of, 196–98
monopodial, 193
Paphiopedilum, 191
Phalaenopsis, 193–95
pots, 188
potting, 189
selection, 185
temperature requirements, 185, 194
terrestrial, 191
Oxalis, 215–16
hedysaroides rubra, 216
martiana aureo-reticulata, 216
ortgiesii, 216
regnellii, 148

P

Peat moss, 82–83
Pebbles, 107
Pelargonium, 164–65
Pentas lanceolata, 216–17
Peristrophe angustifolia, 217
Perlite, 81
Pesticides, 124–31
alcohol treatment, 126
dangers, 124
list of, 131
pest strips, 127
protection against, 124–25
recommended, 127–28
soil, 125
systemics, 125
testing, 129
Pests
alcohol and brush removal, 126–27
common, 129–30
discovering, 129
manual removal, 126–27
washing, 126
Phosphors, 13, 15, 23
Photoperiodism, 36–38
Photosynthesis, 7
Phytochrome, 11
Plant introductions, 2–3
Planter, Aquamatic, 114
Plants, reaction to color, 6–7

acclimatizing, 136
aging of, 116
buying, 132–36
habit of, 133
Miracle Blooming, 137–51
Plastic crate, 107
Pollution, 101–2
effect on gesneriads, 102
effect on orchids, 102
from paints, 102
protection against, 102
Pomegranate, dwarf, 148
Portulaca grandiflora, 217
Pots, 87–88
clay or plastic, 87
decorative, 87
Japanese, 87
sizes, 88
Potting, 88–89
crock, 87
for pot-bound plants, 89
Propagation, 116–23
by division, 122
germination, 119
leaf cuttings, 121
medium, 118
pollination, 117
potting up, 120
seedlings, 119
seeds, 118
soil layering, 120
sowing, 118–19
stem cuttings, 122
when growth appears, 122
Punica granatum nana, 148

R

Reflectors, 30, 40
Roses, miniature, 218
Ruellia, 218

S

Saintpaulia, 138–40
culture, 140
miniatures, 140
species, 140
Sand, 84
Scilla violacea, 218
Seeds, 118
handling of small, 118
propagating medium, 118